Prototyping Augmented Reality

TONY MULLEN

WILEY

John Wiley & Sons, Inc.

Acquisitions Editor: Mariann Barsolo
Development Editor: Gary Schwartz
Technical Editor: John Nyquist
Production Editor: Dassi Zeidel
Copy Editor: Liz Welch
Editorial Manager: Pete Gaughan
Production Manager: Tim Tate
Vice President and Executive Group Publisher: Richard Swadley
Vice President and Publisher: Neil Edde
Book Designer: Caryl Gorska
Compositor: Chris Gillespie, Happenstance Type-O-Rama
Proofreader: Candace English
Indexer: Ted Laux
Project Coordinator, Cover: Katherine Crocker
Cover Designer: Ryan Sneed
Cover Image: Tony Mullen

Dear Reader,

Thank you for choosing *Prototyping Augmented Reality*. This book is part of a family of premium-quality Sybex books, all of which are written by outstanding authors who combine practical experience with a gift for teaching.

Sybex was founded in 1976. More than 30 years later, we're still committed to producing consistently exceptional books. With each of our titles, we're working hard to set a new standard for the industry. From the paper we print on, to the authors we work with, our goal is to bring you the best books available.

I hope you see all that reflected in these pages. I'd be very interested to hear your comments and get your feedback on how we're doing. Feel free to let me know what you think about this or any other Sybex book by sending me an email at nedde@wiley.com. If you think you've found a technical error in this book, please visit http://sybex.custhelp .com. Customer feedback is critical to our efforts at Sybex.

Best regards,

Neil Edde
Vice President and Publisher
Sybex, an Imprint of Wiley

For my family

Acknowledgments

I'd like to thank Acquisitions Editor Mariann Barsolo, Editorial Manager Pete Gaughan, Development Editor Gary Schwartz, Technical Editor John Nyquist, Editorial Assistants Jenni Housh and Connor O'Brien, Production Editor Dassi Zeidel, Copyeditor Liz Welch, and everyone else at Sybex who contributed to putting this book together. I'm also very grateful to the dedicated software developers who contributed their time and effort to create the open source software used in this book, including the ARToolKit, NyARToolkit, Processing, Blender, and JMonkeyEngine developers. I want to single out Adam Clarkson, creator of ARMonkeyKit, in particular for his help with the content of this book.

About the Author

Tony Mullen, PhD, has a broad background in CG and programming. He teaches at Tsuda College in Tokyo, Japan, where his courses include Python programming as well as Blender modeling and animation. He has been a cartoonist and an illustrator; his screen credits include writer, codirector, and lead animator on several short films, including the award-winning live-action/stop-motion film "Gustav Braustache and the Auto-Debilitator" (2007). He is the author of *Introducing Character Animation with Blender; 3D for iPhone Apps with Blender and SIO2; Mastering Blender, Bounce, Tumble, and Splash!: Simulating the Physical World with Blender 3D,* and *Blender Studio Projects: Digital Movie-Making,* all from Sybex.

About the Technical Editor

John R. Nyquist is a Blender Foundation Certified Trainer (BFCT) and has created seven Blender and two ActionScript training videos for CartoonSmart.com, as well as 60 episodes of Bits of Blender. He has worked professionally using Blender/Python, Java, ActionScript, C++, C#, and Lingo for interactive multimedia. John has coauthored two books on Director/Lingo and has served as technical editor for books on Java, Director, and Lingo.

CONTENTS AT A GLANCE

Contents

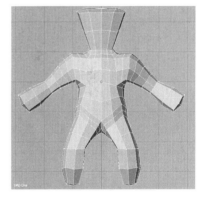

Introduction

Augmented Reality (AR) is a term used for a wide range of related technologies aimed at integrating virtual content and data with live, real-time media. The idea of AR is to mingle what is not really there with what is there as seamlessly as possible, and to present users with an enhanced, or augmented, display of the world around them. The nature of the augmentation could be anything from a textual display of data overlaid on real scenes or objects to complete, interactive 3D graphical scenes integrated into real ones.

AR depends crucially on hardware that is able to capture information about the real world, such as video, position data, orientation data, and potentially other forms of data, and also able to play back a display that mixes live media with virtual content in a way that is meaningful and useful to users.

With the recent ubiquity of smartphones, just about everybody now has in their pockets hardware with exciting AR potential. This has contributed to an explosion of interest in AR development, both for mobile platforms and in general. With the widespread use of webcams on laptops and desktop computers, browser-based AR for marketing and creative purposes has begun to boom. Inexpensive cameras and displays also make it possible to set up on-site AR installations cheaply and easily, as LEGO did with their brilliant AR-based marketing campaign in which AR stations were set up at toy stores to enable customers to hold a box up to the camera and see the completed 3D model in the display, fully integrated into the live camera video.

There are several major varieties of AR, and each is a broad topic in itself. Currently available books about mobile AR mainly focus on AR that uses location (GPS) and orientation (accelerometer) data from a mobile device to annotate or integrate content into live scenery. These applications know what your smartphone camera is viewing because they know where you're standing and which direction your smartphone is pointing. Based on this data, annotations that have been uploaded, either by a centralized service or by other users, can be overlaid on the scene in your camera.

Another, but by no means mutually exclusive, approach to AR is to use the actual image content captured by a camera to determine what is being viewed. This technology is known as *computer vision,* for obvious reasons. The computer processes each pixel of each video frame, evaluating each pixel's relationship with neighboring pixels in both time and space, and identifies patterns. Among other things, the current state of the art of computer vision includes accurate algorithms for face recognition, identifying moving objects in videos, and the ability to recognize familiar *markers*, or specific visual patterns that have been identified in advance to the algorithm, in a very robust way.

Computer vision–based AR can be used in both mobile contexts and non-mobile contexts. It can be used to enhance location- and orientation-based AR methods, and it can also be used to create AR applications that are not tied in any way to a specific location. The computer-vision algorithm can be made to recognize patterns on packaging, products, clothing, artwork, or in any number of other contexts.

This book is concerned with tools and technologies used for computer vision–based AR. Aside from its potential use in marketing campaigns and the like, computer vision–based AR is a lot of fun and, in my opinion, a bit magical. This aspect was what motivated me to begin investigating the subject and ultimately to write this book. I think that the creative potential of this technology has only begun to be explored, and I am eager to see people take it further. This is also why this book is geared less toward professional developers and more toward creative people who want to have fun exploring the possibilities before getting too bogged down in the technical demands of creating stable, ready-to-deploy software.

To these ends, I've tried to keep the technologies discussed in this book as accessible as possible. This is why a large portion of the book is devoted to the Processing programming environment. Processing is perhaps the most accessible programming environment around for creating visual, interactive programs. Processing is open source and cross-platform, and was developed specifically with the needs of artists and creative people in mind, people who are not necessarily highly skilled programmers. Processing has a comparatively gentle learning curve, but is remarkably powerful in spite of its simplicity. In addition to learning the basics of programming in Processing, you'll learn how to create animated 3D content using the open source 3D application Blender. This portion of the book is entirely optional; 3D content files are provided for download if you want to follow the other chapters without making your own.

In the interest of keeping things as accessible as possible, I've also stuck with AR technologies that use markers. Markers are printable patterns that provide AR systems with easy-to-recognize reference points. Because of the need for real-world markers, marker-based AR has some definite limitations. The technology exists to do some very impressive things with *markerless* AR. Markerless AR systems are able to create AR environments that reference other recognizable features of a video stream. For example, a markerless AR system might be made to recognize human faces or other objects, without the need for an explicitly printed marker.

The problem is that, at present, the available markerless AR technologies of which I am aware are not very accessible to nonprogrammers. By contrast, there is a variety of marker-based libraries that I think are comparatively easy to get running. This will certainly change in the future.

The Goals of This Book

This book is intended to give a broad introduction to some of the most accessible and usable tools for computer vision– and marker-based AR content creation. In doing so, a certain amount of programming is unavoidable, but programming is not the primary objective of this book. This book will show you how to get started using a wide variety of tools, each of which has different functions and benefits. Although there are overlaps, each of the tools depends on a different set of programming skills. To get the most out of these tools, you will need to pick up the ball in going further in your study of the programming environments you want to use. Whole shelves exist on the subject of 3D programming in Java or ActionScript, for example, and this book makes no attempt to replace these.

Rather, this book will give you the opportunity to get AR applications up and running on your computer (and potentially on your Android mobile device) and to get the basics of how to go about creating your own content. Depending on the technology, it may be possible to create an interactive AR application yourself quickly. Some of the chapters involve more hands-on programming activities, whereas others provide more cursory glimpses at the technology. You won't need programming skills to follow the content of the book, but you *will* need to pick them up if you want to go further with some of the topics.

Ultimately, the goal of this book is to inspire you to do just that. This book should give you a sense of the possibilities already available to you for creating AR applications in a variety of settings. Perhaps you'll be impressed by the possibilities of physical computing–based AR, and you'll go further in studying the Arduino and Processing environments. Maybe you'll get a great idea for a Flash-based AR game to create, and you'll throw yourself into learning ActionScript. Or maybe this book will inspire you to dive into 3D development in Android. Whatever the case may be, this book is intended to be a first step, not a last step.

Who Should Buy This Book

The title of this book is *Prototyping Augmented Reality*, and the focus of the book is not on creating polished, deployment-ready software, but rather on experimenting with and demonstrating AR applications, hopefully in as quick and simple a manner as possible. For this reason, the main target readership for this book is people who are creative and eager to explore the possibilities of AR for making fun, interactive applications with a sense of merging the real with the virtual. The book is written deliberately to avoid making assumptions of specific programming experience. Even if you've done no programming at all, you should be able to follow along and do some interesting things.

This does not mean that there's nothing here for professional, experienced developers. The value for more experienced developers will lie mostly in being pointed to interesting technologies and libraries. For people with programming chops in Java or ActionScript, this book should serve as a quick springboard into the world of AR. You won't learn much programming you don't already know, but you'll find out exactly where to start hacking to bring your own AR ideas to life. The breadth of the topics covered here also makes it likely that, even if you're a fairly experienced developer, there is something new within that might give you some interesting ideas.

Although I try to avoid assuming programming experience in describing this book, the fact is that programming is central to everything this book is about. Any programming experience you have, even in a completely different language, will be useful. Understanding object-oriented programming concepts will make a lot of things in the book more self-evident, and I do take a basic level of programming literacy for granted. If the idea of a "for" loop mystifies you, much of what you'll find in these pages will be pretty cryptic.

For some of the technologies discussed in this book, programming skills are an absolute must in going further to create your own content. You simply cannot develop AR applications on your own for Android without an understanding of Java, for example. The book's handling of those topics is intended as a gentle introduction to the AR potential of the environment, not as an in-depth programming course.

In short, this book is intended for anybody with an interest in computer vision– and marker-based AR who isn't sure where to start exploring the subject. What you get out of the book will depend a lot on what you bring to it.

What's Inside?

Here is a glance at what's in each chapter:

Chapter 1: Getting Started with Augmented Reality This chapter provides an overview of augmented reality and broadly introduces the libraries that the rest of the book covers in more depth. The topic of marker creation, which is relevant to all the other chapters, is covered here.

Chapter 2: Introduction to Processing This chapter provides a gentle introduction to the Processing programming environment, suitable for nonprogrammers. The basics of programming in Processing are covered with examples using 2D graphics.

Chapter 3: Blender Modeling and Texturing Basics This chapter gives a brief introduction to modeling and texturing using the open source 3D modeling and animation software called Blender.

Chapter 4: Creating a Low-Poly Animated Character This chapter picks up where Chapter 3 leaves off in creating a textured, low-poly animated character for use in AR applications.

Chapter 5: 3D Programming in Processing This chapter returns to Processing to introduce 3D programming and show what to do with an animated 3D character similar to the one you learned to create in Chapter 4.

Chapter 6: Augmented Reality with Processing This chapter carries what you've learned in the previous chapters into the world of AR by introducing special third-party libraries for Processing that enable AR.

Chapter 7: Interacting with the Physical World This chapter introduces the Arduino microcontroller and programming environment for physical computing. You'll learn to create an AR application that incorporates data from the real world via channels other than video only.

Chapter 8: Browser-Based AR with ActionScript and FLARManager This chapter shows you how to put your AR ideas online by using the FLARManager toolset for creating Flash-based browser AR applications.

Chapter 9: Prototyping AR with jMonkeyEngine This chapter introduces ARMonkeyKit, a powerful tool under development for rapid prototyping of 3D AR applications based on the open source jMonkeyEngine.

Chapter 10: Setting Up NyARToolKit for Android This chapter shows you how to install the NyARToolKit development environment for Android and run AR applications on your Android-based mobile device.

Appendix A: From Blender 2.49 to Blender 2.58 This appendix shows you how to translate the modeling, texturing, and animation concepts you learned in Chapters 3 and 4 from Blender 2.49 into Blender 2.58.

Appendix B: File Formats and Exporting This appendix provides a concise digest of 3D file formats used throughout the book and how you can export your content to the appropriate format for the environment with which you want to work.

Online Companion Files

You'll find the project files you need to follow the chapters on the book's companion website, `www.sybex.com/go/prototypingar`. Where licenses allow, software described in the chapters will also be available as a download from the book's website in case the corresponding version later becomes unavailable elsewhere.

How to Contact the Author

I welcome feedback from you about this book or about books you'd like to see from me in the future. You can reach me by writing to `blender.characters@gmail.com`.

Sybex strives to keep you supplied with the latest tools and information you need for your work. Please check the book's website, `www.sybex.com/go/prototypingar`, where we'll post additional content and updates that supplement this book if the need arises.

Prototyping Augmented Reality

CHAPTER 1

Getting Started with Augmented Reality

Augmented reality (AR), in which virtual content is seamlessly integrated with displays of real-world scenes, is an exciting area of interactive design. With the rise of personal mobile devices capable of producing interesting AR environments, the vast potential of AR has begun to be explored. The goal of this chapter is to help you become familiar with the terminology, tools, and technology necessary to begin your own AR explorations and experiments.

In this chapter, you'll learn about the following topics:

- **What is augmented reality?**
- **Tools and technologies**
- **AR necessities**

What Is Augmented Reality?

The term *augmented reality* (AR) is used to describe a combination of technologies that enable real-time mixing of computer-generated content with live video displays. Traditionally, it is distinguished from *virtual reality* (VR) in that VR involves creating complete, immersive 3D environments, and AR uses various hardware technologies to create an annotated, or "augmented," composite based on the real world.

There are several ways that the virtual components and real content can be made to interact. Techniques from image processing and computer vision can be used to make the computer-generated elements interact with the content of the video in a convincing way. Most current computer vision–based methods rely on predefined physical markers to enable the computer vision system to get its bearings in the visible 3D space. In Figure 1.1, you can see an example of AR in which two 3D models are manipulated by use of printed markers. AR systems that do not require specially made markers, known as *markerless* systems, are also possible. Markerless AR is a steadily progressing area of research, and in the near future, robust visual AR systems that do not require markers will surely become widely available.

Figure 1.1
Live video augmented with 3D models

Nonvision-based AR methods are gaining in popularity on smartphone platforms. These methods use a combination of the device's global positioning system (GPS) or other location-tracking data and accelerometer data to determine where the device is located and in what direction it is pointing. Based on this information, tags and annotations are superimposed over the scene. These methods are the basis of several geographical annotation services such as Layar, which is annotated for locations in the Netherlands; mixare, an open source mix augmented reality engine, which currently has data for Switzerland; and the Wikitude World Browser, which enables users from around the world to contribute localized data.

This book is primarily concerned with computer vision–based AR. You'll learn how to incorporate computer-generated 3D content into live video using physical markers. Getting into the details of location- and accelerometer-based AR is beyond the scope of this book. However, I will mention relevant links and references to these technologies where they are pertinent to the topic, such as in Chapter 10, "Setting Up NyARToolkit for Android."

A Brief History of AR

AR technology has its roots in computer interface research in the early days of computer science. Many of the main concepts of AR have been familiar in movies and science fiction at least as far back as movies like *The Terminator* (1984) and *RoboCop* (1987). Both movies feature cyborg characters whose views of the world are augmented by a steady stream of annotations and graphical overlays in their vision systems.

Practical systems using AR as it's currently viewed began to be developed in the next decade. The term *augmented reality* was coined in 1990 by Tom Caudell, a researcher at The Boeing Company. Throughout the early and mid 1990s, Caudell and his colleagues at Boeing worked on developing head-mounted display systems to enable engineers to assemble complex wire bundles using digital, AR diagrams superimposed on a board over which the wiring would be arranged. Because they made the wiring diagrams virtual, the previous system of using numerous unwieldy printed boards was greatly simplified.

Throughout the 1990s, industrial and military AR applications continued to be developed. But the technical requirements for useful AR displays, such as bulky, expensive head-mounted display devices, kept the technology out of reach for most users.

There were experiments incorporating AR technologies with the arts. Julie Martin, wife and collaborator of art technology pioneer Billy Klüver, is credited with producing the first AR theater production in 1994. The work, titled *Dancing in Cyberspace*, uses dancers who interact with virtual content projected onto the stage.

At the end of the 1990s, another major development in AR came about when Hirokazu Kato created ARToolKit, a powerful library of tools for creating AR applications. ARToolKit helped to make AR accessible to a much wider audience of designers and developers, and it provided the basis of much of the technology addressed in this book.

AR in Practice

In spite of the availability of ARToolKit, potential applications of AR have been slow to be explored fully. One big reason for this has been the demanding hardware requirements for achieving the benefits of an AR interface. The user must be looking at a display that has access both to camera data and to data from a computer processor capable of running the AR application. This setup was not standard even for consumer desktop environments just a few years ago, and it was almost unheard of in consumer mobile environments until the rise of smartphones, such as the iPhone and the Android family of phones. These smartphones, and the burgeoning tablet computer market that has followed them, have helped usher in a new era of interest in AR programming. With smartphones and tablets, users have an integrated camera and computer at their fingertips at all times, opening up many interesting new possibilities for AR applications.

Whether by using mobile apps or through browser interfaces on computers with webcams, it has become easier than ever to give users an engaging AR experience on their own devices, and the possibilities don't end there. AR marketing campaigns have been used by Hallmark, Adidas, and many other companies. In 2010, toymaker Lego created a pioneering point-of-sale AR marketing campaign. Computer screens were set up at toy stores carrying Lego toys and shoppers could hold up a box in front of the screen to see a 3D virtual representation of the completed Lego model in the video. In addition to being an incredibly effective point-of-sale campaign, the campaign generated a great deal of attention online, as shoppers posted their own videos of the experience. As discussed in Chapter 7, "Interacting with the Physical World," exploring alternate interfaces through physical computing can expand the possibilities even further.

Several trends are leading to an explosion of interest in AR. One is the steady improvement of computer vision technology, which will enable developers to work with more subtle, less obtrusive, and more robust markers and even completely markerless AR. Another trend is the rapid advance in display technologies for enabling AR. These include head-mounted displays and projector-based displays, as well as handheld mobile devices.

Head-mounted displays are essentially a combination of a camera and display screens that are worn like goggles or glasses. The viewing area may be a fully digital, opaque video screen that displays video from the camera, or it may be transparent in a way that allows the user to see the world directly with data laid over it. Head-mounted displays are ideally suited to AR applications and are becoming lighter, less obtrusive, and less expensive. In the long term, as wearable computers grow in popularity, head-mounted displays are likely to become increasingly commonplace.

Perhaps even more interesting are recent experiments in projector-based AR displays. Projector-based displays use projectors to project images or text directly onto surfaces in the real world. This approach can be extremely versatile in suitable environments. Projector-based displays can be used to present AR environments to large groups of people at once in ways that head-mounted displays or mobile devices cannot. Small, wearable projectors can also be used to create personal AR environments.

Other display methods may be available depending on specific application environments. Onboard AR applications for cars and airplanes can be used to add virtual content to dashboard displays. Online, browser-based AR applications can create engaging, interactive experiences for visitors to a website, as in the case of the Hotels.com online ad shown in Figure 1.2.

The recent rise in popularity of physical computing is also interesting from the standpoint of AR. The last few years have seen incredible developments in accessible and open physical computing platforms. These platforms consist of specific hardware specifications for programmable microcontrollers along with high-level APIs for programming them. Among the best known of these platforms are Wiring, Gainer, and Arduino. Of these, the most versatile and widely used is Arduino. Using a physical computing platform such as Arduino, you can program applications that interact physically with the world using electronic sensors for input. This is a natural fit with AR, and it deepens the sensory possibilities of AR applications. With physical computing, the "reality" with which you can process and program becomes much more than just video.

Figure 1.2

Hotels.com's virtualvacay.com site features interactive AR content.

Prototyping for Innovation

Prototyping refers to creating prototypes or working demonstrations of systems or devices. Prototyping is traditionally associated with innovative hardware constructions. Before manufacturing and mass-producing a new invention, it is desirable and often necessary to have a working implementation, however crude, to demonstrate it. Products ranging from mobile phones to automobiles typically go through a prototyping step in their design to test and demonstrate technical features. In electronics, prototyping by means of a temporary prototyping board (or *breadboard*) enables the circuit designer to set up a working circuit for testing without having to waste materials by soldering a permanent circuit prematurely. The same principles are becoming increasingly true of software. Many people who are not professional programmers nonetheless have interesting and innovative ideas for software. Software prototyping tools such as the Processing programming environment were created for such people. Just as an inventor can prototype a device in order to seek funding and one day achieve mass production, an artist or designer can prototype an application or software environment that can later be implemented professionally in a more robust or faster language.

Interactive systems and environments are exactly the kind of things that can benefit from accessible prototyping tools. Interaction designers may want to be able to put together quick and simple AR demonstrations without having to deal with the low-level headaches of compiling and building software.

A huge amount of room for innovation exists in the field of AR. My goal is to bring the basic tools of AR to as broad an audience of creative people as possible and to encourage experimentation and exploration. For this reason, I've tried to cover a range of different application contexts and display modes.

Tools and Technologies

A variety of software technologies is available for developers interested in working with AR, ranging from commercially available proprietary solutions to open source projects with little or no professional support and even combinations of both. In this book, I've selected tools that are reasonably accessible, inexpensive or free, minimally restrictive, and versatile while also enabling nontrivial programming. Much of what is covered in the book is connected with the NyARToolkit Java class library, which is based on the original ARToolKit.

However, depending on your needs, other software solutions are well worth investigating. In this section, I take a quick look at a few that you might want to check out.

ARToolKit

ARToolKit is the original C/C++ library that was the basis for many of the AR development resources that followed. ARToolKit was originally developed by the University of Washington's Human Interface Technology Laboratory (HITLab) as an open source library and released under the GNU General Public License (GPL). ARToolKit is now maintained by HITLab and HIT Lab NZ at the University of Canterbury, New Zealand. Proprietary versions of the software suitable for creating closed source applications is available from ARToolworks, Inc. ARToolworks has adapted the original ARToolKit to be useful on a variety of platforms and offers numerous solutions with professional support. For example, ARToolKit for Apple's mobile operating system, iOS, is available under a proprietary license from ARToolworks.

Quick Mockups with BuildAR

A quick and easy way to set up a basic AR viewer is the BuildAR application from HIT Lab NZ, available at `www.buildar.co.nz`. BuildAR is a proprietary application available for

Windows, with a freely downloadable trial version that enables you to add a 3D model and control its rotation, translation, and scale. BuildAR is suitable for some prototyping and demoing of limited AR applications. The commercial version comes with useful tools for training markers. BuildAR requires no programming at all, which is both its strength and its weakness. It's the easiest way to get an AR scene up and running on your Windows computer, but it is fairly limited in what you can do.

DART

The Designer's Augmented Reality Toolkit (DART) is a set of software tools for prototyping AR applications using the Adobe Director multimedia programming environment. You can download the software and find installation instructions and other documentation at `www.cc.gatech.edu/dart/`. Users familiar with the Director environment should definitely look into DART, as it can be used to prototype AR environments in a similar manner to some of the software discussed in this book. The website also claims that it is well suited to interacting with other programming languages.

Markerless AR with PTAM

Parallel Tracking and Mapping (PTAM) is a set of development tools for markerless AR. The source code is available at `http://ewokrampage.wordpress.com`. Getting PTAM up and running requires experience in building and compiling C projects, but the ability to set up AR scenes without markers opens up many interesting possibilities. Users with C/C++ experience should look into PTAM.

AR Necessities

For doing any kind of visual AR, a decent computer (anything built in the last three years should be adequate for the purposes of this book) with a camera is a must. Many computers have cameras built in nowadays, and these will work fine for many of the projects in this book. However, because they are built into the computer the cameras are difficult to aim and place, so even if your computer has a webcam, you might prefer to invest in an inexpensive USB webcam.

As for what kind of computer you use, there are advantages and disadvantages to all of the major platforms. For this book I've made every effort to track down cross-platform solutions, but this hasn't always been possible. Depending on a variety of factors— including your operating system, your specific computer manufacturer, your graphics card, and others—you may find that some of the Java libraries mentioned in this book need special handling to work on your platform. In a few cases, there are nontrivial restrictions on which Java library items will work on specific platforms. I will clarify any restrictions as they come up.

Getting the Software

Throughout this book, you'll be introduced to a variety of software tools, large and small. I'll describe where you can download the necessary software as it is pertinent. In most cases, installing what you need will be straightforward, but in the later chapters you'll encounter some cases where it is a bit more complicated to get your programming environment set up correctly. In these cases, I'll walk you through the steps.

Most of the software used in the projects in this book is open source, released under an Open Source Initiative (OSI)–approved license. You can download it all freely, and it is freely distributable. In cases where I mention software that has different licensing restrictions, I will make those clear. Some of the software packages, such as the Eclipse integrated development environment (IDE) and the Processing programming environment, are major projects that are widely used and very well supported by developers. Large, OSI-approved open source projects can be relied on to remain available well into the future. In other cases, I may describe a small library or modification to a library that has been created by an individual and may only be available from that person's personal website or blog. In these cases, I will make sure that the software also remains permanently available on the Sybex website for this book (`www.sybex.com/go/prototypingar`).

The World of Java

Much of the software discussed in this book is based on the Java programming language (the biggest exception to this is Chapter 8, "Browser-Based AR with ActionScript and FLARManager," which deals with ActionScript). If you have experience programming in Java, you're going to feel very comfortable. If not, I think that the progression from the Processing environment to Java that this book follows is a great way to ease into Java programming. *Processing* is essentially a simplified and streamlined subset of Java built for ease of use by nonprogrammers. When you've gotten comfortable with Processing, the leap to Java is not so intimidating. Of course, a thorough introduction to Java programming is far beyond the scope of this book, but you should be able to pick up where the book leaves off and study Java itself with other resources.

The benefit of Java from the standpoint of this book is the ease with which Java applications can (usually) be ported from platform to platform. With the Java-based software described in this book, you should not need to be concerned too much with the low-level details of your software-building environment. The ActionScript code described in Chapter 8, likewise, is very portable across platforms.

Peripheral Hardware

In addition to a computer and a camera, several other significant pieces of hardware will be required for you to follow along completely with some of the advanced projects in this book.

Chapter 7 introduces physical computing with Arduino. This chapter is heavily hardware based. You will need a minimum of an Arduino microcontroller unit, a breadboard for circuit prototyping, jump wires, a 180-Ohm resistor, and an electronic pressure sensor. You will also need either a couple of small alligator clips or a soldering iron and solder. You can buy all of this online (not counting the soldering iron and solder, which you probably should buy only if you plan to use it for other things as well). In Chapter 7, I'll go into more detail about where to order these things.

Chapter 10 deals with programming AR for the Android environment. For this, an Android handset is highly recommended. The Android SDK handset emulator does not have simple built-in access to a USB camera, so being able to access the device's camera is a big advantage.

Markers

The variety of AR discussed in this book uses specific types of markers, originally designed for ARToolKit. The computer vision algorithms used here recognize the markers, and they are able to calculate the orientation of the markers in space based on the shape of the markers' projected outline in the camera view. A marker can be printed or displayed in any way that a camera can see it. Figure 1.3 shows a marker displayed on a mobile device.

Figure 1.3

An AR marker displayed in a browser on an iPod touch

ARToolKit markers are square, with an image in the middle and a very thick, black, square outline around the image. Outside the square is typically a white edge. Most of the code samples from packages derived from ARToolKit use one of a handful of widely available marker patterns, such as the classic Hiro marker shown in Figure 1.4. This one and the Japanese kanji symbol marker are available from numerous sources online and are included among the downloadable support files for this book.

You'll probably want to create your own marker designs. This involves two steps. The first step is to create the graphical design itself. The second step is to "train" the system on the design. This step produces what is called a pattern file (often named using the extension `.patt` or `.pat`), which can then be loaded into your AR application so that the application can recognize the pattern.

Figure 1.4

The classic Hiro marker

Creating the graphic can be done by hand. See the following website for information on the exact dimensions if you want to do this: `www.artoolworks.com/support/library/Creating_and_training_new_ARToolKit_markers`.

However, it is much handier to use the online Marker Maker site at `www.roarmot.co.nz/ar/`, shown in Figure 1.5. Using this service, you can submit your own JPEG file, and the system will automatically create a properly formatted marker PDF file.

Figure 1.5

The ARToolKit Marker Maker site

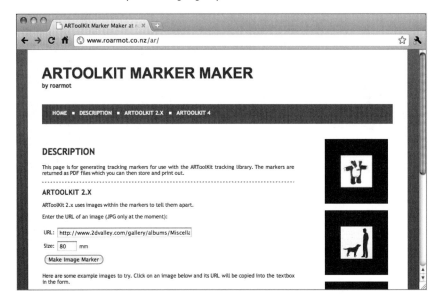

Training the pattern is somewhat trickier, but an excellent online resource exists for this as well. To train the pattern, first print the pattern on paper or display it in the manner you want to display it in your application—on a tablet or smartphone screen, for example. Go to `http://flash.tarotaro.org/blog/2009/07/12/mgo2/` and click the ARToolKit Marker Generator Online Multi link. The website's Flash application will request access to your webcam, which you should grant. Hold your pattern in front of the camera until the application recognizes it as a marker candidate and draws a red outline around the marker's edge, as shown in Figure 1.6. For the purposes of this book, leave the options at their default values, and then click Get Pattern. The pattern will be generated, as shown in Figure 1.7. You can either continue and make more before saving them all, or you can click Save Current and save the pattern file to a directory. Save the resulting pattern files somewhere safe. You'll learn how to use them in your applications later in this book.

One final note regarding AR markers: In a few years, when markerless AR gains currency, these markers will be regarded as crude, unsightly, and hopelessly dated. So I strongly recommend you resist the temptation to get them tattooed on your skin.

Figure 1.6

Recognizing a marker with the online Marker Generator

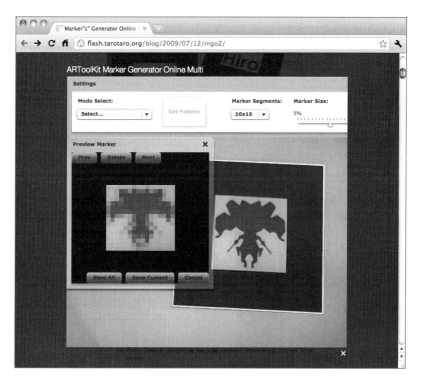

Figure 1.7

Generating the pattern

Other Useful Items

There are a few more items I've found helpful in AR prototyping, although they aren't strictly necessary. For easy rotation of AR markers, it's nice to have some kind of small turntable or lazy Susan. I wasn't able to find anything suitable readymade, so I built my own using the swivels shown in Figure 1.8 (easily purchased at any good hardware store or online). I picked up some Styrofoam and rubber pieces from the local hobby shop and jury-rigged the turntable you see in Figure 1.9.

Figure 1.8

Lazy Susan swivels

Figure 1.9

A homemade turntable

Finally, mounting some markers on cardboard and Popsicle sticks makes them easy to manipulate. The computer vision algorithms are very sensitive, and even slightly obscuring the marker can render it unrecognizable to the algorithm. A Popsicle stick gives you a nice handle and keeps your fingers out of the way of the marker content, as shown in Figure 1.10.

You now have the basic necessities to get started experimenting with AR. In the next few chapters, you'll take a bit of a detour to learn some simple programming with Processing and 3D content creation with Blender. In Chapter 6, "Augmented Reality with Processing," you'll get a chance to put your markers to use.

Figure 1.10

Markers on Popsicle sticks

CHAPTER 2

Introduction to Processing

The first hurdle in learning any complex piece of software is to become familiar with the interface.

In this chapter, you'll learn about the following topics:

- **The Processing programming environment**

- **Drawing in Processing**

- **Working with classes**

The Processing Programming Environment

Processing is an open source, Java-based programming environment for creative people who are not primarily computer programmers. Its biggest strength is that it is comparatively easy to learn, and it enables creators to get started quickly producing sophisticated graphical and interactive applications while minimizing the headaches often associated with compiling and building software. On the other hand, because it is basically an extension of the Java programming language, it has, in principle, access to all the power of Java. In general, the syntax of Processing is straightforward to anyone who has any programming experience at all in a procedural programming language such as Java or C. If you have a basic understanding of variables, functions, and control structures, such as for loops, then programming in Processing should come as second nature for you. If not, you will learn about those things as you go.

Processing has libraries available for working with Arduino, for implementing AR applications, and for building for the Android platform, making it a good place to start for many prototyping tasks related to this book. You should be aware of some important limitations in how these libraries can be used in conjunction with each other—at present, it's not quite the one-stop solution it might one day be. Later in the book, you'll deal with more advanced use cases where Processing can't be easily used, but it's an easy entrance point for programming simple AR projects.

Installing and Running Processing

You need to download and install Processing for your own platform from `www.processing` `.org`. The download and installation process is relatively straightforward. In the case of the Windows platform, you have two choices: either the standard download or expert edition (labeled "Without Java"). The expert download is for users who already have the Java Development Kit installed on their computer. If you're not sure whether you do, choose the standard download.

> As of this writing, some of the Java dependencies that Processing relies on can be inconsistent when Java is installed independently on the 64-bit version of Windows 7. If you are using this operating system, I highly recommended that you install the standard (Java included) version of Processing, even if Java is already installed on your computer.

Click the installation executable, and follow the steps to install Processing for your platform. When you've finished, click the icon to start Processing.

You should see a window open like the one shown in Figure 2.1. This is the Processing integrated development environment (IDE). This is the interface in which you'll write and execute your code. The main white area of the window is the code editing area. It is already open to a new sketch (Processing programs are called *sketches*) named according to the current date. In the bar above this, you'll see the Run, Stop, New, Open, Save, and Export buttons. The black area below is the standard output area where you'll see error messages and where you can print values for debugging.

Figure 2.1

The Processing IDE window

The location of the menu bar depends on your operating system. In Windows, the menu bar is along the top of the Processing window, as shown in Figure 2.1. On the Mac, the menu bar runs along the top of your screen, as is standard on Macs. In the menu bar, you'll see the Processing, File, Edit, Sketch, Tools, and Help menus.

Your First Processing Program

Running a Processing program is incredibly simple. In fact, you can create a windowed application with just a single line of code. Enter the following into the editor, and click the Run button:

```
size(600, 400);
```

The result should look something like Figure 2.2. The new window that opens is your sketch. The window is 600 pixels wide and 400 pixels high, as specified by the arguments of the size() function.

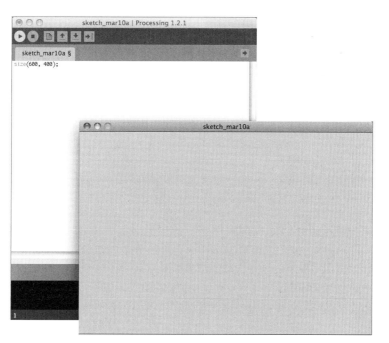

Figure 2.2

Running a Processing sketch

Of course, there's nothing in the window. All you've done so far is determine the size of your sketch. To put some content in the window, add the following lines below the line where you called the size() function:

```
background(0);
fill(255, 255, 0);
stroke(255, 0, 255);
strokeWeight(10);

ellipse(300, 200, 200, 200);
```

When you run this code, the sketch shown in Figure 2.3 will appear: On your screen, you'll see a yellow circle with a thick magenta outline on a black background. The code for this should be nearly self-explanatory even for a novice programmer, but there are a few points worth noting.

Figure 2.3

Running a
Processing sketch

The first line of the code after the size() function is the background() function, which fills the background with a color. Like many functions in Processing that take colors as arguments, the background() function can be called with one numerical argument, two arguments, three arguments, or four arguments. If you call it with one argument, as in this example, the color is assumed to be grayscale and the argument represents its grayscale value (using a default range of 0–255, which can be modified to whatever range you want to use). In this case, the argument of 0, then, means black. If you call background() with two arguments, the first argument is the grayscale value and the second argument is the alpha (opacity) value. If you call background() with three values, they can represent red, green, and blue components (using the default RGB color mode) or hue, saturation, and brightness (using the HSB color mode setting). Calling background() with four arguments adds an alpha value to the three-argument call.

The same argument pattern comes up in many other cases where colors are passed to a function. The next two lines of the code are further examples of this way of passing color information to a function. The fill() function takes the same kinds of arguments to determine the fill-in color of the next shape to be drawn, and the stroke() function determines the color of the outline around the next shape drawn. In this case, the fill value is yellow, denoted by the maximum values for red and green and no blue; the stroke value is magenta, denoted by the maximum values for red and blue, and no green. Both colors are drawn at full opacity because there is no alpha argument.

The strokeWeight() function sets the thickness of the outline, and the ellipse() function draws the circle. The first two arguments of this function determine the center point of the ellipse, and the third and fourth arguments determine the width and height of the ellipse. If these last two values are the same, of course, a circle is drawn.

Interactive Mode

In order for your Processing sketch to change over time or react to input, you must use *Interactive mode*. This involves calling your code from within two special functions, setup() and draw(). You use the setup() function when you include code that is intended to run only once: when your sketch is first executed. This function determines the starting state of the sketch; hence its name. The draw() function, by contrast, is called repeatedly as the sketch runs. The contents of this function determine how the sketch window is redrawn as values change as the sketch runs. For a simple example, create a new sketch by choosing File → New from your Processing menu bar (either at the top of the sketch window or at the top of your screen, depending on your operating system). In the editor window, enter the following code:

```
int i = -50;
void setup(){
    size(300, 300);
    fill(255);
    stroke(0);
    strokeWeight(3);
}
void draw(){
    background(100);
    ellipse(150, i, 100, 100);
    i++;
    if(i > 350){
        i = -50;
    }
}
```

When you run this sketch, you should see a white circle with a black outline moving downward over a gray background, as illustrated in Figure 2.4.

Figure 2.4

A sketch with animation

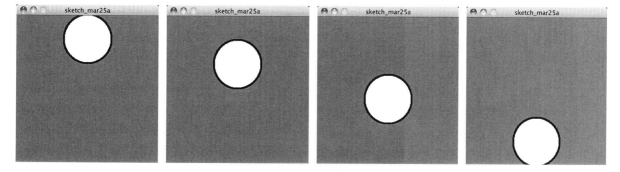

Let's take a quick look at the code. The very first line is a declaration of the variable *i*:

```
int i = -50;
```

This will be the integer that will determine the vertical location of the circle to be drawn. This value will be used to count pixels, and because pixels are discrete units, an integer value is most appropriate. Integer-valued variables are declared with the `int` declaration.

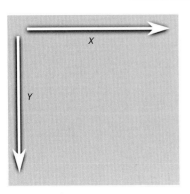

The value assigned is –50, which will initialize the center location of the circle 50 imaginary pixels above the top edge of the sketch window.

Why is this? A standard 2D Processing sketch like the one described here is drawn into the sketch window according to an x,y coordinate system running downward and to the right from an origin point in the upper-left corner of the window, as illustrated in Figure 2.5.

Coordinate values of less than zero or greater than the window size can be used, but they will "draw" the element beyond the edge of the visible window and it will not be displayed onscreen.

The next section is the `setup()` function:

Figure 2.5

The Processing 2D coordinate system

```
void setup(){
size(300, 300);
fill(255);
stroke(0);
strokeWeight(3);

}
```

You've seen the content of this function already in this chapter, so you should know what it does. The only difference is that now it is enclosed in a `setup()` function definition, so Processing knows that it is running in interactive mode and that this code will be executed only once, when the sketch begins. Note that either function can be empty, and you define either function without defining the other function.

The `draw()` function is where the action happens. First the gray background is drawn:

```
void draw(){

background(100);
```

Then the ellipse is drawn:

```
ellipse(150, i, 100, 100);
```

Note that the *i* variable is used to position the circle vertically. Since the circle has a diameter of 100 pixels, positioning the circle's center 50 pixels above the top edge of the window initializes the circle just off the screen.

The next line of code increments the variable:

```
i++;
```

If you're familiar with the syntax of any of the most commonly used programming languages, you'll recognize this. It has the same meaning as i = i + 1; that is, take the value of *i* and increase it by 1.

The last part of the sketch is a conditional control structure. If the value of *i* goes above 350, it is reset to –50. This places the circle back up above the top edge of the sketch after it drops off the bottom of the sketch:

```
        if(i > 350){
            i = -50;
        }
    }
```

Consider the reasons why the various function calls are placed as they are in this sketch. For example, intuitively it might seem that setting the background color would be something you could do just once at the beginning of the sketch. Why do you think the `background()` call is in the `draw()` function here? Experiment with changing this and see what happens.

As an exercise, adapt this sketch to make a simple drawing program that uses a sequence of circles to draw curly lines that follow the movements of your mouse. Use the special Processing variables *mouseX* and *mouseY* to access the mouse's screen position. These special variables always automatically contain the values corresponding to wherever the mouse is located on the screen. Using these variables makes it incredibly simple to incorporate mouse information into your sketch. The function call `noStroke()` can be used to draw the circle without an outline. Consider varying the opacity of the circle for an airbrush-like effect. A solution for this exercise is shown in the "Simple Airbrush" sidebar at the end of the chapter.

Drawing in Processing

Processing is first and foremost a programming environment for putting graphical elements onto a display quickly and easily. For this reason, getting familiar with drawing functions is a big part of learning the basics of Processing. Fortunately, it's very easy and the Processing reference web page (both online and included locally as part of your Processing download) is a great resource for looking up everything you need to know.

Primitive Shapes

There are seven basic 2D shape primitive functions in Processing: `point()`, `line()`, `triangle()`, `quad()`, `rect()`, `ellipse()`, and `arc()`. Each of these functions requires a different set of arguments to define the shape's parameters.

The simplest is `point()`, which takes only two arguments representing x and y values and draws a single pixel (the color determined by the current `stroke()` color value) at that point. The `line()` function takes four arguments to represent the x and y coordinates of each end of the line, and the `triangle()` and `quad()` functions take six and eight arguments, respectively, representing the coordinates of the shape's corner points.

The rect() function takes four arguments to create a rectangle. By default, the first two arguments represent the center point coordinates and the third and fourth arguments represent the width and height of the rectangle. A special function, rectMode(), can be called to change the rectangle draw mode so that the first two arguments represent the top-left corner (rectMode(CORNER)) or so that the third and fourth arguments represent the "radius," or distance of the edges from the center point of the rectangle (rectMode(RADIUS)). The CORNERS rect mode interprets the first two arguments as one corner and the third and fourth arguments as the coordinates of the opposing corner. The default rect mode is CENTER.

The ellipse() function that you saw in the previous example works analogously, and the ellipseMode() function can take the same four mode arguments—CORNER, CORNERS, RADIUS, and CENTER. Their meaning is analogous to the rectangle case.

The arc() function draws a portion of an ellipse extending from one angle to another angle. This function takes six arguments. The first two arguments represent the position of the arc, the second two represent the width and height of the ellipse, and the fifth and sixth arguments represent the angles that the arc extends from and to. Angles in Processing are represented in radians, and the last two arguments for this function must be given in radians. Because most people prefer to think of angles in degrees, however, the radians() function can be used to convert degrees to radians. Furthermore, angles for the arc() function are considered to rotate clockwise beginning with the zero angle directly to the right of the center, as shown in Figure 2.6.

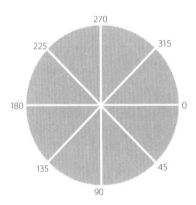

Figure 2.6

Angles for the arc() function

Therefore, the code here yields the arc shown in Figure 2.7:

```
size(600,400);
arc(300, 200, 300, 300, radians(90), radians(200));
```

Figure 2.7

An arc

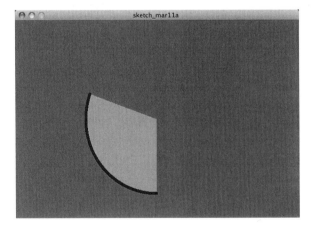

Working with HSB Color

The default color mode in Processing is RGB, where the three numerical values stand for red, green, and blue components of the color, respectively. To understand better how the HSB color mode can be useful, try typing in the following sketch and running it:

```
void setup(){
    size(500, 500);
    colorMode(HSB, 1);
}
void draw(){
    for(int x=0; x <= 500; x++){
        stroke(x/500.0, mouseX/500.0, 0.7);
        line(x, 0, x, 500);
    }
}
```

Let's look more closely at what's new here. In the `setup()` function, the call to `colorMode()` is introduced. This function does two things here. The first argument changes the color mode from RGB to HSB. As mentioned previously, doing so will make the color arguments of subsequent functions represent hue, saturation, and brightness, rather than red, green, and blue. This function is very useful if you want to cycle through colors of the rainbow or smoothly adjust the brightness or saturation of the color. Using HSB colors, you can cycle through the color spectrum by simply incrementing the hue value. The second argument of the `colorMode()` function determines the range to be used for color arguments. The default range for color arguments is from 0 to 255, as you saw in previous examples. In this case, however, it will be more intuitive to use a range between 0 and 1, so the second argument here is 1:

```
colorMode(HSB, 1);
```

The rainbow background is filled in this sketch by drawing a sequence of 1-pixel-wide vertical lines and graduating their hue. Because the background is 500 pixels wide, it is necessary to draw 500 lines. This is done with a `for` loop with x ranging from 0 to 500. The `stroke()` function is called to set the color of each line. The first argument represents hue, and the value is `x/500.0`. When x is closer to 0 (closer to the left edge of the window) the value of the argument is 0. As x approaches 500 (the right edge of the window), the argument approaches 1. Thus, from right to left, the hue value ranges from 0 to 1, running through the entire range of available hues. The second argument here is `mouseX/500.0`. This ranges from 0 to 1 depending on where you move the mouse—from 0 when the mouse is at the left of the window to 1 when the mouse is at the right of the window. This controls saturation, or the "purity" of the colors. At 0 saturation, all colors are gray. Finally, the third argument sets the brightness. This can also range from 0 (black) to 1 (maximum brightness for each color):

```
stroke(x/500.0, mouseX/500.0, 0.7);
```

Simple Trigonometry

Being familiar with basic trigonometric functions is very useful when you're programming graphics-related software. The next sketch shows how to use Processing's built-in
trigonometric functions *cos()* and *sin()*. Type the following and run it:

```
int angle = 0;
float rads = 0.0;
void setup(){
    size(500, 500);
    colorMode(HSB, 1);
}
void draw(){
    background(0.5);
    rads = radians(angle);
    noFill();
    stroke(0.0, 0.0, 1.0);
    arc(250, 250, 200, 200, 0, rads);
    stroke(0.0, 0.0, 0.0);
    line(250, 250, 250 + cos(rads)*100, 250);
    line(250, 250 + sin(rads)*100, 250, 250);
    angle++;
    if(angle == 360){
        angle = 0;
    }
}
```

When you run this sketch, you should see an animation of a white arc being drawn at
increasing angles along with black lines whose lengths change in relation to the angle.

Now let's take a closer look at the code. The first few lines declare some variables. The
angle variable is an integer, and it will represent the angle of the arc in degrees. The *rads*
variable is a floating-point variable, and it will represent the angle in radians:

```
int angle = 0;
float rads = 0.0;
```

When the draw() function is called and the background drawn, the next thing to do is
to pass the value in radians of the current angle to the *rads* variable. The angle will incre-
ment by one degree each time the window is redrawn (this incrementing is performed
later in the draw() function):

```
rads = radians(angle);
```

The next couple of lines set the draw mode to noFill and the stroke to white. Note
that, in HSB color mode, if the second color value (saturation) is zero, then the color is
grayscale by definition, and the third value determines where the value lies between

black (0) and white (1). In this case, the first value (hue) does not matter. Finally, the arc is drawn using the value of *rads* as its angle argument:

```
noFill();
stroke(0.0, 0.0, 1.0);
arc(250, 250, 200, 200, 0, rads);
```

The next few lines set the stroke color to black and draw two lines: one representing the cosine value of the angle and one representing the sine value of the angle:

```
stroke(0.0, 0.0, 0.0);
line(250, 250, 250 + cos(rads)*100, 250);
line(250, 250 + sin(rads)*100, 250, 250);
```

Finally, the angle value is iterated by one degree with each redraw of the window. When it hits 360, it is reset to 0:

```
angle++;
if(angle == 360){
    angle = 0;
}
```

You can make use of the changing angles to position objects around a circle. Try inserting the following code after the line `line(250, 250 + sin(rads)*100, 250, 250);`:

```
noStroke();
fill(abs(sin(rads)), 1.0, 1.0);
ellipse(250+(cos(rads)*50), 250+(sin(rads)*50),
    5+abs((sin(rads)*5)), 5+abs((cos(rads)*5)));
```

This code draws an ellipse that rotates around the shape of the arc. Using sines and cosines enables you to locate points on a circular trajectory based on an angle. This is how they are used in the first two arguments of the `ellipse()` function. The number 250 is added to the x and y values to make them relative to the center of the 500×500–pixel window. The width and height of the ellipses is also tied to the sine and cosine values of the angle.

Putting Things Together

You can combine the example code from the previous sections with a few more whistles and bells to get more of a sense of how cosines and sines can be used to derive simple harmonic motion and how `for` loops can be used to control changing values. Experiment on your own with incorporating the different things you've learned so far into more complex sketches. The complete example you'll find in the download material for this chapter (go to www.sybex.com/go/prototypingar) is reprinted here:

```
//declare the variables
int angle = 0;
float rads = 0.0;
```

```
//setup function
void setup(){
    size(500, 500);
    colorMode(HSB, 1);
    rectMode(CENTER);
}
//repeating code
void draw(){
    rads = radians(angle);
    for(int x=0; x <= 500; x++){
        stroke(x/500.0, abs(cos(rads)), 0.7);
        line(x, 0, x, 500);
    }
    noFill();
    stroke(0.0, 0.0, 1.0);
    arc(250, 250, 200, 200, 0, rads);
    stroke(0.0, 0.0, 0.0);
    line(250, 250, 250 + cos(rads)*100, 250);
    line(250, 250 + sin(rads)*100, 250, 250);

    noStroke();
    fill(abs(sin(rads)), 1.0, 1.0);

    ellipse(250+(cos(rads)*50), 250+(sin(rads)*50),
        5+abs((sin(rads)*5)), 5+abs((cos(rads)*5)));

    ellipse(250+(cos(rads)*100), 250+(sin(rads)*100),
        10+abs((sin(rads)*10)), 10+abs((cos(rads)*10)));

    ellipse(250+(cos(rads)*150), 250+(sin(rads)*150),
        15+abs((sin(rads)*15)), 15+abs((cos(rads)*15)));

    ellipse(250+(cos(rads)*200), 250+(sin(rads)*200),
        20+abs((sin(rads)*20)), 20+abs((cos(rads)*20)));

    stroke(0.0, 0.0, 1.0);

    fill(0.0, 0.0, cos(rads));
    rect((cos(rads)*200) + 250, 50, 20, 20);

    fill(0.0, 0.0, 1.0 - abs(cos(rads)));
    rect((-cos(rads))*200 + 250, 450, 20, 20);

    fill(0.0, 0.0, sin(rads));
    rect(50, (sin(rads)*200) + 250, 20, 20);
```

```
fill(0.0, 0.0, 1.0 - abs(sin(rads)));
rect(450, (-sin(rads)*200) + 250, 20, 20);

angle++;
if(angle == 360){
    angle = 0;
}
}
}
```

When you run this sketch, you should see an animation of
the arc being drawn at increasing angles along with other elements whose position and shapes change with the angle, as
shown in Figure 2.8. The background is a rainbow spectrum
from left to right that fades to grayscale when the angle is a
right angle pointing straight up or down.

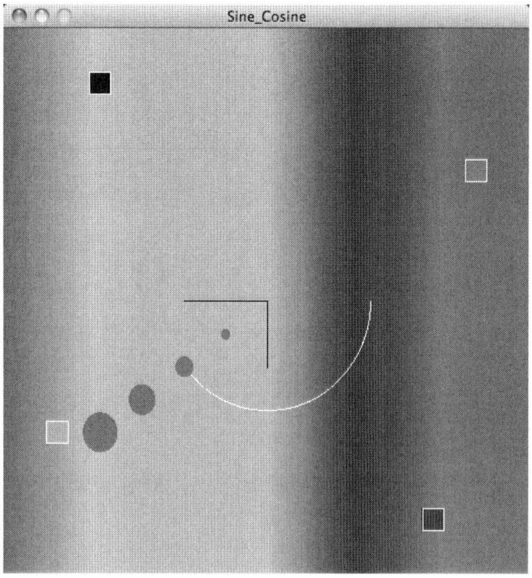

Figure 2.8

A sample sketch
demonstrating
angles, shapes,
and color mode

Working with Classes

Processing is built on top of the Java programming language and can seamlessly interface with Java libraries. Like Java itself, Processing is an object-oriented language. This
means that you can create complex custom data structures called *classes* and organize your
program based on the interactions between instantiated *objects* of these classes. If you're
unfamiliar with object-oriented programming, this may sound more complicated than
it actually is. The following example should help you understand the basics of classes. It
also introduces some other basic programming concepts such as working with arrays and
user interaction with the mouse.

To get started, create a new sketch in Processing. Save it with the name **Bouncers**. The
completed sketch will create a bull's-eye–like spot wherever you click on the window, which
will then bounce up and down from the point where you clicked. A total of five of these
spots will be created. If you click more than five times, then a previously placed spot will
disappear and a new spot will show up where you clicked.

Because each target is bouncing independently of the others, each different spot needs
to maintain location data about where it is on the bounce (that is, it needs to know its
current y coordinate value). This is exactly the kind of thing that is handled easily and
intuitively with classes and objects. You'll create a class to represent the spots. This class
will contain information about how to draw the spot, and it will also contain class variables to hold data that is unique to instances (objects) of the class.

To define a class to which the sketch has access, you'll create a new file in the same
sketch. Do this simply by adding a tab to the sketch. Click the arrow icon at the right
of the tab's bar near the top of your Processing window and choose New Tab, as shown
in Figure 2.9. You'll be prompted to give the new tab a name. Enter **Spot,** as shown in

Figure 2.10. The resulting window with both tabs is shown in Figure 2.11. You can choose the file you want to edit by clicking on the corresponding tab.

Figure 2.9

Adding a tab

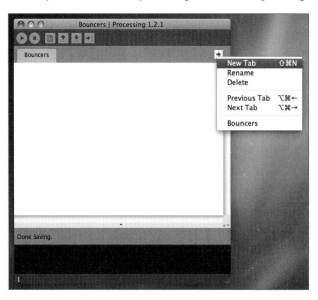

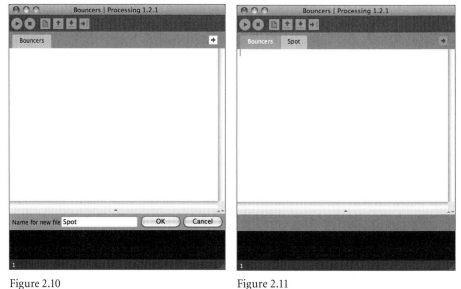

Figure 2.10

Naming the new tab

Figure 2.11

The sketch with two tabs

Now that you've got the files set up as they should be, enter the code in the Spot file to define a class called Spot as follows:

```
class Spot{
    int x, y;
    int rate = 1;
```

```
        int initialY;
        boolean fall = true;
        boolean active = false;
         Spot(int xpos, int ypos){
           x = xpos;
           y = ypos;
           initialY = y;
        }
        void display(){
           noStroke();
           fill(255);
           ellipse(x, y, 95, 95);
           fill(0);
           ellipse(x, y, 80, 80);
           fill(255);
           ellipse(x, y, 65, 65);
           fill(255,0,0);
           ellipse(x, y, 50, 50);
           fill(255);
           ellipse(x, y, 25, 25);
           fill(0);
           ellipse(x, y, 10, 10);
        }

      }
```

In the Bouncers file tab, enter the following code. This is the main code for the sketch:

```
      int height = 400;
      int width = 500;
      int spottotal = 5;
      int spotcount = 0;
      Spot[] spots;

      void setup(){
         size(width, height);
         spots =  new Spot[spottotal];
      }
      void draw(){
         background(180);
         for(int i = 0; i < spotcount; i++){
           spots[i].display();
           if(spots[i].active){
              if(spots[i].fall){
                 spots[i].y = spots[i].y + spots[i].rate;
                 spots[i].rate++;
              }else{
                 spots[i].y = spots[i].y - spots[i].rate;
```

```
                    spots[i].rate--;
                }
            }
            if(spots[i].y > height -45){
                spots[i].fall = false;
            }
            if(spots[i].y < spots[i].initialY){
                spots[i].rate = 1;
                spots[i].fall = true;
            }
        }
    }
    void mousePressed(){
        if(spotcount == spottotal){
            spotcount--;
            for(int i = 0; i < spotcount; i++){
                spots[i] = spots[i+1];
            }
        }
        spots[spotcount] = new Spot(mouseX, mouseY);
        spotcount++;
    }
    void mouseReleased(){
        spots[spotcount-1].initialY = mouseY;
        spots[spotcount-1].active = true;
    }
```

When you've entered the code for both of these files, save your sketch and run it. You should see a gray background. Clicking on the window will place up to five spots that then bounce up and down, as shown in Figure 2.12.

Let's go over this class definition in more detail. Look again at the Spot file, where the Spot class is defined. The top-level function call is typical of all class definitions:

Figure 2.12

The Bouncers sketch

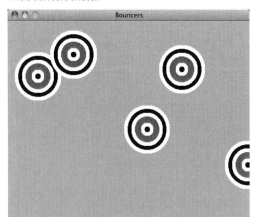

```
class Spot{
    ...
}
```

This declares a class called Spot, which you will be able to access and use later in the main sketch. You can have multiple class definitions in the same file, but in this case you'll need only one. All the code defining this class goes between the curly brackets following this function call.

The following few lines declare variables that will be used by objects of the class. Each object will have its own set of variables. These include the spot's x and y coordinates, its speed (the *rate* variable), its starting y position, and two Boolean (true/false) values. The first one, *fall*, represents whether the spot is on its way down (or, if false, on its way up). The second Boolean represents whether the spot is moving yet; the spot begins to move when the user releases the mouse button.

```
int x, y;
int rate = 1;
int initialY;
boolean fall = true;

boolean active = false;
```

The next chunk of code is the *constructor method*. This is a function (properly called a *method*) that creates a new object instance of the Spot class. It takes two arguments representing an x and a y location and passes them to the Spot object's internal variables:

```
Spot(int xpos, int ypos){
    x = xpos;
    y = ypos;
    initialY = y;
}
```

The next section of code defines a method called display() for the class. This is defined just like an ordinary function, but in fact it is a method that pertains specifically to objects of the Spot class. Each object can call its own instance of the method, as you'll see later when you look at the main code for the sketch. The internal code of this method should all be familiar. It simply draws some concentric ellipses of black, white, and red to give the bull's-eye appearance.

```
void display(){
    noStroke();
    fill(255);
    ellipse(x, y, 95, 95);
        ...

}
```

That's all there is to the class definition. Now turn your attention to the main sketch code in the Bouncers file tab. The code starts out by declaring some boilerplate variables. The height and width of the sketch window come first. Then comes *spottotal*, which determines the maximum number of spots that will be allowed on the screen at once. The next variable, *spotcount*, initializes the number of spots on the screen as 0. Finally, the line Spot[] spots; declares a variable, *spots*, which represents an array of objects of the Spot class. An array is an ordered collection of objects that can be iterated through quickly. In this case, the five spots will be stored together in this array:

```
int height = 400;
int width = 500;
int spottotal = 5;
int spotcount = 0;

Spot[] spots;
```

Next is the setup code. This is all familiar by now, and there's not much to it. The only thing new is the line where a concrete value is assigned to the *spots* variable. Although the variable was already declared, the actual array was not created. With this line, an array is created to hold five Spot objects:

```
spots = new Spot[spottotal];
```

In the draw() function, the sketch iterates through the existing spots using a for loop ranging from 0 to the value of *spotcount*:

```
for(int i = 0; i < spotcount; i++){
```

Using the *i* index for each of the spots in the array, that spot's own display() method is called to draw the spot to the screen using the following syntax:

```
spots[i].display();
```

The next block of code runs only on the condition that the spot has been put into motion by the user releasing the mouse button:

```
if(spots[i].active){
```

After this, the sketch checks each of the active spots to see whether they are falling downward or bouncing upward. If a spot is falling downward, its y coordinate is updated accordingly and its speed (*rate* variable) is incremented. If it is bouncing upward, the y value is updated and the speed is decreased:

```
if(spots[i].fall){
    spots[i].y = spots[i].y + spots[i].rate;
    spots[i].rate++;
}else{
    spots[i].y = spots[i].y - spots[i].rate;
    spots[i].rate--;
}
```

The next chunk of code determines whether the spot has hit the bottom of the window. If it has, then the *fall* variable is set to false, causing the spot to bounce back upward:

```
if(spots[i].y > height -45){
    spots[i].fall = false;
}
```

When the bouncing spot hits the original height from which it was dropped, it falls back downward (energy loss is not represented here, so it's a simple and unrealistic bounce, but the speed adjustment makes for a reasonably convincing bounce):

```
if(spots[i].y < spots[i].initialY){
    spots[i].rate = 1;
    spots[i].fall = true;
}
```

That's all there is to the draw() function. However, there are two more functions that I haven't discussed yet: mousePressed() and mouseReleased(). These are both built-in functions, and shrewd readers can probably hazard a pretty good guess about when they are called. The mousePressed() function contains code that you want to execute when the user presses the mouse button, and the mouseReleased() function contains code that you want to call when the user releases the mouse button.

Starting from the last two lines of code in the function, you can see that clicking the mouse button creates a new Spot object at the mouseX and mouseY position, puts it in the array at the *spotcount* index, and increments *spotcount*. The first chunk of code in the function is a conditional if statement that tests whether the maximum number of spots (5) has been reached. If it has, it decreases the count by 1 and pushes each element of the array down 1 (effectively deleting the oldest spot) before going on to add the new spot:

```
void mousePressed(){
    if(spotcount == spottotal){
        spotcount--;
        for(int i = 0; i < spotcount; i++){
            spots[i] = spots[i+1];
        }
    }
    spots[spotcount] = new Spot(mouseX, mouseY);
    spotcount++;
}
```

Finally, the mouseReleased() function assigns the initial y value and makes the new spot active, thus dropping the spot when the user releases the mouse button. Note that the *spotcount* value has already been incremented, so you use *spotcount*-1 to index the recently created spot.

```
void mouseReleased(){
    spots[spotcount-1].initialY = mouseY;
    spots[spotcount-1].active = true;
}
```

You can now run the sketch. If any parts of the sketch aren't clear at this point, try experimenting with values to see how that changes the behavior of the sketch. As an exercise, try writing a similar sketch in which, rather than bouncing up and down, the spots rotate in circles around a central point in the window. Between this example and the example in the previous section, that shouldn't be too hard to do.

SIMPLE AIRBRUSH

A solution to the exercise from the first section is shown here:

```
int i = -50;
void setup(){
    size(300, 300);
    "11(255, 10);
    noStroke();
    background(100);
}
void draw(){
    ellipse(mouseX, mouseY, 30, 30);

}
```

You now know the basics of programming in Processing, a very powerful prototyping environment. To do the kind of AR covered in this book, you'll also need some basic knowledge of how to create 3D content and work with it in Processing. The next chapter takes a break from programming and introduces you to the basics of modeling suitable 3D content with Blender.

CHAPTER 3

Blender Modeling and Texturing Basics

At some point, creating any kind of 3D experience usually involves building textured, potentially animated models to populate the 3D world. Interactive AR experiences are no exception. In this chapter, you'll take a break from programming to learn the basics of working with Blender, the open source 3D content creation software. With a bit of effort, you can learn to create whatever kind of 3D content you need. This chapter will get you started by walking through the creation of a 3D-modeled, textured character.

In this chapter, you'll learn about the following topics:

- Modeling with Blender

- Baking a smooth AO texture

- Creating a finished texture with GIMP

Modeling with Blender

Blender is an open source application for modeling, texturing, animation, and many other tasks in 3D content creation. Blender is free and open source and can be quickly downloaded at www.blender.org. It is a very stable, feature-rich application and, in most respects, ranks with other state-of-the-art consumer 3D applications. It's a great application for creating the sorts of 3D assets you'll use in your AR applications.

This chapter and the next one will walk you through all the steps you'll follow to create an animated character suitable for the AR environments described in the book. If you already know how to model, texture, rig, and animate with Blender, then you can skip ahead to Chapter 5, "3D Programming in Processing."

Which Version to Use?

There's just one wrinkle in using Blender for the purposes of this book, and that's deciding which version of the software to use. Blender has recently undergone some significant changes, many of which were connected with the user interface. For this reason, the previous stable version Blender 2.49b and the current stable version 2.58 (versions in between these were alpha- and beta-level test versions) are quite different. If you have no background in Blender, the differences aren't trivial.

In general, I recommend that those new to Blender simply start with learning version 2.58 at this point. However, the specific needs of this book present a dilemma. Each of the development environments in this book requires the content to be exported in specific formats in order to be used in AR applications. Among the formats you may need to export to are Collada (.dae), FBX, OBJ, Metasequoia, Ogre XML, and MD2. The problem is that much of Blender's export functionality is in the form of third-party Python scripts, some of which have not yet been fully updated for the 2.58 release. On the other hand, a few of the exporters have been improved or introduced recently and are not available for Blender 2.49.

You can open older content in a newer version of Blender, so if you create your animated model in 2.49, you can upgrade easily to Blender 2.58 when the necessary exporter becomes available, or if the necessary exporter isn't available for Blender 2.49. However, animations created in and saved for Blender 2.58 will break if you try to open them in Blender 2.49. For this reason, I'm going to show you how to do the modeling in Blender 2.49.

There's been a lot of excitement about the improved interface and event handling code introduced in the Blender 2.5 series, and I know that many new users are eager to go straight to learning Blender 2.58. Furthermore, third-party export scripts are progressing rapidly, and it's very likely that, by the time you're reading this, whatever exporter you need will exist for Blender 2.58, possibly even in a better form than the current 2.49 exporter. For this reason, you'll find an overview of key differences between Blender 2.49

and 2.58 in Appendix A, which will enable you to reconstruct the steps in this chapter in Blender 2.58.

Also, you'll find an in-depth rundown of the necessary file format and export information in Appendix B, including which development environments require which file formats and what export functionality is available for each version of Blender. You'll also find out where to get third-party export plug-ins and how to use them. If there's a specific development environment in which you're interested, you might want to check that appendix first to see what restrictions there might be on Blender versions.

Modeling a Simple Alien in Blender 2.49

For now, you'll work in Blender 2.49. If you haven't already, download and install Blender 2.49b for your system (this is a slightly bug-fixed release of 2.49) from `http://download .blender.org/release/Blender2.49b`. You can always download any version of Blender as far back as version 1.0 by following the "older versions" link from the main download page.

When you open Blender for the first time, you'll see a work area that looks like Figure 3.1. The window taking up the upper two-thirds of the work area is the 3D Viewport. Holding down the middle mouse button (MMB) and dragging your mouse over this area will rotate your view of the space. Holding down Shift+MMB will pan, and holding down Ctrl+MMB will enable you to zoom in and out.

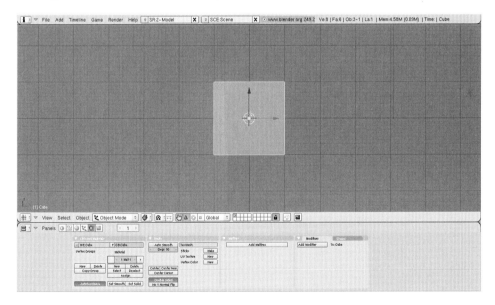

Figure 3.1

Starting Blender 2.49

A quick way to enter common view angles is to use your keyboard's numeric keypad. To use this, make sure that Num Lock is enabled on your keyboard. Pressing 1 on the numeric keypad puts you in Front view, pressing 3 puts you in Side view, and pressing 7 puts you in Top view. For the work you'll do in this chapter, this should be all you need.

If you don't have a numeric keypad or you prefer not to use it, there are several alternatives; the most straightforward is to select the view angle from the View menu as shown in Figure 3.2. As you can see, Front, Side, and Top views can all be accessed through this menu. You can also toggle between Orthographic and Perspective views using this menu. Read about user preferences in the online user manual at www.blender.org to find out about other quick alternatives to using the numeric keypad.

Figure 3.2

Entering Front view with the menu

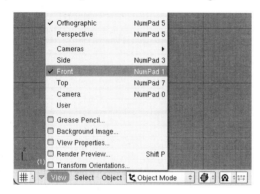

To model the alien character, follow these steps:

1. Enter Front view in the 3D Viewport. Ensure that the default cube is selected by right-clicking on it. Select Edit Mode from the drop-down menu in the header bar at the bottom of the window, as shown in Figure 3.3. When you are in Edit mode, the vertices of the mesh object are displayed and the structure of the object can be edited.

Figure 3.3

Select Edit Mode.

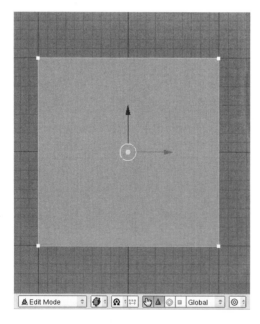

2. Press the W key to bring up the Specials menu, as shown in Figure 3.4. Select Subdivide Smooth. Accept the default value by pressing Enter. This subdivides the mesh by adding edges and vertices, while also smoothing the overall shape of the new mesh to something like a ball, as shown in Figure 3.5. This will be the basis for the torso of the character.

Figure 3.4

Subdivide Smooth

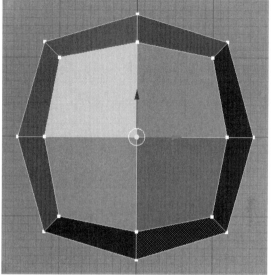

Figure 3.5

The subdivided shape

3. To begin extruding the leg, first toggle into Wireframe view by pressing the Z key. This makes it possible to see and select all of the vertices of the model. In the solid view, only vertices that are visible (that is, vertices on geometry that faces the user view) can be selected. Now, you want to be able to select both front and back faces simultaneously, so you must be in Wireframe view. First, deselect all vertices by pressing the A key. Use the Box Select tool by pressing B and then dragging your mouse to form a box around the lower-right faces of the object, as shown in Figure 3.6. Note that although only one selected face is visible, two faces are actually selected—the front face and the rear face.

4. Begin extruding the leg by pressing the E key and choosing Region from the Extrude menu, as shown in Figure 3.7. Move the extruded faces downward

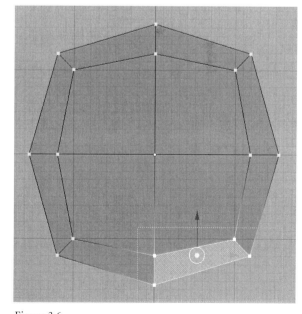

Figure 3.6

Selecting vertices to extrude

and slightly away from the center, and press the left mouse button to complete the move. Press the S button to scale the faces, scaling it down slightly with the mouse, as shown in Figure 3.8.

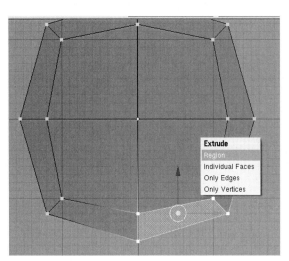

Figure 3.7
Extruding the region

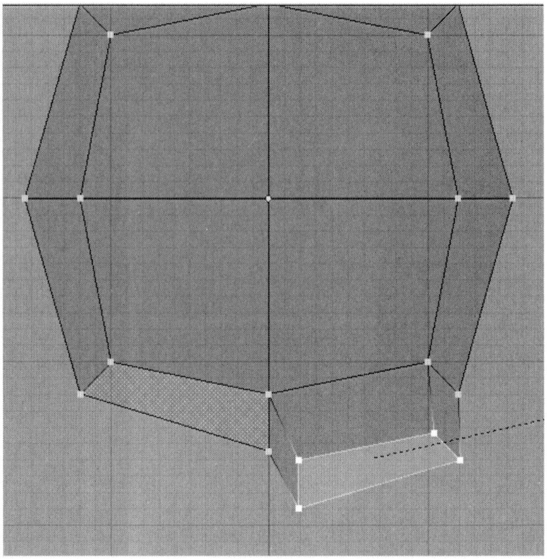

Figure 3.8
Scaling the extruded face

5. Extrude the leg again, as shown in Figure 3.9. Scale the extruded faces vertically by pressing the S key to scale, followed by the Z key to constrain the scaling to the z-axis, followed by 0; then press Enter. Scaling the vertices to a factor of 0 along the z-axis has the effect of flattening the faces downward, as you can see in Figure 3.10.

Figure 3.9
Extruding again

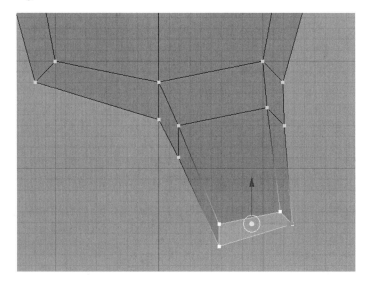

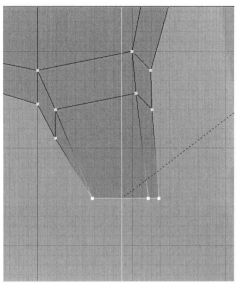

Figure 3.10

Flattening the geometry at the knee

6. For modeling symmetrical objects, such as humans and animals, it is best to model only half of the object and let Blender's Mirror modifier take care of the other half. The Mirror modifier copies the model's geometry along a chosen axis. Before adding a Mirror modifier, delete the existing left side of the model. First deselect all vertices by pressing the A key. Then box-select the vertices to delete, as shown in Figure 3.11, by pressing B and dragging your mouse to surround the vertices with the box. Delete the vertices by pressing the X key and choosing Vertices from the Erase menu, as shown in Figure 3.12. The resulting half-model should look like the one shown in Figure 3.13.

Figure 3.11

Selecting the left-side vertices

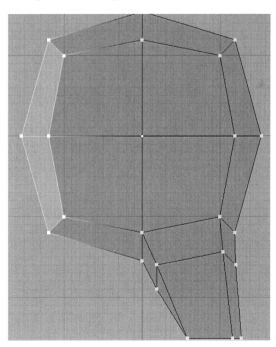

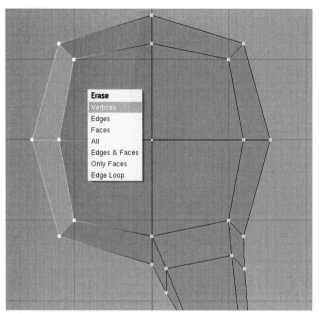

Figure 3.12
Deleting the vertices

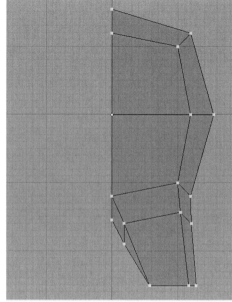

Figure 3.13
The remaining half of the model

7. Add the Mirror modifier by locating the Modifiers tab in the Editing buttons area. The buttons area is the window that covers the lower third of the workspace in the default Blender configuration, when you first open the application. You can switch to the Editing buttons area by pressing F9 over this window or by pressing the ▣ icon in the buttons area header. Add the Mirror modifier by choosing Mirror from the Add Modifier drop-down menu, as shown in Figure 3.14. The Mirror modifier will appear in the panel, as shown in Figure 3.15. Select the Do Clipping option to ensure that the left side and the right side of the model stay merged together along the centerline of the model. The model should now appear as shown in Figure 3.16. In Transparent view, by default, the mirrored side of the model shows up as a gray wireframe.

Figure 3.14
Adding a Mirror modifier

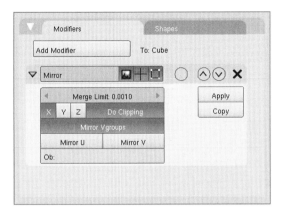

Figure 3.15
The Mirror modifier

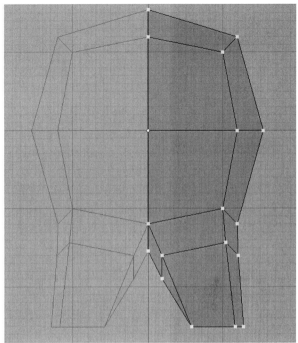

8. Before doing any further modeling, it's a good idea to resize the model along the y-axis (front to back) to make the proportions more like a humanoid figure. To do this, first enter Side view by either pressing 3 on the numeric keypad or by choosing Side from the View menu in the 3D Viewport header, as described previously. Select all of the vertices by pressing the A key. Press the S key to start scaling, followed by the Y key to constrain scaling to the y-axis. Then scale the object with your mouse, as shown in Figure 3.17.

Figure 3.16
The Mirror modified mesh

Figure 3.17
Resizing along the y-axis

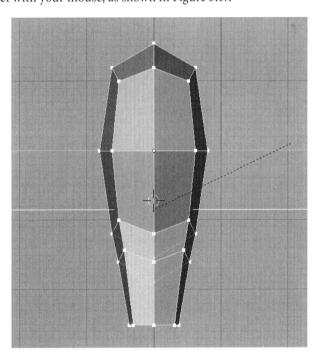

9. Return to Front view by pressing 1 on the numeric keypad (or using the View menu), and deselect all vertices by pressing the A key. Box-select the end of the leg, as shown in Figure 3.18, to continue modeling. Extrude with the E key, and scale with the S key to complete the leg, as shown in Figure 3.19.

Figure 3.18

Selecting the ends of the legs

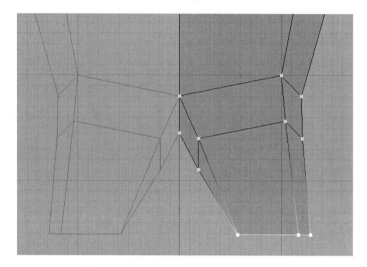

Figure 3.19

Extruding to form the lower legs

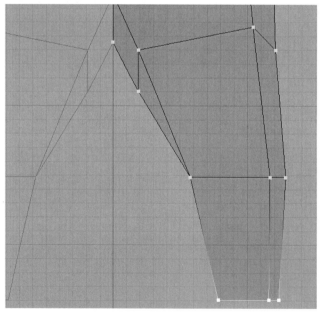

10. Now turn your attention to the upper body. Begin extruding arms by first deselecting all vertices with the A key and then box-selecting the vertices that will become the shoulder, as shown in Figure 3.20. Make a few more extrudes as shown in Figure 3.21 and Figure 3.22 to begin to form the arm.

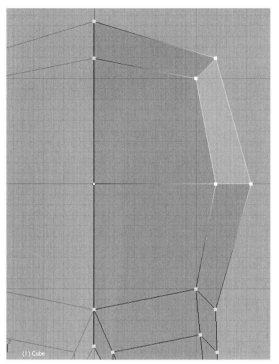

Figure 3.20

Selecting vertices to extrude for arms

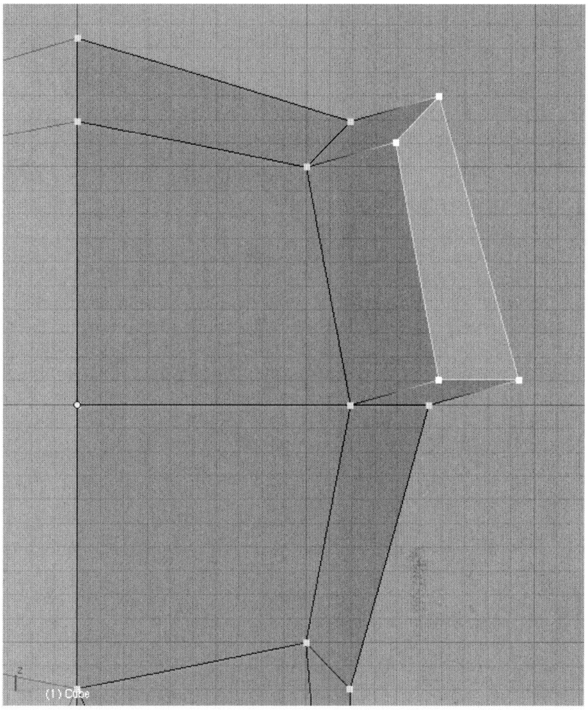

Figure 3.21

Extruding the arm

Figure 3.22

Extruding the arm again

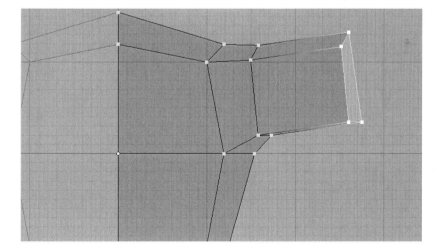

11. Before completing the arms, let's adjust the angle and shape of the arm and begin forming the shoulder. Reposition and scale the extruded end, as shown in Figure 3.23. To move the vertices, press the G key (it stands for "grab") and use your

mouse to position the elements; then press the left mouse button to complete the transformation. To rotate the vertices, press the R key (for "rotate"), rotate the element with the mouse, and then press the left mouse button to complete the transformation. To scale the selected faces, use the S key. When you have the shoulder as you like it, extrude the end of the arm twice more—once to the elbow point and once more to the end of the arm—as shown in Figure 3.24.

Figure 3.23

Forming the shoulder

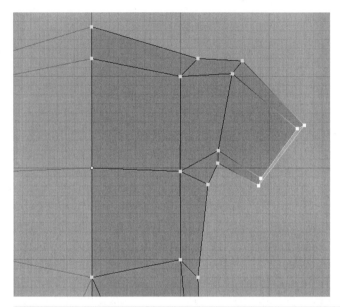

Figure 3.24

Extruding the rest of the arm

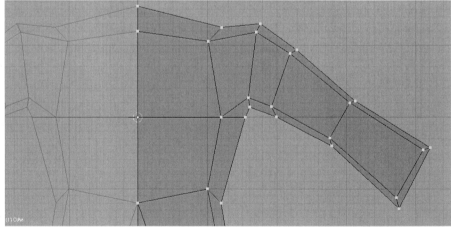

12. Next, deselect all vertices with the A key, select the top faces as shown in Figure 3.25, and extrude with the E key. Left-click to confirm the operation. Scale the extruded faces down by pressing the S key to form the neck, as shown in Figure 3.26. Extrude once more, and scale up to form the alien's head, as shown in Figure 3.27.

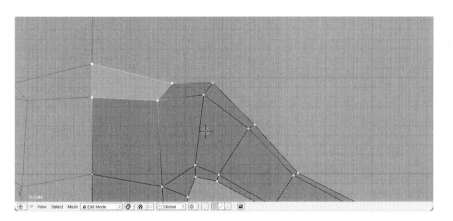

Figure 3.25
Selecting vertices
to extrude for
the head

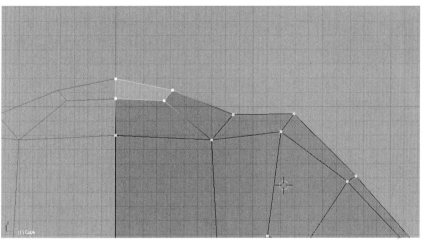

Figure 3.26
Extruding and
scaling the base
of the neck

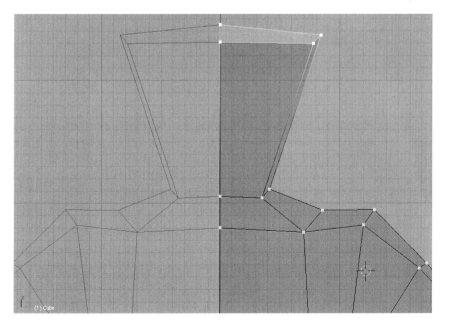

Figure 3.27
Extruding and
scaling the head

13. The mesh should now look something like Figure 3.28. Press the Z key to view in solid mode and the A key to deselect all of the vertices. The basic shape is pretty much finished, but it would be helpful to bend the knees and elbows to make posing a bit easier later. First work on the knees. To bend the knees, select the loop of edges around the knee by holding down the Alt key and pressing the right mouse button over any edge in the loop. Switch to Side view by pressing the 3 key on the numeric keypad. With the edge loop selected, press the G key (to grab) followed by the Y key to constrain the move to the y-axis. Use your mouse to move the knee loops slightly forward, as shown in Figure 3.29. Follow the same procedure to bend the elbows, as shown in Figure 3.30. You can enter Top view by pressing the numeric keypad 7 key or using the View menu.

Figure 3.28

The mesh so far

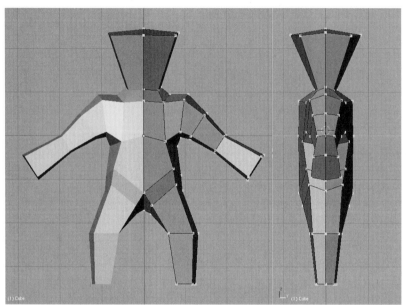

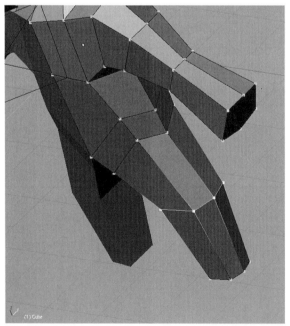

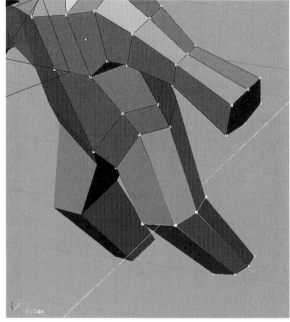

Figure 3.29

Bending the knees

Figure 3.30
Bending the elbows

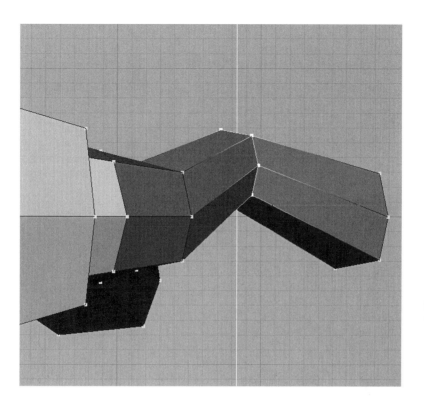

You've now finished the main modeling of the low-poly character that you'll be animating in Chapter 4, "Creating a Low-Poly Animated Character," and using for your AR experiments. Some of the environments in which you'll be working are extremely restrictive in terms of what kind of 3D processing load they can handle, and only models with a very low number of vertices can be used. Smoothing techniques like subdivision surfacing are too computationally intensive. This model's geometry should be sufficiently lightweight for most uses described in this book.

However, although it's necessary for the model to be very low-poly, it would still be nice for it to *look* a bit more refined. To do this, we'll make a second model, which has a higher poly count and uses subdivision surfacing and smooth surface rendering to generate a surface texture. We can then create a mapping from the higher-poly model to the low-poly model to generate a low-resolution surface texture for the low-poly model. The effect won't be perfect, but for the purposes of prototyping AR applications, it's a good compromise.

To do this, you must branch the model into two copies. One copy you'll leave as is, and that copy will be your low-poly model. The other copy you'll continue to refine a bit and then texture.

To create the copies, first press the Tab key to enter Object mode. Duplicate the object by pressing Shift+D then right-clicking the mouse to cancel moving the duplicated object. You now have two objects, although it's hard to see because they occupy the same space. Put the duplicated mesh out of the way where you can't see it by pressing the M key to bring up the layer dialog box, shown in Figure 3.31. Click the second little square from the left on the top row to put the duplicated mesh onto Layer 2. The Layer buttons in the 3D Viewport header should now look like this: ▓▓▓▓▓▓▓▓. Note that there are little dots in the upper-left two layers, indicating that there are objects in both Layers 1 and 2. Also note that the upper-left box is shaded, indicating that only Layer 1 is currently visible in the 3D Viewport.

Figure 3.31

Putting the duplicated mesh on a new layer

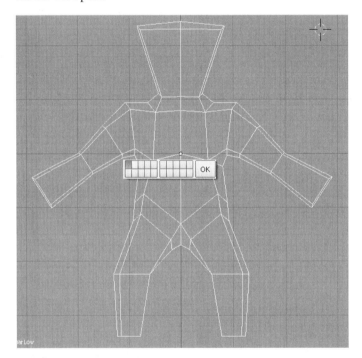

The remainder of this chapter will deal with modeling and texturing the higher-poly model. You'll go back to the other mesh in the next chapter.

To refine the model, follow these steps:

1. Select the object by right-clicking on it. Press Tab to enter Edit mode, and toggle selection on for the entire model by pressing the A key. Use the Subdivide Smooth tool to add more geometry and to round out the shape of the character. You access this tool by pressing W and choosing Subdivide Smooth, as shown in Figure 3.32. Use the default subdivision value. The result is shown in Figure 3.33. The additional geometry will help the model maintain its shape better when a Subsurf modifier is added.

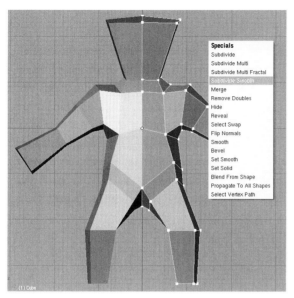

Figure 3.32

Subdividing the mesh

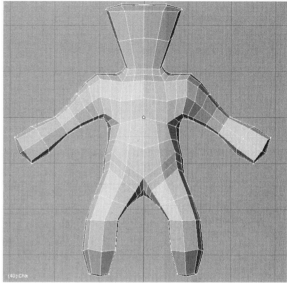

Figure 3.33

The subdivided mesh

2. In the Modifiers panel in the Editing buttons area (the same place you added the Mirror modifier), choose Subsurf from the Add Modifier drop-down menu and add a Subsurf modifier, as shown in Figure 3.34. You can leave all the default values as they are. After adding the Subsurf modifier, locate the Links and Materials panel and click Set Smooth, as shown in Figure 3.35, to set the surface lighting on the model to smooth. Set Smooth works on only selected faces, so be sure that the entire model is selected.

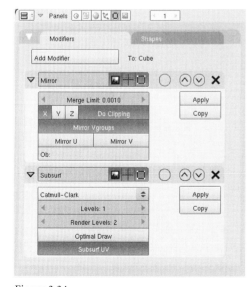

Figure 3.34

Adding a Subsurf modifier

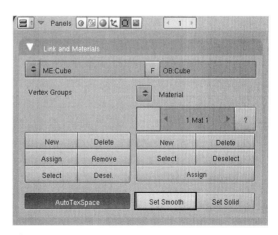

Figure 3.35

The Set Smooth button

3. Next, we'll model a belt for the character, just for the sake of adding a bit more detail. Geometric details are brought out nicely by ambient occlusion, as you'll see in the next section, so this belt will make the ambient occlusion (AO) texture a bit more interesting. To do this, you'll need to make a few cuts around the belt area. Press Ctrl+R to activate the Loop Cut tool; then hover your mouse over one of the edges perpendicular to the loops you want to cut. Roll the mouse wheel (or use the + key) to turn the single cut into a double cut. You'll see two placement lines drawn in purple to indicate where the cuts will be made, as shown (in gray scale) in Figure 3.36. Press the left mouse button to confirm the cut. The resulting new geometry should appear as shown in Figure 3.37. Flatten each of the two new loops, as shown in Figure 3.38. First press the A key to deselect all vertices, then select the loop to flatten by holding down Alt and right-clicking on any edge in the loop. Press S to scale, followed by Z to constrain to the z-axis, followed by 0 to flatten the edge, then Enter. Do this to both of the newly cut loops, which results in a straight horizontal strip of faces, as shown in Figure 3.39.

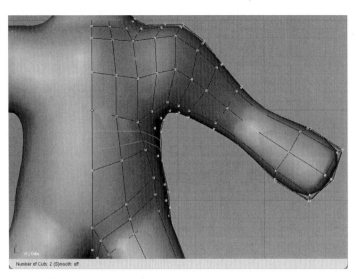

Figure 3.36

Making a double cut with the cut tool

Figure 3.37

The newly cut loops

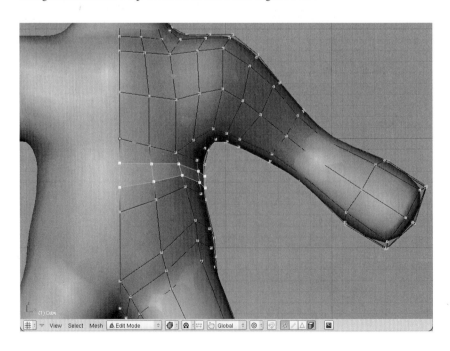

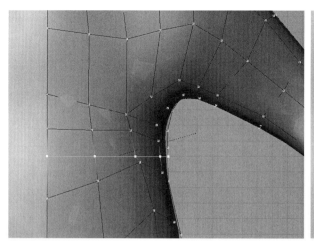 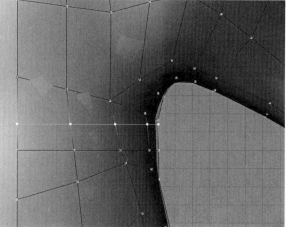

Figure 3.38
Flattening the new loops vertically

Figure 3.39
The face loop to extrude a belt

4. Select the face loop by selecting one edge loop (Alt+right-click) and then selecting the other edge loop (Shift+Alt+click). With the face loop of the belt selected, press the E key and choose Region to extrude the belt shape, as shown in Figure 3.40. Cancel out of moving the extruded vertices by pressing the right mouse button immediately after extruding. Press Alt+S and use the mouse to inflate the faces slightly, as shown in Figure 3.41. Inflate works differently from simply scaling the mesh. When a mesh

is inflated, each face expands only in the direction of its own normal. That is to say, faces move in the direction that they are facing rather than scaling in all directions.

Figure 3.40

**Extruding the
region for the belt**

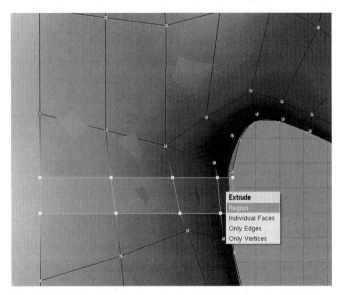

Figure 3.41

**Slightly inflating the
extruded region**

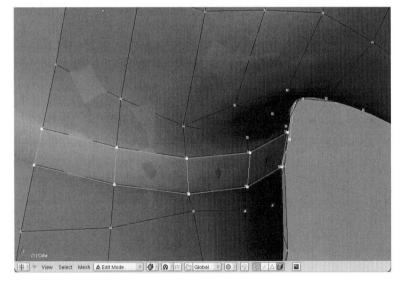

5. Extrude again with the E key, as shown in Figure 3.42, and once again cancel the transformation by pressing the right mouse button. Inflate again with Alt+S to give the belt its full thickness, as shown in Figure 3.43. Note that the Subsurf modifier has the effect of rounding off shapes. If a subsurfaced shape is too round or puffy-looking, the solution is to add more geometry to hold the shape in place. Do that by extruding one more time and inflating just slightly to give the belt a flat surface, as shown in Figure 3.44.

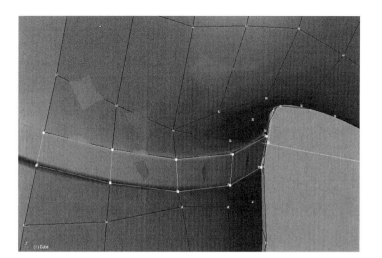

Figure 3.42
Extruding again

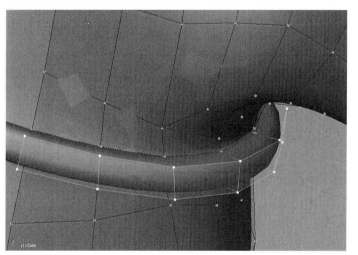

Figure 3.43
Inflating the belt region

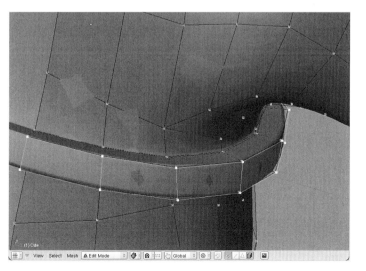

Figure 3.44
Extruding and inflating to define the belt's shape

6. You're finished with the mesh modeling, so you can now apply the Mirror modifier by switching back to Object mode with the Tab key and then pressing the Apply button shown in Figure 3.45. Applying a modifier makes the modified mesh "real" and deletes the modifier. When you apply the Mirror modifier, the resulting mesh (in Object mode) will appear as shown in Figure 3.46.

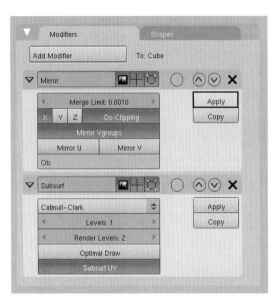

Figure 3.45

Applying the Mirror modifier

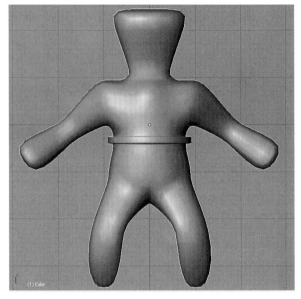

Figure 3.46

The finished mesh

Now that you've completed the modeling of the mesh, the next step is to create a texture for the mesh. The texture will include an ambient occlusion effect, which is the subject of the next section.

Baking a Smooth AO Texture

Ambient occlusion (AO) is a lighting effect that is calculated entirely from the geometry of a mesh. The idea behind AO is that, regardless of lighting conditions, certain parts of an object are likely to receive more light than others. Broad, outward-facing surfaces are usually well lit, whereas nooks, crannies, and corners tend to be occluded. Since these factors are dependent only on the shape of the mesh, AO can be calculated without reference to lights. The result is a highly diffuse (soft) lighting effect that can be used in conjunction with a wide variety of other lighting effects.

AO takes a comparatively long time to calculate and even the faster variations of AO are usually too slow to be calculated for real-time uses. In Blender, it is possible to *bake* the AO effect to a texture. This means that it can be calculated once, rendered to an image, and rendered quickly after that (image textures are quick to render).

To bake an AO effect to your model, follow these steps:

1. The first step in texturing a mesh is to UV unwrap the surface geometry of the mesh. This means to create a 2D representation of the mesh that can be made to align with an image texture. To do this, you need to indicate where the 3D surface should split in order to be flattened out. This is done by marking seams. For this model, seam marking is very simple. You'll just make a single loop seam that divides the front of the model from the back of the model. Enter Edit mode and select the loop, as shown in Figure 3.47, by holding down Alt and right-clicking on any edge in the seam. With the edge selected, mark the seam by pressing Ctrl+E to bring up the Edge menu and choosing Mark Seam, as shown in Figure 3.48. The seam will show up highlighted in orange.

2. To perform UV unwrapping on a model, at least one UV texture slot must be created for the model. Add a UV texture slot to the model by clicking the New button to the right of the UV Texture label in the Mesh panel of the Editing buttons, as shown in Figure 3.49. The UV Texture slot will be displayed on the same panel, as shown in Figure 3.50.

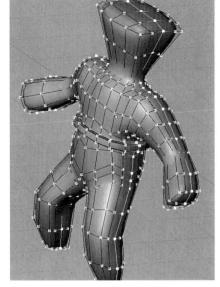

Figure 3.47

Selecting the edge loop around the character

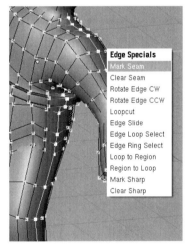

Figure 3.48

Marking the seam

Figure 3.49

Adding a new UV texture

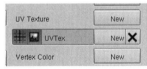

Figure 3.50

The new UV texture slot

3. To open a UV/Image editor when in the default desktop configuration, move your mouse over the horizontal border of the 3D Viewport, right-click, and choose Split Area, as shown in Figure 3.51. In the newly created window, choose UV/Image Editor from the Window Type menu in the corner of the header, as shown in Figure 3.52.

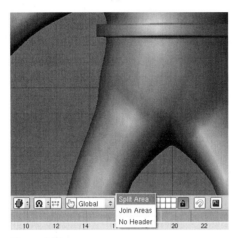

Figure 3.51

Splitting the 3D View

Figure 3.52

Switching to a UV/Image Editor window type

4. Be sure that you are in Edit mode and the entire model is selected. (Use the A key to toggle selection of all vertices.) Put your mouse over the UV/Image editor, and press the E key to unwrap the mesh. Click Unwrap in the pop-up menu. The mesh should unwrap into two islands representing the front and the back of the mesh, as shown in Figure 3.53. The layout of the unwrapping may be different than shown here, but it should be roughly similar. If the unwrapping looks drastically different, it may be that your model's topology is different from what was described in the previous section. Go back and fix your model if necessary.

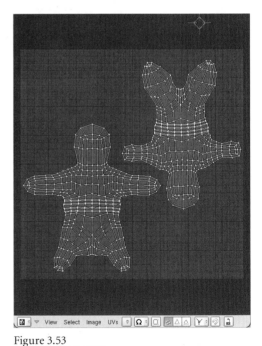

Figure 3.53

The UV unwrapping in the UV/Image editor

5. From the Image menu in the UV/Image editor header, select New, as shown in Figure 3.54. A dialog box will pop up where you can enter the settings for the image. Enter **512** for the Width and the Height fields; choose UV Test Grid, as shown in Figure 3.55; and click OK. This will generate an image texture and display it in the UV/Image editor, as shown in Figure 3.56. You can see how the texture maps onto your 3D object by choosing Textured in the Draw Type drop-down menu in the header of the 3D Viewport, as shown in Figure 3.57. When you do this, the mesh will be drawn as shown in Figure 3.58, and you can see exactly how the image texture is applied to the surface.

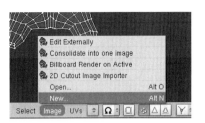

Figure 3.54

Creating a new image

Figure 3.55

New Image settings

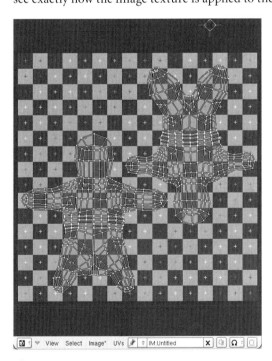

Figure 3.56

The test grid texture

Figure 3.57

Selecting textured draw type

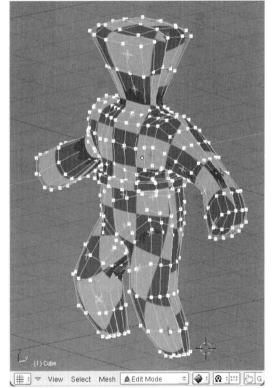

Figure 3.58

Mesh displayed in textured draw type

6. Enter the World buttons subcontext of the Shading buttons context by either clicking on the ⬤ icon followed by the ◉ icon, or by pressing the F5 key four times. In the Amb Occ tab, click the Ambient Occlusion button to activate AO, as shown in Figure 3.59. You can leave all the default settings as they are.

Figure 3.59
Turning on ambient occlusion

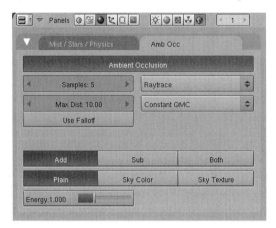

7. Navigate to the Render subcontext of the Scene buttons context by clicking on the 🖼 icon followed by the 🖼 icon, or by pressing F10. In the Bake panel, choose Ambient Occlusion and Normalized, as shown in Figure 3.60. Baking textures is closely analogous to rendering, except that it "renders" to a texture on the surface of the object in 3D space rather than to a final image of the scene. When only Ambient Occlusion is selected, only the AO values are rendered to that texture. The Normalized option sets the value of the brightest part of the texture to white and the darkest part of the texture to black, so that the final texture ranges across the full grayscale spectrum rather than just between two middling grays. Click the Bake button to bake the texture, and wait for the AO texture to render completely. The image in the UV/Image editor will be redrawn to look something like Figure 3.61. When the baking ends, save this image as a PNG file from the Image menu in the header. Don't forget where you've saved this file. Tab into Object mode. Your 3D object should look something like Figure 3.62. You should save your file (with the extension .blend) by choosing File → Save if you haven't done so already.

Figure 3.60
Baking AO to the texture

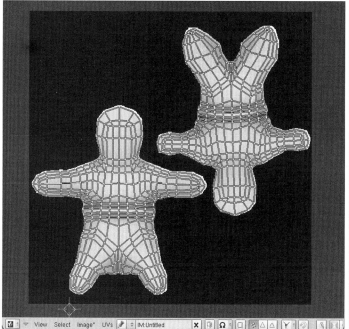

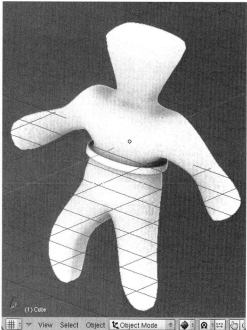

Figure 3.61

The baked AO texture

Figure 3.62

The model with AO baked on

Now you've got a UV-mapped 3D object with a nicely rendered ambient occlusion texture. In the next section, you'll step out of Blender briefly to complete the texturing with the GIMP 2D image editing application.

Creating a Finished Texture with GIMP

As you can see, UV texturing is all about the mapping between a 2D texture and a 3D object. Blender has some nice tools for editing these textures directly. (See the online manual for the Texture Paint functionality for more information on this.) In general, however, you're better off using a dedicated 2D image editor for your texture work. The commercial standard application for this is Photoshop, and the open source standard is GIMP. For the purposes of 3D texture work, I don't know of any real advantages one has over the other, so the free GIMP is the obvious choice for me. Before you work through this section, you will need to download and install GIMP from `www.gimp.org`. There are ports of GIMP available for all major operating systems.

Before you fire up GIMP, there's one more thing you need to do in Blender. In the UV/Image editor header, from the UVs menu, select Scripts → Save UV Face Layout, as shown in Figure 3.63. The default values should be fine, so leave them as they are. This will open a file browser for you to choose where you wish to save the exported image. By default, it will export a Targa file showing the UV layout. Make a note of where you save this file. The file will be named automatically after the name of your blend file and the name of the mesh object, separated by an underscore. It will be saved to a TGA file, which can be opened by GIMP. Note that TGA files cannot typically be viewed as images in the Windows preview.

Figure 3.63

**Saving the
UV face layout**

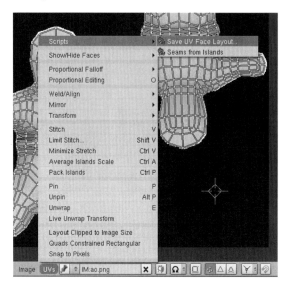

Once you've got that file saved, you're ready to start GIMP and follow these steps to create the finished texture for your model:

1. Open the AO texture file you saved using GIMP. Make sure that the layers dialog box is visible by selecting Windows → Dockable Dialogs → Layers. The GIMP interface should look something like Figure 3.64. The default name for the first layer is Background, so this is the name of the layer that contains the AO texture image for now.

Figure 3.64

**Opening the
AO texture in GIMP**

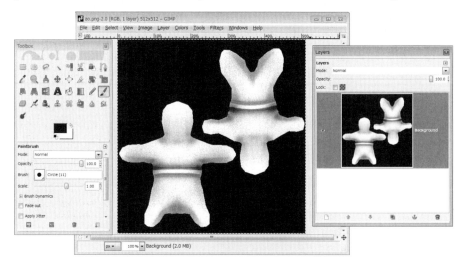

2. Open the image file with the UV face layout as a layer. Do so by pressing Ctrl+Alt+O or by choosing Open As Layers from the File menu, as shown in Figure 3.65. The GIMP file will now appear as shown in Figure 3.66, with the two images stacked one on top of the other in the Layers dialog window.

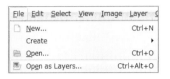

Figure 3.65

Opening a file as a layer in GIMP

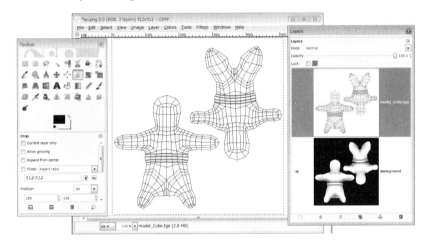

Figure 3.66

The two layers in Normal layer mode

By default, layers are displayed in Normal layer mode, which in this case means that the top layer is drawn as an opaque image over the lower layer. We want to use the UV face layout as a reference while working on other layers, so it's necessary to use a different layer mode that leaves the lower layers visible. Left-click on the top layer (the UV face layout) to select it; then choose Divide from the Mode drop-down menu. This will cause the black lines of the layer to show up drawn in white and the white areas of the layer to be transparent so that the lower layer is visible, as you can see in Figure 3.67.

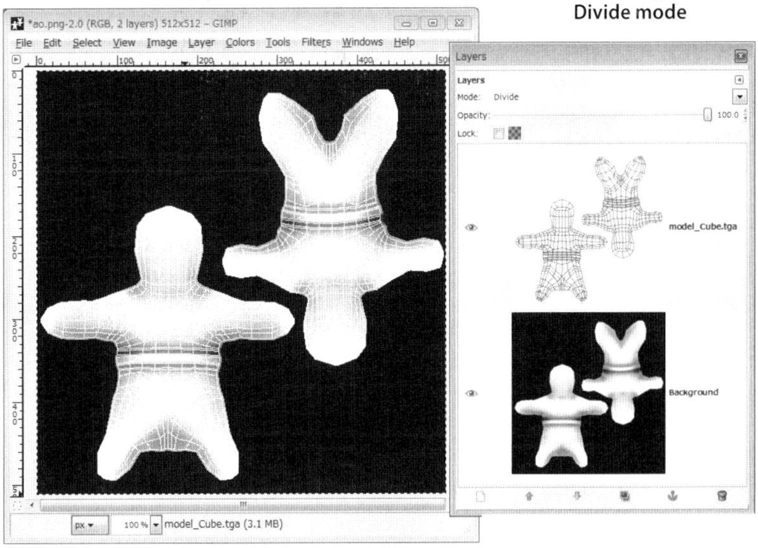

Figure 3.67

The UV layer in Divide mode

3. You'll do the coloring for the texture on still another layer. To create a new layer, click the icon indicated in Figure 3.68. In the New Layer dialog box, give the layer the name **Color**, as shown

in Figure 3.69. Check White for the Layer Fill Type and then click OK. The new layer will appear above whatever layer had been selected when you added it. Using your mouse, drag the new layer to the bottom, as shown in Figure 3.70.

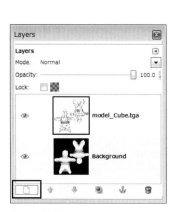

Figure 3.68 _____
Adding a new layer

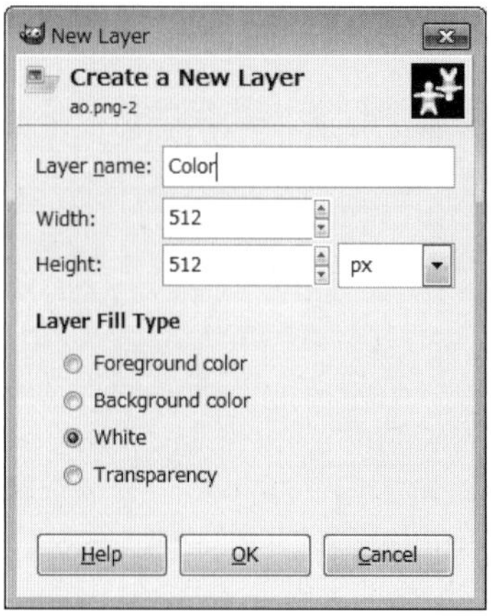

Figure 3.69 _____
The New Layer dialog box

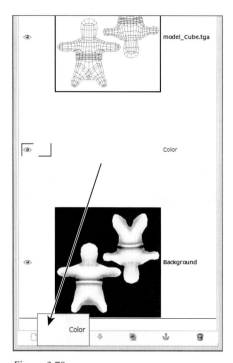

Figure 3.70 _____
Dragging the new layer to the bottom

4. Now the Color layer is obscured behind the AO texture layer (still called Background). Select the AO texture layer and change the mode to Multiply, as shown in Figure 3.71. You won't notice any difference in the way the image is displayed at first because the bottom layer is all white. However, when you start adding color, the effect of the Multiply layer mode will be clear.

5. Select the Color layer and choose the Bucket Fill tool from the Toolbox, as shown in Figure 3.72. Click the Foreground Color button shown in Figure 3.73 to open the Color Picker dialog box shown in Figure 3.74. Set the foreground color to solid green (or whatever color you like for your alien). Then simply click anywhere on the image to bucket-fill the layer with this color, as shown in Figure 3.75 (in gray scale, of course).

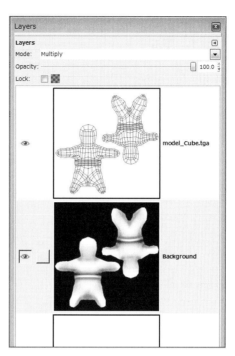

Figure 3.71

Setting the AO (Background) layer to Multiply mode

Figure 3.72

The Bucket Fill tool

Figure 3.73

The Foreground Color button

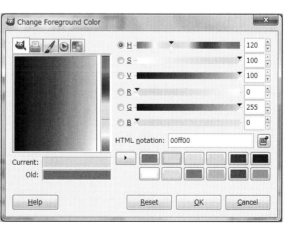

Figure 3.74

The Color Picker dialog box

Figure 3.75

Bucket-filling the layer with a solid color

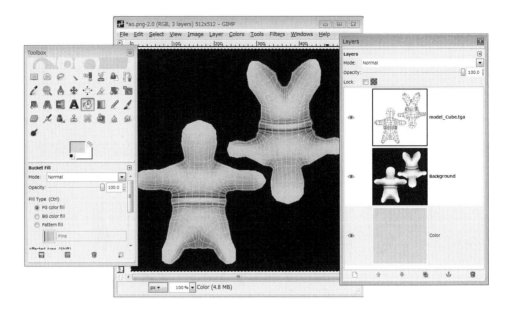

Figure 3.75

Bucket-filling the layer with a solid color

6. Select the Lasso tool on the Toolbox, as shown in Figure 3.76. Using a series of mouse clicks, surround the belt area with the Lasso tool, as shown in Figure 3.77. When you've closed the lassoed area around the belt by double-clicking, return to the Bucket Fill tool, select a different foreground color (I'm using solid yellow), and do a bucket fill into the belt area, as shown in Figure 3.78. After this, you can add whatever other decorative colored parts you like. I've added a pair of white eyes.

Figure 3.76

Selecting the Lasso tool

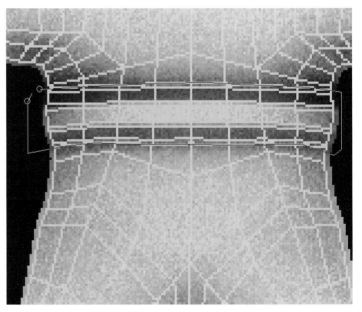

Figure 3.77

Enclosing the belt area with the Lasso tool

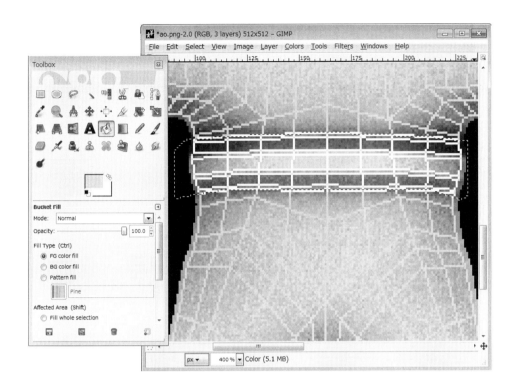

Figure 3.78

Filling the belt with a solid color

7. Before you export the final image, you need to make the UV face layout layer invisible. Layer visibility is toggled on and off using the eye-shaped icon to the left of the thumbnail in the Layers dialog box. Toggle the UV layer off, as shown in Figure 3.79. Notice that I've renamed the layers UV, AO, and Color to be more intuitive. When you have set the UV layer to be invisible, simply save the file as a PNG file by choosing File → Save As; then name the file **texture.tif**. Choose Merge Visible Layers, and leave the defaults for the second dialog box that comes up. This will automatically export the image to PNG format. Note that layers will be lost in this saved image. If you plan to go back and do more editing with separated layers, save the file as an XCF file, which is GIMP's native file format. Your finished PNG image file will look something like Figure 3.80.

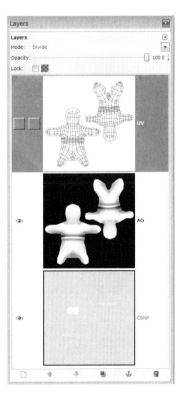

Figure 3.79

Setting the UV layer to be invisible

Figure 3.80

**The final
color texture**

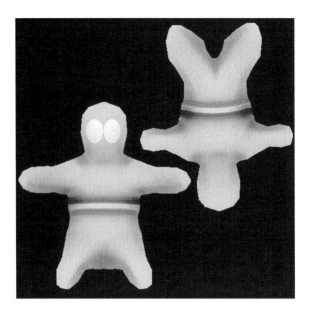

8. Now let's return to Blender. You want to use the newly created PNG file you just
   exported from GIMP as the object's texture, rather than the previously baked AO
   texture. To do this, simply choose Replace from the Image menu in the UV/Image
   editor header, as shown in Figure 3.81. This will open a file browser. Navigate to the
   texture file you just created in GIMP and select it. The new texture will immediately
   replace the old one in the model, as shown in Figure 3.82.

Figure 3.81

**Replacing the
active texture**

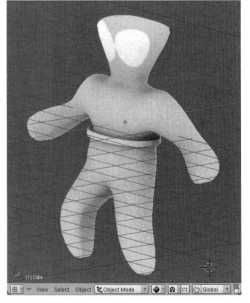

Figure 3.82

The textured model

9. Next, you'll assign the model a material. Doing so will enable it to be rendered and its texture to be baked onto the low-poly model later. A material is also necessary in some cases for exporting a textured mesh. To add a material, first enter the Material buttons subcontext of the Shading buttons context by clicking the 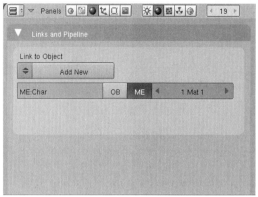 icon followed by the red ⬤ icon, or by pressing F5. If there is no material already associated with the object, add a new material by clicking Add New in the Links And Pipeline panel, as shown in Figure 3.83.

Figure 3.83
Adding a material

10. In the Texture panel of the Material buttons, click Add New to assign a texture to the material, as shown in Figure 3.84. A texture slot labeled Tex will be created automatically. Enter the Texture subcontext of the Shading buttons by clicking the 🔲 icon. Select Image from the Texture Type drop-down menu in the Texture panel, shown in Figure 3.85.

Figure 3.84
Adding a texture to the material

Figure 3.85
Selecting the texture type

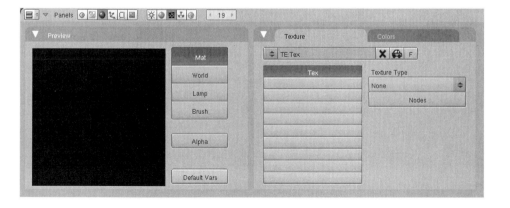

11. Load the `texture.tif` file in the field on the Image panel of the texture, as shown in Figure 3.86. Aside from this, you can leave the default values for the rest of the texture settings as shown in the figure. Return to the Material buttons, and set the options for the material as shown in Figure 3.87. Set the material to Shadeless in the Material tab of the Material panel and set the Map Input value to UV, as indicated in that figure.

Figure 3.86

Settings for the Image texture

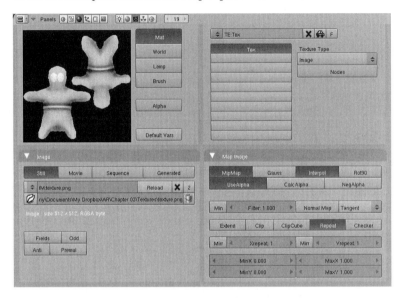

Figure 3.87

Settings for the textured material

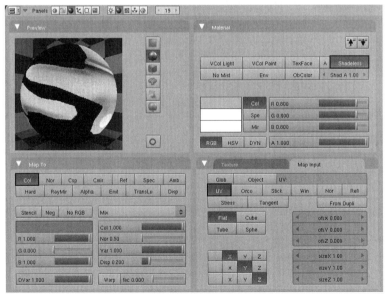

When you've finished this, save your file and take a break. The higher-poly model is finished. In the next chapter, you'll turn your attention back to the low-poly model to prepare it for use as an animated element in an AR application.

CHAPTER 4

Creating a Low-Poly Animated Character

Rigging and animating in Blender are important skills to have if you want to add animated 3D objects to your AR applications. In this chapter, you'll learn how to set up a minimal character rig and walk cycle. However, many of the programming environments you'll deal with are restrictive in terms of the size and complexity of 3D assets. For this reason, before you begin animating, you'll see how to create a simplified version of the model you made in Chapter 3, "Blender Modeling and Texturing Basics," that is suitable for animating in low-memory situations.

In this chapter, you'll learn about the following topics:

- Texturing your low-poly alien
- Rigging the model
- Keying a simple walk cycle

Texturing Your Low-Poly Alien

In Chapter 3, you created a finished, fairly refined (albeit simple) character model complete with subsurfacing, some detailed modeling (the belt), and a nice texture including baked ambient occlusion. Unfortunately, that's a bit more model than the Processing 3D environment can handle. Subdivision surfaces are not supported in Processing, and the number of vertices of that model (especially if you applied the Subsurf modifier) can bring Processing to its knees, particularly with the overhead required by the AR processing. Resources are also precious on mobile platforms such as Android (which you'll take a look at in Chapter 10, "Setting up NyARToolkit for Android")—and this isn't even with animation. As you'll see in Chapter 5, "3D Programming in Processing," the approach you'll take to 3D animation in Processing 3D involves importing a separate 3D model file for each frame of the animation. A model with too many vertices will cause real problems.

Fortunately, you've already modeled a low-poly version of your character, which should be sufficiently lightweight to be used in the various programming environments described in this book. For most of the examples in the book, I've used a super low-poly version of my own Shootin' Annie character. The super-low-poly model was based on a higher-poly model, as you can see in Figure 4.1. The texture of the low-poly model is also lower resolution and, as you can see, it's clearly suitable only for small displays. The low-resolution texture was created (almost) automatically by baking the texture straight from the higher-poly model onto the low-poly model. In this chapter, you'll do the same thing with the models you created in Chapter 3, before keying a quick-and-dirty walk cycle.

Figure 4.1

The original Shootin' Annie model and the super-low-poly version

To texture your low-poly alien character, follow these steps; remember to save your work frequently:

1. If you don't have your blend file from Chapter 3 open already, open it now. In the 3D Viewport, switch to the layer where you placed your low-poly model using the layer buttons in the header (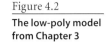). You should see only the low-poly model in the 3D Viewport, as shown in Figure 4.2. Right-click the object, and then go to the Mirror modifier on the object and click Apply, as shown in Figure 4.3.

2. With the model selected, enter Edit mode by pressing the Tab key or by choosing Edit mode from the drop-down menu in the 3D Viewport header. Just as you did with the higher-poly model in Chapter 3, select the edge around the model separating the front of the model from the rear of the model by Alt+right-clicking on an edge in the loop. Press Ctrl+E, and choose Mark Seam from the Edge Specials menu, as shown in Figure 4.4.

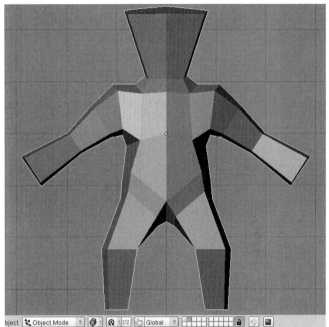

Figure 4.2

The low-poly model from Chapter 3

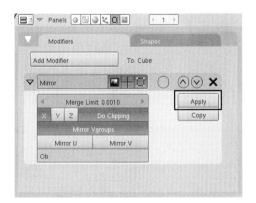

Figure 4.3

Applying the Mirror modifier

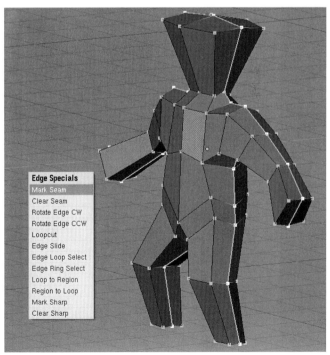

Figure 4.4

Marking a seam

3. Press the A key to select the entire model. Add a UV texture as shown in Figure 4.5. In the UV/Image editor, unwrap the mesh by pressing E just as you did with the higher-poly model in Chapter 3. Create a new image by choosing New from the Image drop-down in the UV/Image editor header. Set the values for the new image in the dialog box as shown in Figure 4.6. Be sure to click UV Test Grid. Note that the dimensions are 256×256, which is lower resolution than the image you used to texture the higher-poly model. The new image should appear in the UV/Image editor and on the model, as shown in Figure 4.7.

Figure 4.5

Adding a UV texture

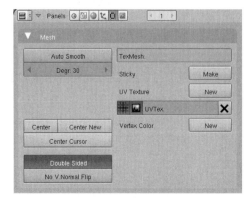

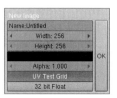

Figure 4.6

Settings for the new image

Figure 4.7

Adding a new image

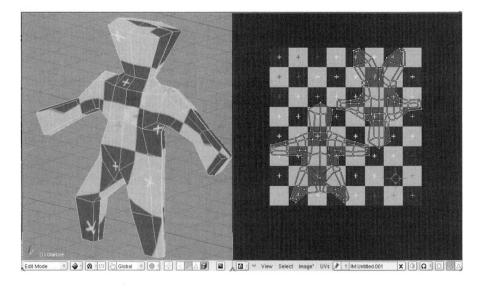

4. Hold down the Shift key and click on the Layer 1 button in the header to display the contents of the layers that contain both the higher- and low-poly models, as shown in Figure 4.8. First select the higher-poly mesh, and then hold down the Shift key and select the low-poly mesh. This makes the low-poly mesh the *active* object (the last single selected object is always the active object).

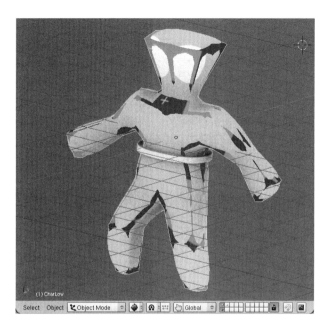

Figure 4.8

Looking at both models at once

5. On the Bake panel of the Render buttons, select Textures and Selected To Active, as shown in Figure 4.9; then click Bake. As the option name suggests, doing so redraws the texture from the selected object onto the texture on the active object, trying to map one texture to the other as directly as possible. The resulting texture on the low-poly model (after the higher-poly model has once again been put away on an unseen layer) is shown in Figure 4.10.

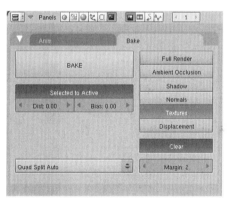

Figure 4.9

Baking textures from Selected To Active

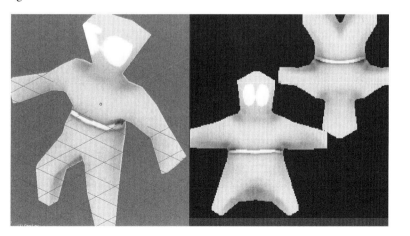

Figure 4.10

The low-poly model textured

As you can see, the resulting textured model is far from a perfect re-creation of the higher-poly textured model. But the smoothed AO effect is present, and the detail of the belt is reasonably mapped to the flat geometry in a convincing manner. For a model that uses minimal resources, this is a decent alternative to the higher-poly model. Follow the same steps to add a textured material to this model as you did at the end of Chapter 3 to add a textured material to the higher-poly model.

Figure 4.11 shows material settings for the new material for the low-poly model, and Figure 4.12 shows texture settings with the newly baked texture UV-mapped to the new material. For details on how to set up the material and texture, review Chapter 3.

Figure 4.11

Material settings for the low-poly model

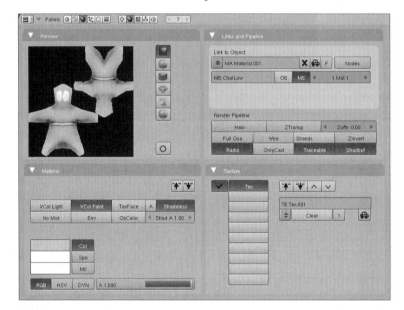

Figure 4.12

Texture settings for the low-poly model

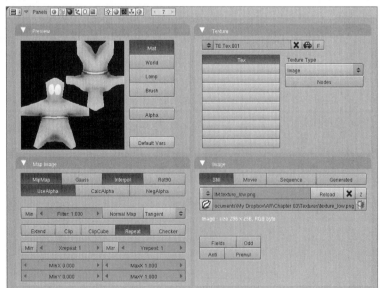

Rigging the Model

The typical way to do character animation in Blender is to create an *armature,* which is then used to deform the mesh into desired poses. An armature is analogous to the skeleton of the character, and in fact, its components are called *bones*. Armature bones are rigid and can be connected at joints. Each bone has some of influence on certain vertices in the mesh, and depending on these levels of influence, the vertices move when the bone is moved for posing.

Advanced armature setups, or *rigs*, can be complex. They can be designed to enable extremely versatile posing, or constrained to allow only realistic poses. For high-quality rigs, a great deal of attention is paid to the interface of the rig for the animator. Such a rig can have hundreds of bones serving a wide variety of functions, some of which deform the mesh directly, some of which are visible to the animator, and some of which perform various other functions.

For the purposes of this book, however, the kind of rig we want is almost the opposite of this situation. The rig we use here should be simple and minimal. It should be capable of producing the brief animation we'll be exporting, and it needn't be capable of much more than that, making it an ideal exercise for first-time riggers. To rig the model with such an armature, follow these steps:

1. In Object mode, add a new Armature object by pressing Shift+A and choosing Add → Armature, as shown in Figure 4.13. The new object will appear in the 3D Viewport at the location of the 3D cursor. To place it into the center of the space, press Alt+G and click Clear Location in the dialog box immediately after adding the object (don't worry if you can't see the Armature object at this point).

2. If you don't see the Armature object, it's probably because it is positioned inside the mesh. To be able to see the armature, click the Editing button and in the Armature panel select X-Ray under Editing Options, as shown in Figure 4.14. In the same panel, select X-Axis Mirror to enable automatic symmetrical editing for the armature. The first bone of the armature should now be visible, as shown in Figure 4.15.

Figure 4.13

Adding an Armature object

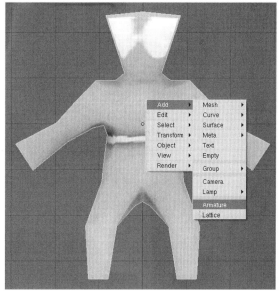

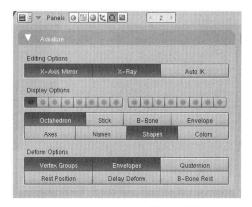

Figure 4.14

Armature settings

Figure 4.15

**The mesh and
the armature**

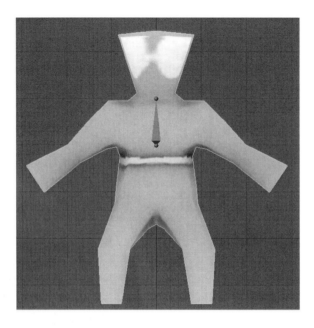

3. Make sure the armature is selected by right-clicking on it. With the mouse over the
   3D Viewport, press Tab to enter Edit mode (or choose Edit mode from the drop-
   down menu in the 3D Viewport header). Press Shift+E to do a mirrored extrude, and
   draw the tips of the extruded bones to the shoulder area of the character, as shown
   in Figure 4.16. Press E to do an ordinary extrude from the shoulder to the elbow area
   (all child bones of the originally mirror-extruded bones will be mirror-edited automatically). Press E once more to extrude the forearms from the elbows to create the
   arms, as shown in Figure 4.17.

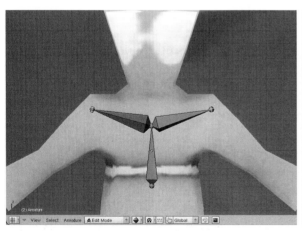

Figure 4.16

Mirror-extruding shoulders

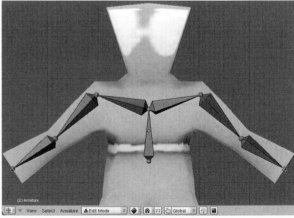

Figure 4.17

Extruding arms

4. Right-click on the tip of the first bone in the armature. Press the E key followed by the Z key to extrude a bone directly upward to the base of the head, and then press the E key again, followed by the Z key again, to extrude another bone to the top of the head, as shown in Figure 4.18.

5. Right-click on the base (the small sphere at the thick end) of the first bone; then press Shift+E to do a mirrored extrude to extrude the hips, as shown in Figure 4.19. Because you extruded these bones from the base of the first bone rather than from the tip, they are not automatically parented to the first bone. It would be better to have them parented to this bone so that the whole armature will move when the first bone moves. Select the hip bone you just extruded by right-clicking on the middle of the bone, and go to the Armature Bones panel in the Editing buttons area. In the drop-down menu to the right of the Child Of label, choose Bone, as shown in Figure 4.20. Then select the tip of the hip bone again and use the E key to continue to extrude the rest of the legs, as shown in Figure 4.21.

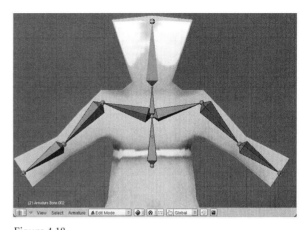

Figure 4.18
Extruding the neck and head

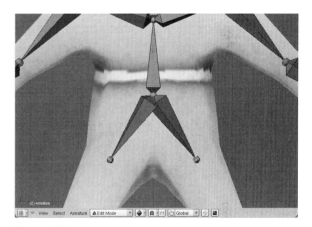

Figure 4.19
Extruding the hips

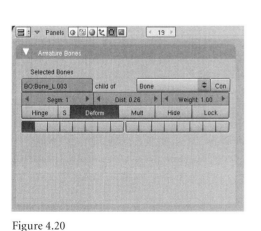

Figure 4.20
Parenting the hip bone to the back bone

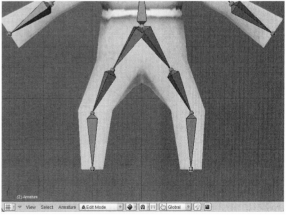

Figure 4.21
Extruding legs

6. Because the armature was modeled entirely in Front view, it is flat. The character mesh is not perfectly flat; rather, it is bent at the arms and knees. To make the armature better conform to the character's shape, first select the elbow joint by clicking on the small sphere between the upper and lower bones. To get a better viewing angle, either press 3 on the numeric keypad or rotate the view with the middle mouse button so that you can see the model from the side. Press G followed by Y and move the elbow joint back to match the shape of the mesh, as shown in Figure 4.22. Press the left mouse button to confirm the change. Do the same in the opposite direction for the knees, as shown in Figure 4.23.

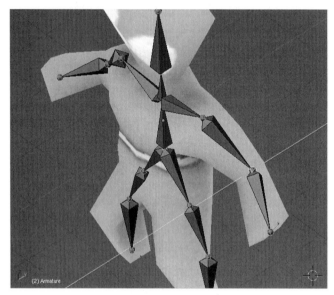

Figure 4.22

Moving the elbows back

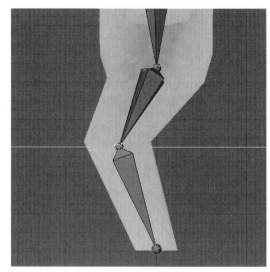

Figure 4.23

Moving the knees forward

7. Before you attach the armature to the mesh and begin animating, there's one more step you should always take. Select all of the bones by pressing the A key and press Ctrl+N to recalculate the bone roll angles. Choose Clear Roll (Z-Axis Up), as shown in Figure 4.24. Doing so will fix bone roll inconsistencies that often arise during armature editing. If you don't recalculate the bone roll angles, you can find your animations going haywire, so this is an important step.

8. Press Tab to enter Object mode. Right-click on the Mesh object to select it; then hold down the Shift key and right-click on the Armature object. Press Ctrl+P to bring up the Make Parent To menu and choose Armature, as shown in Figure 4.25. Next you'll see the Create Vertex Groups menu. Choose Create From Bone Heat, as shown in Figure 4.26. This automatically associates vertices in the mesh to the appropriate bones. In a model like the alien here, you shouldn't need to do any further modification of the bone influences.

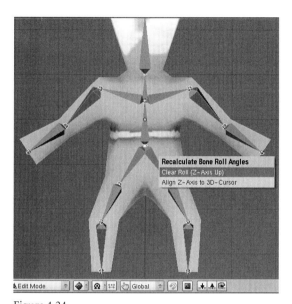

Figure 4.24
Recalculating bone roll angles

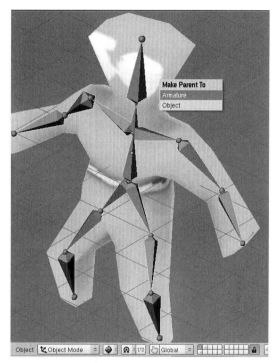

Figure 4.25
Parenting the mesh to the armature

The model is now fully rigged. You can test it to make sure the mesh is deforming nicely by posing the armature. To do so, select the Armature object and choose Pose Mode from the Mode drop-down menu in the 3D Viewport header, as shown in Figure 4.27. You can now select and rotate bones as though you were posing a doll or puppet, and the mesh should deform accordingly.

Figure 4.26
Creating vertex groups from bone heat

Figure 4.27
Entering Pose mode

Keying a Simple Walk Cycle

Animation in Blender is a matter of placing 3D elements, *keying* their placement to fix it at a particular point on the timeline, and then changing their placement and keying it differently at a different point in time. For character animation, the 3D elements used are typically armature bones. You pose the armature, key the pose for the point in time, and then key other poses at different points in time.

There are several editors in Blender that are used in various ways to look at animation values over time. For simple animations like the one you'll be doing in this section, the Action editor is the main editor you will use.

To animate a simple walk cycle using the Action editor, follow these steps:

Figure 4.28

Opening an Action editor

1. Open an Action editor window. You can do this in the same window area where you previously were using the UV/Image editor, because you will no longer need the UV/Image editor. Choose Action Editor from the Window Type menu in the left corner of the header, as shown in Figure 4.28. Select Add New from the drop-down menu shown in Figure 4.29. Give the new action a meaningful name by entering **Walk** in the AC field on the Action editor, as shown in Figure 4.30.

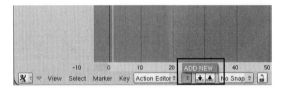

Figure 4.29

Adding a new action

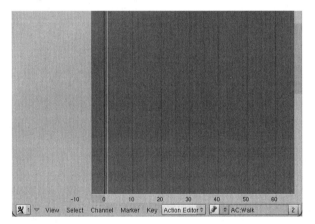

Figure 4.30

The Action editor window

2. Split the Action editor window by right-clicking over the window's vertical border and choosing Split Area, as shown in Figure 4.31. Make the second window a low, horizontal shape, and choose Timeline from the Window Type menu, as shown in Figure 4.32. In the Timeline window, enter **20** in the End field to set the animation to loop after 20 frames. Enter **1** in the field to the right to set the current frame to 1, as shown in Figure 4.33.

Figure 4.31

Splitting the Action editor

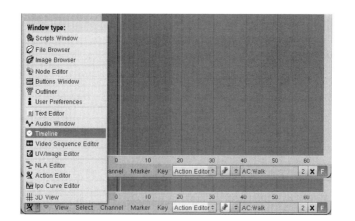

Figure 4.32
Opening a Timeline

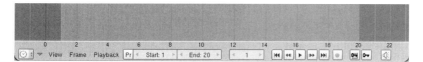

Figure 4.33
A Timeline window

3. With the armature still in Pose mode, select the upper bone of the left leg and press the R key to rotate it, followed by the X key to constrain the rotation to the global x-axis. With the mouse, rotate the leg forward, as shown in Figure 4.34, and then confirm the rotation with the left mouse button. Enter Side view by pressing 3 on the numeric keypad. Select the right leg and rotate it to the rear, as shown in Figure 4.35.

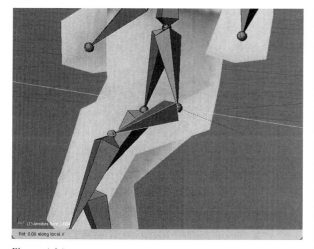

Figure 4.34
Rotating the left leg forward

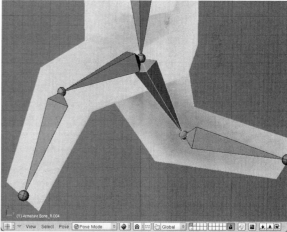

Figure 4.35
Rotating the right leg back

4. Do the same, but in reverse, with the arms. Select the left arm and rotate it back around the x-axis, as shown in Figure 4.36 (press the R key followed by the X key, and then press the left mouse button to confirm). Rotate the right arm forward in the same manner, as shown in Figure 4.37.

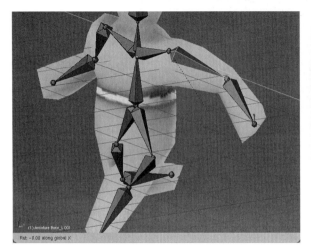

Figure 4.36
Rotating the left arm back

Figure 4.37
Rotating the right arm forward

5. Select each of the four bones you just posed by holding down the Shift key and right-clicking on each one. Press the I key to bring up the Insert Key menu and key the bones' location and rotation by choosing the LocRot entry in the menu, as shown in Figure 4.38. You should see channels for each bone appear in the Action editor with keys on frame 1 represented by yellow diamonds, as shown in Figure 4.39.

Figure 4.38
Keying the four bones

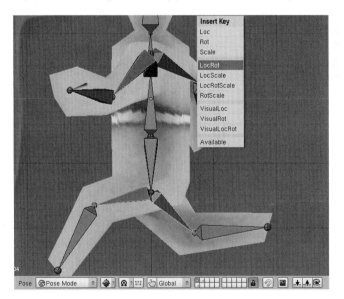

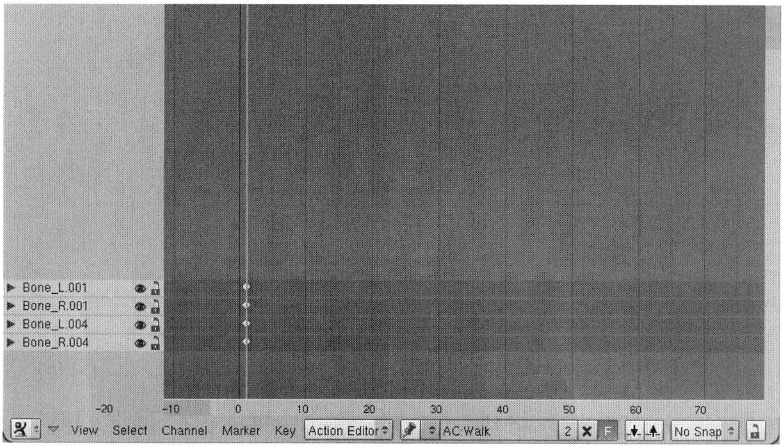

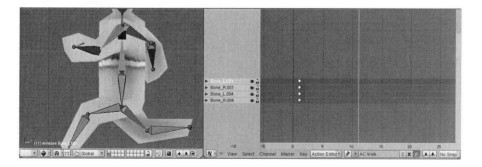

Figure 4.39

**The keys in the
Action editor**

6. Advance 10 frames, as shown in Figure 4.40, by pressing the up arrow key on your keyboard (or by pressing the right arrow key 10 times). You want to reverse the walking pose for this frame, and there's a simple way to do that. With the four posed bones still selected, click the [icon] button in the 3D Viewport. This "copies" the poses for the selected bones to a special type of pose clipboard. You can then "paste" the pose *in reverse* by clicking the [icon] icon. Do so, and then key the pose by pressing I and choosing LocRot. They keys should appear as shown in Figure 4.41.

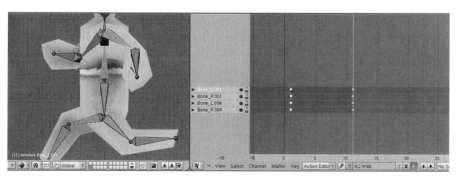

Figure 4.40

**Advancing
10 frames**

Figure 4.41

Reversing the pose

7. To make the walk cycle repeat frame 20 smoothly, you want to copy the poses of frame 1 to frame 21. Do this by first pressing the A key to deselect all keyframes. Then, box-select the first set of keyframes with the B key, as shown in Figure 4.42. Press Shift+D to duplicate the selected keyframes and move them. Hold down the Ctrl key while you move the keyframes to constrain them to whole numbered frames, and offset them 20 frames (DeltaX: 20 in the header), as shown in Figure 4.43.

Figure 4.42

Box-selecting the first set of keyframes

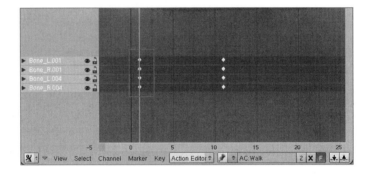

Figure 4.43

Duplicating the keyframes and moving them 20 frames

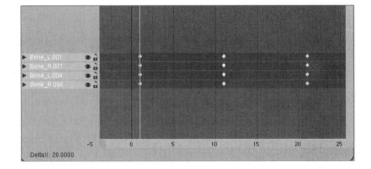

You can now press the triangular play icon in the Timeline to play back the full animation. It's as simple a walk cycle as you can get, but if you've managed to get it looking good, then you've done well as a Blender beginner.

To use the model or animation in an AR application, you'll need to export the object to the appropriate format. Which format you choose depends on the environment in which it will be used. How you export the animated model also depends on which Blender version you're using. (Although this chapter has dealt with Blender 2.49, there are some cases already where you're better off opening what you've done here directly in Blender 2.58 and exporting from there.)

The work you'll be doing in Processing in Chapter 5 and in Chapter 6, "Augmented Reality with Processing," requires OBJ files. This is a good example of why I chose to start with Blender 2.49—as of this writing, Blender 2.58's OBJ export functionality does not yet support animated meshes. To export your animated model in OBJ format, select the model object and choose File ⇒ Export ⇒ Wavefront (.obj) from the File menu at the top of your Blender work area, as shown in Figure 4.44. Choose a directory to which you'll export the files. There will be a total of 40 files written: one OBJ file for each frame and one MTL (material) file for each OBJ file. In the OBJ Export dialog box, choose Animation, Triangulate, and Normals and leave the other values at their default settings, as shown in Figure 4.45.

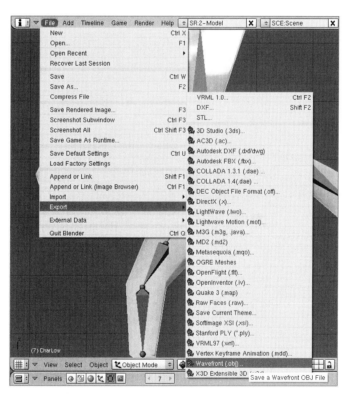

Figure 4.44

Selecting the OBJ exporter

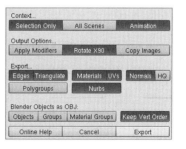

Figure 4.45

The OBJ Export dialog box

All the information about file-format exporting you need to know for this book is collected in Appendix B, so if you're unsure about which file format to use for an environment or how best to export to that file format, refer to that appendix.

Now you should be ready to get back to Processing and begin to play around with your animated Blender model in the Processing environment.

CHAPTER 5

3D Programming in Processing

In Chapter 2, "Introduction to Processing," you learned the basics of working with Processing in two dimensions. For integrating virtual content into the 3D space of live-action video, as in AR, it's necessary to use Processing's 3D programming capabilities. In this chapter, you'll be introduced to 3D programming and you'll learn how to work with 3D assets similar to the ones you created in Chapters 3, "Blender Modeling and Texturing Basics," and 4, "Creating a Low-Poly Animated Character."

In this chapter, you'll learn about the following topics:

- The P3D and OpenGL environments

- Working with OBJ files

- Simple animation with OBJ arrays

The P3D and OpenGL Environments

Processing enables you to program in 3D using a selection of 3D environments. Processing's native 3D environment, P3D, is the simplest to work with and, if it suits your goals, it's the best place to start. If necessary (and for the purposes of this book, it is necessary), you can also program using Processing's integrated OpenGL environment.

3D Primitives

Just as when programming for 2D, you can use primitive shapes in the 3D environment. In addition to the 2D primitives that can be used, there are two three-dimensional primitives—sphere and box—for use exclusively in the 3D environment. Here is a very basic example of a program using a 3D primitive:

```
void setup(){
    size(500, 500, P3D);
}
void draw() {
    background(255);
    sphere(100);

}
```

The first difference between this program and the programs you dealt with previously is in the arguments to the size() function. In this case, note that there is a third argument, called P3D. This tells Processing to use the Processing 3D environment (P3D) and treat the window as a view into a three-dimensional space.

The output of this program is shown in Figure 5.1. As you can see, the default drawing mode, just as in 3D, uses the stroke option, resulting in a wireframe-style 3D rendering. Furthermore, the sphere is centered at the upper-left corner of the window, at the origin of the x and y coordinates. Unlike 2D primitives such as ellipses, there are no location arguments for 3D-primitive functions. The only argument represents the radius of the sphere. This is because placing objects in 3D works a bit differently than placing them in 2D.

Figure 5.1

A simple 3D program

Positioning Objects in Space

To control the location, rotation, or scale of a 3D object, you must translate, rotate, or scale the frame of reference (model coordinate space) in which the object is drawn. By default, the origin of this coordinate space (which corresponds to the center of the sphere object) is placed at the origin of the 2D space (the corner of the window). To place the sphere in the middle of the window, add a translate command as follows just before the line where the sphere() function is called:

```
translate(250, 250, 0);
```

This command translates the origin to the middle of the window plane. The z coordinate is the depth. The 0 value is the distance at which the object appears at exactly the size (in pixels) that the radius argument determines. Below 0, the object moves deeper into the scene and away from the viewer. With a z value above 0, the object moves closer to the viewer and appears larger (see Figure 5.2).

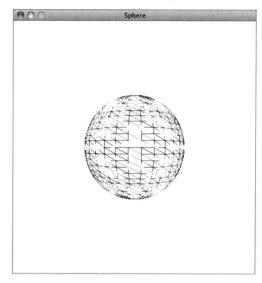

Figure 5.2

Translating the sphere to the center

Now try adding the boldface code shown here to your program:

```
int y = -100;
void setup(){
  size(500, 500, P3D);
  noStroke();
}
void draw() {
  background(255);
  lights();
  translate(250, y, 0);
  sphere(100);
  y++;
  if(y > 600){
    y = -100;
  }
}
```

This added code does a few things. The *y* variable works similarly to the example in Chapter 2, enabling the object to be animated along the y-axis. Using this variable as the second argument to `translate()` and then incrementing it causes the ball to drop from above the top of the window to off the bottom of the window. It should be clear by now how this works.

Lighting and Drawing Commands

The other new things are the `noStroke()` command and the `lights()` command. The first turns off stroke drawing, so the object is no longer displayed as a wireframe. The second produces general-purpose, directionless lighting so that solid 3D objects can be seen. The result should look something like Figure 5.3.

The `lights()` function is fine if all you want to do is be able to see a 3D object, but it doesn't allow much control over the lighting conditions. Another alternative is to use directional

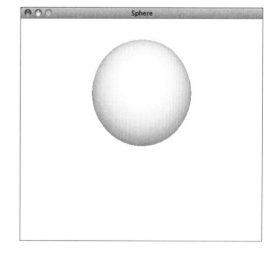

Figure 5.3

The solid lighted sphere

lights. Add the boldface code that follows to see an example of how those work. (Note that the call to lights() has been deleted.)

```
int y = -100;
float dirY;
float dirX;


void setup(){
    size(500, 500, P3D);
    noStroke();
    fill(255, 0, 255);
}
void draw() {
    background(255);
    if(mouseY <= y){
        dirY = -(1.0-(mouseY/float(y)));
    }else{
        dirY = float(mouseY-y)/float(height-y);
    }
    dirX = (mouseX / float(width) - 0.5) * 2;
    directionalLight(255, 255, 255, -dirX, -dirY, -0.5);
    translate(250, y, 0);
    sphere(100);
    y++;
    if(y > 600){
        y = -100;
    }

}
```

The first thing this code does is add two new variables, *dirX* and *dirY*. These will be used to specify the x and y coordinates of the direction that the directional lights are pointing. The light will be set to point away from the mouse cursor's position to give the effect of the light source coming from the mouse location. The equations for defining *dirX* and *dirY* result in a value range between –1 and 1. Note the arguments to the directionalLight() function. The first three arguments determine the color of the light (in this case white). The last three arguments are float values ranging from –1.0 to 1.0 for each coordinate. These determine the component along each axis describing the direction of the light. Here, the light points away from the mouse along the x- and y-axes, and it points away from the viewer (in the negative direction on the z-axis). The lines of code above this argument calculate this value based on the location of the mouse and, in the case of the y value, the location of the sphere in the window. Finally, note that in the setup() function, a call to fill() has been added. This sets the fill color for primitives, just as in the two-dimensional case. Here it means that the sphere is drawn in purple. The result is shown, in gray scale, in Figure 5.4.

Figure 5.4

The ball with directional light

Working with OpenGL

The P3D environment conforms most closely to the kind of 3D programming that Processing was meant to handle, doing well with fairly lightweight 3D content and providing intuitive controls. For this reason, in most cases you should consider it your first choice for your 3D programming in Processing. However, certain libraries and tasks require more powerful and flexible 3D functionality. For these cases, you should use the Processing OpenGL library. Some of the libraries you'll be using to do augmented reality require this library, so from this point on, all examples will use OpenGL rather than P3D.

A few caveats are in order. As previously stated, Processing is a prototyping language that is best suited for quickly creating interactive, executable demonstration software. The Processing OpenGL environment is not a good substitute for an industrial-strength OpenGL programming solution if you intend to create finished software for deployment. The amount of 3D geometry that Processing can handle and the render speed that it can produce can quickly become serious bottlenecks, and low-level OpenGL programming is not well supported in Processing. OpenGL also makes certain assumptions about your graphics hardware. If you have trouble, you may need to look into the specifications of your own graphics-processing unit and ensure that the drivers from the manufacturer are up-to-date.

Assuming there are no hardware problems, switching to OpenGL is very simple. First, make sure that you have imported the OpenGL library. Do so by choosing Sketch → Import Library → OpenGL, as shown in Figure 5.5. (In Windows, the menu is positioned along the top of the Processing window itself.) This will automatically add the following line of code to your sketch:

```
import processing.opengl.*;
```

Of course, you can also type in this line of code directly and the effect will be exactly the same.

Then, change the argument to the `size()` function call from P3D to OPENGL (this is case-sensitive, so use all caps), as shown here:

```
size(500, 500, OPENGL);
```

In this example, the sketch should execute identically when using OpenGL as it did for P3D. If it doesn't, now is the time to investigate your graphics card, and make sure that it has OpenGL support.

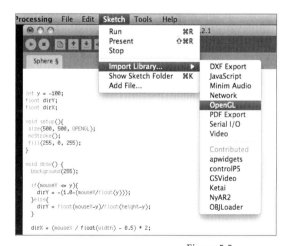

Figure 5.5

Importing the OpenGL library

Working with OBJ files

In the previous example, you created a very simple 3D scene with just a moving sphere. In fact, Processing can handle only fairly simple 3D scenes. You wouldn't want to use Processing to try to create a 3D game, for example. However, it is possible to work with more sophisticated models than just primitives, and you can even work with textured models. The easiest way to do this is to use the OBJLoader library in Processing and import 3D models from Wavefront OBJ files.

OBJ files are text-based files that describe the coordinates of vertices and the edges and faces that connect the vertices. An OBJ file can be accompanied by a material file with the `.mtl` extension, which represents material and texture-mapping information for the object. The Processing OBJLoader library can handle these files as well.

Using OBJLoader

The OBJLoader library is not part of the standard Processing download. To use it, you must download it and install it. You can get the library here:

`http://code.google.com/p/saitoobjloader/downloads/list`

You must download and extract the file. When you've extracted it, move the top-level directory into the `libraries` subdirectory of your `Processing` directory. Processing typically creates your `Processing` directory automatically in the `Documents` (or `My Documents`) directory. The `Processing` directory is the same directory where your sketches are stored by default. If you haven't used any third-party libraries yet, there won't be a `libraries` directory in your Processing directory, so you'll have to create it. Now, look inside the extracted directory. You should find four subdirectories: `examples`, `library`, `reference`, and `src`. Under `library`, you will find a JAR file with the name of the library itself. Make sure that the directory you placed in the `libraries` directory has exactly the same name as this file (minus the `.jar`). In the case of OBJLoader version 023, the latest OBJLoader version as of this writing, the directory is called `OBJLoader_023` and the JAR file is called simply `OBJLoader.jar`. You must rename the directory by deleting the `_023` from the directory name; otherwise, Processing will not correctly find the library. Finally, if Processing is running when you do all this, be sure to restart Processing after you've installed the library.

In Appendix B, you can read in detail about how to export OBJ files from Blender. For the next example, you can either use the OBJ file you created or you can find the OBJ file `sa.obj` and corresponding `sa.mtl` files among the support files that accompany this book. Start a new Processing sketch. Add the OpenGL library as you did in the previous section, and add the OBJLoader in the same way. If you can't find the OBJLoader library under the Contributed portion of the Import Library menu option, then there was a problem with the installation. Make sure the library is in the right place and that the directory has the same name as the JAR file.

Copy the rest of the code as shown here (the first two lines should already have appeared when you imported the libraries):

```
import processing.opengl.*;
import saito.objloader.*;

OBJModel model ;
float rotX, rotY;
void setup(){
    size(800, 600, OPENGL);
    model = new OBJModel(this, "sa.obj", TRIANGLES);
    model.enableDebug();
    model.scale(80);
    model.translateToCenter();
    noStroke();
}
void draw(){
    background(200);
    lights();
    translate(width/2, height/2, 0);
    rotateX(rotY);
    rotateY(rotX);
    model.draw();
}
void mouseDragged(){
    rotX += (mouseX - pmouseX) * 0.01;
    rotY -= (mouseY - pmouseY) * 0.01;
}
```

If you run this code as is, you will get an error. You have not yet made the necessary data files accessible to the sketch. Any time your Processing sketch depends on external data files, whether they be images, text files, or 3D models, it is necessary to include the files in the sketch's data directory. The easy way to do this is simply to drag the file icons directly into the sketch editor window. In this case, you need the OBJ file, the accompanying material file, and the image file for the color texture of the material. This means that you need to add the files sa.obj, sa.mtl, and shootinanniecolor.jpg, as shown in Figure 5.6. When you do so, the three files will automatically be copied into the data directory of your sketch directory. You can check that this is true by opening the sketch directory by choosing Sketch → Show Sketch Folder, as shown in Figure 5.7. The sketch directory should open up in its own window, as shown in Figure 5.8. The PDE file is the Processing sketch file itself, and as you can see, the other files are there in the data directory.

Figure 5.6

Dragging data files into the sketch

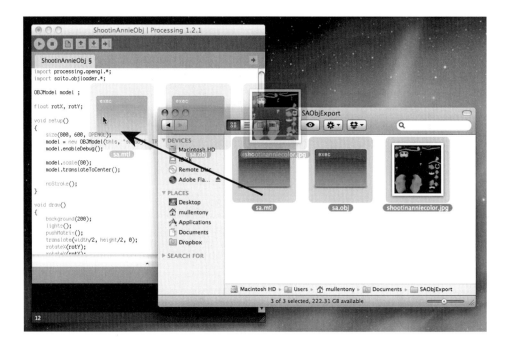

Figure 5.7

Opening the sketch directory

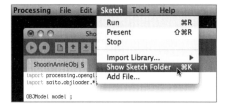

Figure 5.8

The sketch directory in the Finder

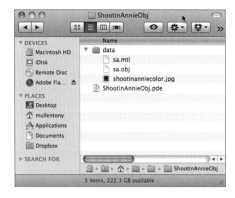

Once you've added the data files, you can run the sketch and it should appear as shown in Figure 5.9. You can rotate the object by dragging with your mouse.

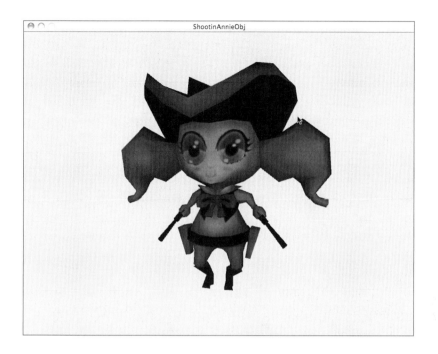

ShootinAnnieObj

Figure 5.9

The OBJ file in your sketch

Let's take a closer look at some of the new code that was introduced here. The first line of code that might be unfamiliar is

```
OBJModel model ;
```

If you recall the discussion of classes and objects in Chapter 2, though, it should be clear that we're declaring a variable for an object of class OBJModel. You don't need to worry about defining the class, though. That's taken care of by the OBJLoader library.

In the setup() function, you actually create the object called model. This is done with the OBJModel constructor. You don't need to worry much about the first and third arguments here. The first argument simply associated the new object with the current sketch, and the third argument ensures that the structural information in the OBJ file is interpreted as triangle data. The second argument is the name of your OBJ file:

```
model = new OBJModel(this, "sa.obj", TRIANGLES);
```

The next couple of lines call some methods related to the model object. Recall that the syntax for methods is a period following the object name, followed by the method itself. The first method called, enableDebug(), turns on debugging information for the object. This will output text diagnostics to the Processing console at the bottom of the sketch window. The second method scales the object. OBJ models exported from Blender will generally appear small in the Processing space so, in this case, I've scaled the model up a factor of 80 to fill the window. Finally, the translateToCenter() method is called to ensure that the center of the space is calculated as the geometric center of the model. In this case, doing so has the effect of moving all the vertices of the model downward slightly, because the original model, exported from Blender, has its origin at the feet of the model. Note that this method does *not* place the model in the middle of the Processing window. The origin of the 3D space is still in the upper-left corner of the window at this point:

```
model.enableDebug();
model.scale(80);
model.translateToCenter();
```

The next few lines of code are from the draw() function. These are the transformation functions that move the model into place. They need to be called each time the model is drawn to the screen. Note that these functions are actually transforming the entire space into which the model will be drawn. If you work with multiple models independently, it's necessary to employ a matrix stack to organize the transformations for drawing each object. (To find out more about the matrix stack in Processing, read the documentation on the pushMatrix() and popMatrix() functions.) After you translate the space to the middle of the window, the space is rotated around the y- and x-axes by the *rotY* and *rotX* values, respectively. Initially, both values are set to 0:

```
translate(width/2, height/2, 0);
rotateX(rotY);
rotateY(rotX);
```

The mouseDragged() function is a built-in Processing function that is used to define what happens when the mouse button is held and the mouse moves. In this case, the x- and y-axes' rotations are dependent on the difference between the current mouse position and the mouse position in the previous frame (accessed using the special built-in Processing variables pmouseX and pmouseY):

```
void mouseDragged(){
    rotX += (mouseX - pmouseX) * 0.01;
    rotY -= (mouseY - pmouseY) * 0.01;
}
```

Going back to the draw() function, you finish by calling the draw() method for the model object. This draws the object to the screen:

```
model.draw();
```

OBJ Draw Modes

The OBJLoader library implements a number of methods that affect the way the model is drawn. To get a sense of some of these, add the following code to the end of the sketch you just wrote. This code mainly adds a keyPressed() function to your sketch, which will demonstrate different draw modes in real time. This code is adapted directly from the example code included with the OBJLoader library. I also recommend that you go through the other examples for that library and study them:

```
boolean texture = true;
boolean stroke = false;

void keyPressed(){
   if(key == 't') {
      if(!texture) {
         model.enableTexture();
         texture = true;
      } else {
         model.disableTexture();
         texture = false;
      }
   }
   if(key == 's') {
      if(!stroke) {
         stroke(255);
         stroke = true;
      } else {
         noStroke();
         stroke = false;
      }
   }
   else if(key=='1')
      model.shapeMode(POINTS);
   else if(key=='2')
      model.shapeMode(LINES);
   else if(key=='3')
      model.shapeMode(TRIANGLES);

}
```

When you run the sketch now, you'll see that pressing the T key while the sketch is running toggles between textured and untextured drawing. Pressing the S key toggles between stroke drawing and nonstroke drawing. Pressing the 1, 2, or 3 number keys switches between POINTS draw mode, which draws only vertices as colored points in space; LINES draw mode, which draws only edges; and TRIANGLES draw mode, which draws triangle faces that can have material properties and textures. To see points and lines, you need to remove the `noStroke()` command from your code.

A Closer Look at OBJ files

OBJ files are text files that contain 3D data. By default, your operating system will probably not know what to do with an OBJ file type, but you can open these files directly in a text editor such as WordPad or TextEdit. If you do this with `sa.obj`, you'll see a file that begins with some commented content (lines of code beginning with the # sign are ignored), and then continues as follows:

```
mtllib sa.mtl
g default
v 0.081989 -0.190131 0.414445
v -0.081989 -0.190131 0.414445

...
```

The file then continues on for many lines to list the x, y, z positions for all vertices and information about textured vertices and normals, edges, and faces. The first line, after the comments, points to the material library file, `sa.mtl`. This file contains information about the material properties. The file must have the same name as is listed here, and it must be in the same directory as the OBJ file.

If you open the MTL file, you can see that there is also information here about external files on which the material depends. In this case, the image `shootinanniecolor.jpg` is listed as the `map_Kd` value. This image must be accessible to the sketch. If you find that your OBJ models are not showing up as expected in the sketch, it can be helpful to double-check the content of these files and make sure that they match up with the data resources available to the sketch:

```
newmtl Material_001_color

...

map_Kd shootinanniecolor.jpg
```

If you're looking at different OBJ and MTL files, don't get too hung up on them looking exactly the same as this one. There are different attributes that may be included depending on your model's properties and on the way you exported it. In general, you shouldn't need to concern yourself directly with the content of these files. The OBJLoader should handle all of that for you.

Simple Animation with OBJ Arrays

The previous example shows how to import an OBJ file into a processing sketch. In this section, you'll see a simple example of an animated OBJ.

There are a couple of things you should be aware of. Processing is not really intended primarily as a 3D game engine, and it is not optimized for 3D animation. The example I show here is a bit of a hack, and it is suitable for only short, animated loops using small models with very small numbers of vertices. The reason for this is that I am loading each frame of the animation as a separate OBJ file and putting them into an array. You can see an overview of the frames rendered from the Blender viewport in Figure 5.10.

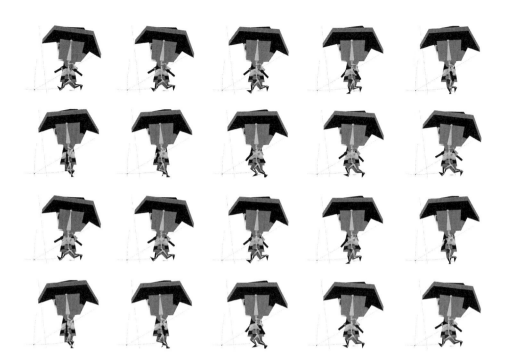

Figure 5.10

The animated frames for the Annie walk cycle

To set up an animated sequence using an array of OBJ files, start a new sketch and enter the following code:

```
import processing.opengl.*;
import saito.objloader.*;
OBJModel[] anim;
int animFrames = 20;
int animFrame;
boolean animOn= false;
float rotX;
float rotY;


void setup(){
   size(600, 600, OPENGL);
   anim = new OBJModel[animFrames];
   String filename = "";
   for(int i = 1; i <= animFrames; i++){
      if(i < 10){
         filename =
            "sa_00000"+ i + ".obj";
      }else{
         filename =
            "sa_0000"+ i + ".obj";
      }
```

```
        anim[i-1] =
            new OBJModel(this, filename, "relative", TRIANGLES);
        anim[i-1].enableDebug();
        anim[i-1].scale(50);
    }
    noStroke();
}


void draw(){
    background(200);
    lights();
    translate(width/2, height/2, 0);
    rotateX(rotX);
    rotateY(rotY);
    if(animOn){
        anim[animFrame].draw();
        animFrame++;
        if(animFrame == animFrames){
            animFrame = 0;
        }
    }else{
        anim[animFrame].draw();
    }
    rotY = rotY + 0.005;
}


void mousePressed(){
    animOn = true;
}


void mouseReleased(){
    animOn = false;
}
```

Rather than use the sa.obj model, I use the super low-poly animated model that you saw in Chapter 3. Make sure that all the OBJ files from sa_000001.obj to sa_000020.obj have been copied into the sketch's data directory, along with all the appropriate MTL files. (This is a bit inefficient. All of the OBJ files could easily point to a single MTL file in this case, but there isn't an option for doing so when exporting animated OBJ files from Blender—and it's too troublesome to change by hand.) Also, be sure the texture image is accessible.

When you run the sketch, you should see the character appear just as previously. This time, the character will rotate slowly around the y-axis, and when the mouse button is pressed, she'll walk with a simple walk cycle.

Let's take a look at the parts of the code that are new. Some variables are necessary for the animation. First, an array of OBJModel objects is declared. This is similar to the array of objects you saw in Chapter 2. The next variable, *animFrames*, is really a constant that simply stores the number of frames in the animation loop. The second integer, *animFrame*, will represent the current frame as the animation loop runs. The last variable here, *animOn*, is a Boolean variable, which means that it represents one of two possible values: true or false. These will be used to switch the animation on and off:

```
OBJModel[] anim;
int animFrames = 20;
int animFrame;

boolean animOn= false;
```

In the setup() function, a new array of OBJModel objects with 20 elements is created:

```
anim = new OBJModel[animFrames];
```

Just as in the previous example, you need to access the OBJ file from the data directory by name. However, in this case, you want to iterate through the numbers 1 to 20 and access the corresponding numbered file. To do this, you create a String type variable called *filename*, which is initialized to the empty string using "":

```
String filename = "";
```

Next is a for loop iterating from 1 to 20. In the case that the iteration number is less than 10 (that is, it's a one-digit number), then the filename needs an extra 0. You create the filename by appending the iteration number between sa_00000 and .obj. When used with a String type object, the + symbol is the string concatenation operator:

```
for(int i = 1; i <= animFrames; i++){
    if(i < 10){
        filename =
"sa_00000"+ i + ".obj";
    }else{
        filename =
"sa_0000"+ i + ".obj";
}
```

Then the appropriate element of the array is created using the OBJModel constructor and the *filename* variable. Note that the array index is i–1. This is because Processing arrays are indexed from 0, whereas the OBJ files are numbered starting with 1. The maximum index for this array is 19:

```
anim[i-1] =
    new OBJModel(this, filename, "relative", TRIANGLES);
```

The actual animation happens in the draw() function, of course. In this case, the animation is dependent on the *animOn* variable. Since it's a Boolean, it can be used as is in an if/then clause. If it's true, *then* the model object in the current frame is drawn and the frame is incremented. When the current frame hits 20, it's reset to 0, repeating the cycle:

```
if(animOn){
    anim[animFrame].draw();
    animFrame++;
    if(animFrame == animFrames){
        animFrame = 0;
    }
}
```

Finally, the mousePressed() and mouseReleased() functions are implemented as follows, controlling the value of animOn:

```
void mousePressed(){
    animOn = true;
}
void mouseReleased(){
    animOn = false;
}
```

That's about it for the basic 3D programming skills in Processing that you'll need for what follows. In the next chapter, you'll take what you've learned here and step into the world of augmented reality.

CHAPTER 6

Augmented Reality with Processing

Here's where the real fun begins. In this chapter, you'll finally get down to the business of running AR applications in Processing. To do this, you'll turn to a few more important third-party libraries and delve a little further into 3D programming in the Processing environment.

In this chapter, you'll learn about the following topics:

- The NyAR4psg library
- Digging into the sample code
- Controlling transformations with multiple markers

The NyAR4psg Library

Now that you're comfortable working with 3D content in the Processing environment and you've got your markers and marker files created as described in Chapter 1, "Getting Started with Augmented Reality," you're ready to take the step of putting it all together in an AR environment. To do this in Processing, you need the NyAR4psg library.

The NyAR4psg library is a port of a wider project called NyARToolkit, originally created by Ryo Iizuka. NyARToolkit is a collection of ports of the original GPL-licensed ARToolKit. NyARToolkit includes ports for Java, Android, C#, ActionScript 3, Silverlight 4, C++, and Processing, although they are not all at the same level in terms of stability. Later in this book, you'll look at some of the other ports, and once you're comfortable working with AR in general, you'll find it straightforward to work with any of the ports in other programming environments familiar to you. The project website of the NyARToolkit project can be found at

    http://nyatla.jp/nyartoolkit/wiki/index.php?FrontPage.en

A description of the Processing port is found at

    http://nyatla.jp/nyartoolkit/wiki/index.php?NyAR4psg.en

The main download site you should use for most NyARToolkit ports is

    https://sourceforge.jp/projects/nyartoolkit

However, you don't need to download anything from these sites right now. In the case of the Processing port, some third-party products that you'll want to use aren't included in the official package available at SourceForge, so you'll download them from another source.

As mentioned previously, different ports vary in their state of development. The official NyAR4psg library does not have multimarker support, meaning that an application can recognize only a single physical marker at a time. Multimarker applications are more interesting because they enable a greater degree of interaction, as you'll see later in this chapter. Fortunately, because this is an open source project, third-party developers can contribute useful features. In the case of the NyAR4psg library, developer Charl Botha has contributed very useful multimarker capabilities, and the improved library is available from his website at

    http://cpbotha.net/2010/06/05/processing-nyartoolkit-multiple-marker-
    tracking

You can follow the link to the downloads page to obtain the latest version of the software, which includes the entire NyARToolkit for Processing along with the multimarker modifications. The most recent version of the modified library supports the P3D environment in addition to OpenGL, so you can compare the performance of the two on your own machine and use whichever one works better for you. The library is also available at this book's web page (www.sybex.com/go/prototypingar). Note that Botha's multimarker version of the NyAR4psg library includes the entire library, so it isn't necessary to download the original library as well.

In order for NyAR4psg to work properly, you'll also need the GSVideo library. This library provides necessary video capture and playback functionality. You can download that at http://gsvideo.sourceforge.net. Be sure to choose the version appropriate to your platform.

Installing and Testing the Library

Install the libraries exactly as you did the OBJLoader library in Chapter 5, "3D Programming in Processing." In the case of GSVideo, uncompress the zip file and place the resulting GSVideo directory in the libraries directory in your Processing directory. (By default, this should reside in your Documents or My Documents directory, depending on your OS.) In the case of NyAR4psg, the uncompressed directory should have the name NyAR2. This should also be placed in your Processing/libraries directory. Figure 6.1 shows the directory structure as it appears in Mac OS X.

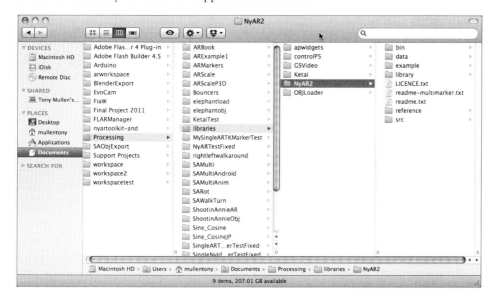

Figure 6.1

The NyAR2 library in its proper place

Inside the NyAR2 directory, you'll find the usual subdirectories. First, look in the data directory to find the files pattHiro.pdf and pattKanji.pdf. These are the test markers you'll use to test the library. Print them or display them in another way. You'll find an image called multimarker.png at this book's web page. This image can be used to display both markers simultaneously on a smartphone screen. In addition to the markers, of course, you'll need a camera connected to your computer. This can be either a built-in webcam or a stand-alone USB camera.

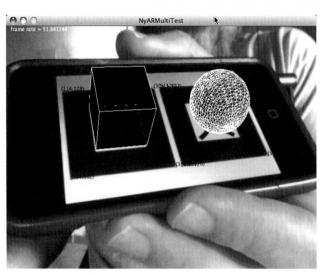

Figure 6.2

Testing the multimarker NyAR4psg library

Next, look in the example directory and find the NyARMultiTest directory. Don't use the example applications in the other directories because they are intended to work with the unmodified NyAR4psg library. For the multimarker library, NyARMultiTest is the only example that will run properly. In this directory, you'll find a Processing sketch called NyARTest.pde. Double-click on the icon to open the sketch in Processing, and then click the Run button. A sketch window should open showing a real-time video stream from your webcam. Hold the markers up so that they're shown in the video. The image of each marker must be completely visible, without shadows or obstructions. You should see a black cube with yellow edges appear on the Hiro marker and a black sphere with cyan edges appear on the Kanji marker, as shown (in gray scale) in Figure 6.2. (Here the two markers are displayed as a single image on a mobile device.)

HEADS UP FOR VERSION INCONSISTENCIES!

As this book was edited for technical accuracy, a new version of GSVideo was released, introducing some version inconsistencies with the NyAR2 library. If run using the most recent version of GSVideo, the NyARMultiTest example will execute without errors, but the screen you see will be only gray, without any video capture displayed. To get the camera to display properly, you must add the line of code cam.play(); after the following line in the sketch code:

```
cam=new GSCapture(this, width, height);
```

If you have any trouble doing this, read the console at the bottom of your Processing window. Make sure you have the libraries correctly installed in Processing/libraries, and also make sure that the names of the directories containing the libraries are identical to the names of the JAR files in the subdirectories named library. Experiment with both the OpenGL and P3D programming modes.

Common problems at this point include graphics-driver issues and Java version problems. If you have persistent problems getting this to work on your computer, start by looking at the questions and answers on the developer's website for the multimarker NyAR4psg library and the GSVideo library, both provided earlier. Another problem that might arise is connected with the dimensions of your webcam. If your webcam has other dimensions besides the standard VGA display, the sketch will probably crash. Keep reading to find out how to deal with that. Another good resource for technical questions is the Processing forum at `www.processing.org`.

Digging into the Sample Code

The best way to learn about new libraries in Processing is to study the code examples included with the library. All libraries should have code examples included that cover their functionality, and it can be a lot of fun and very inspiring to go through the examples to see the capabilities of the libraries. The GSVideo library is a great example of this, and I highly recommend checking out the examples included for that library. However, for the purposes of this book, the only Processing library code you really need to understand can be found in the NyARMultiTest example.

The example sketch itself includes extensive explanatory comment text from the developer. This may well be all you'll need to understand the code, and I recommend you always read the developer comments in the library sample code. (This is another reason why the modified NyAR4psg library is preferable for most readers of this book—the original version's comments are in Japanese.) For the sake of completeness, I'm going to run through the example line by line and fill in any blanks so that you completely understand what's going on.

The first few lines of code should be familiar already:

```
import codeanticode.gsvideo.*;
import jp.nyatla.nyar4psg.*;
import processing.opengl.*;
```

These are where necessary libraries are imported. The example leaves in the `import` command for the OpenGL library, but this is necessary only if you use `OPENGL` as the argument for the `size()` function. In this case, you can delete the line `import processing.opengl.*;` and there will be no problem, because the example uses the P3D environment.

The next several lines declare some specialized variables:

```
GSCapture cam;
NyARMultiBoard nya;
PFont font, font2d;
```

The first of these variables is a `GSVideo` class variable, so it requires the GSVideo library. This creates an object to capture images from the camera. The variable *cam* will hold an image representing a captured video frame for each iteration of the `draw()` function. This provides the live-action backdrop for the sketch.

The `NyARMultiBoard` class is from the NyAR2 library. The variable *nya* holds an object of this class. This object handles the computer-vision and marker management work that is integral to the AR application. The `NyARMultiBoard` class stores the pattern information you provide, recognizes the markers, calculates their locations and rotations, and enables you to access their data within the application.

Finally, two PFont objects are created. These are Processing fonts, and they are used to write characters to the screen. One of the fonts will be used to draw text within the 3D space, and another, smaller version of the same font will be used to draw text in 2D.

The next few lines should also be pretty familiar. This sketch uses the P3D environment, as you can see from the third argument to size(). The dimensions here are important: They're the dimensions of a standard VGA webcam display. If your camera has different dimensions than this, you'll need to adjust these values to conform to the camera's dimensions. The application will crash if you try to set the display to a different size than your camera's data provides for pixel data.

The colormode() function sets the color values to range from 0 to 100 rather than the default 255, but this line appears to be left in the code by mistake. Later in the code, you can see stroke() calls that use values of 200 and 255, which indicate that the programmer intended the range to be 0 to 255. Because RGB and 255 are the default values for the color mode parameters, it would be more appropriate not to call the colormode() function at all here. You should delete this line of code.

The two lines following the colormode() function call create the fonts that will be used for text:

```
void setup() {
    size(640,480,P3D);
    colorMode(RGB, 100);
    font = createFont("FFScala", 32);
    font2d = createFont("FFScala", 10);
```

Next, a new GSCapture object is created and assigned to the variable that has already been declared for that purpose. The arguments associate the object with the current sketch and set its dimensions to be the size of the display (which, as mentioned earlier, must match the dimensions of the real-life camera). The next line, cam.play();, activates the camera:

```
cam=new GSCapture(this,width,height);
cam.play();
```

Next, two new arrays are introduced. The first is an array of strings called *patts*. This holds the filenames of the pattern files for the markers to be used. You can look in the sketch's data directory to confirm that both of these files are present. You can have as many strings here as you have distinct marker types. The second array is an array of doubles representing the width of the markers in millimeters. This array must have a value for each value in the *patts* array.

```
String[] patts = {"patt.hiro", "patt.kanji"};
double[] widths = {80,80};
```

Now that these values have been set, these variables are used as arguments for the `NyARMultiBoard` constructor to create the new `NyARMultiBoard` object `nya`. The fourth argument contains the name of the camera-calibration file, which must also be present in the sketch's data file. For the purposes of this book, you can simply use the default camera-calibration file, which gives good results for a wide variety of commonly used webcams and mobile cameras.

```
nya=new
        NyARMultiBoard(this,width,height,
        "camera_para.dat",patts,widths);
```

You can achieve better pattern recognition for specific cameras by creating custom calibration files. For information on how to do this, please see the documentation at `www.artoolworks.com/support/library/Calibrating_your_camera`.

The next line simply prints the version of the NyAR4psg library to the Processing console at the bottom of the sketch window:

```
        print(nya.VERSION);
```

After this, two more lines set parameters relevant to marker recognition. The first line sets the grayscale threshold, which is used to distinguish light from dark in the image once it's been converted to gray scale. Somewhere approximately midway between 0 and 255 is appropriate here, and you can tweak this value for various lighting conditions. The next line sets the confidence threshold. A marker is considered to be detected if the algorithm recognizes it with a level of confidence above this value. If the value is set to 1.0, the marker will never be detected. If the value is set to 0.0, almost anything could be mistaken for a marker and treated as a detected marker. The value should be somewhere between these values in order to limit detections to actual markers as strictly as possible while still being forgiving enough to withstand the slight ambiguity in the image.

```
        nya.gsThreshold=120;//(0<n<255) default=110
        nya.cfThreshold=0.4;//(0.0<n<1.0) default=0.4
    }
```

The next chunk of code is for drawing the little labeled dots that indicate the corner positions. The argument is a two-dimensional array of integers that holds x and y coordinates for each of the four corners of the marker. This value can be accessed directly from the `nya` object, as you will see shortly.

```
        void drawMarkerPos(int[][] pos2d){
```

To define this function, first the font, stroke color, and fill color are set:

```
        textFont(font,10.0);
        stroke(100,0,0);
        fill(100,0,0);
```

Still in the definition of the `drawMarkerPos()` function, we iterate from 1 to 4 to draw an ellipse at each corner. The first index for `pos2d[][]` represents the corner index, and the second index is 0 for the x coordinate and 1 for the y coordinate. The ellipses are 5 pixels in height and width.

```
for(int i=0;i<4;i++){
    ellipse(pos2d[i][0], pos2d[i][1],5,5);
}
```

Next the corners are iterated through once more to draw the position text labels. The `text()` function has three arguments: The first is the string content of the text itself (the + operator concatenates strings), and the second and third arguments are the x and y coordinates of where the text is written on the screen.

```
fill(0,0,0);
for(int i=0;i<4;i++){
    text("("+pos2d[i][0]+
        ","+pos2d[i][1]+
        ")",pos2d[i][0],pos2d[i][1]);
}
}
```

Now begins the `draw()` function. As usual, this contains the main repeating functionality of the sketch. It begins by checking whether camera data is available. If not, it returns immediately and the rest of the function is not executed.

```
void draw() {
    if (cam.available() !=true) {
        return;
    }
```

The `read()` method is called for the `cam` object. This tells `cam` to read the camera data into an image:

```
cam.read();
```

We want to draw the image from the camera into the sketch window. To do this, it's first necessary to ensure that the 3D depth test is disabled. Depth testing is how Processing determines which 3D geometry obscures which other geometry; with depth testing, objects "closer" to the viewer are drawn over objects "further" from the viewer. When depth testing is disabled, this step is omitted and everything is drawn to the screen in the order that its `draw` command is called. In this case, we want the 2D image from the camera to behave as a background and for everything else to be drawn on top of it, so depth testing is disabled with the `hint()` function. The `hint()` function is a bit of a hack in Processing, and it is used to control various rendering attributes that do not have a more consistent implementation in Processing. The image is drawn (beginning at the upper-left corner) and depth testing is turned back on. (This step is redundant and probably left over from previous code, because depth testing will be turned off again for text in the next few lines, but the redundancy doesn't hurt anything.)

```
hint(DISABLE_DEPTH_TEST);
image(cam,0,0);
hint(ENABLE_DEPTH_TEST);
```

The rest of the function depends on the recognition algorithm detecting a marker in the cam image. The detect() method is called for nya to determine this. This method returns a true value if at least one marker is detected:

```
if (nya.detect(cam)){
```

The next block of code iterates through the defined markers (nya.markers.length returns the number of defined marker patterns) and draws the little ellipses and the position tags for each corner of the marker, using the drawMarkerPos() function defined previously:

```
hint(DISABLE_DEPTH_TEST);
for (int i=0; i < nya.markers.length; i++){
   if (nya.markers[i].detected){
      drawMarkerPos(nya.markers[i].pos2d);
   }
}
```

To draw the 3D content, you must turn depth testing back on:

```
hint(ENABLE_DEPTH_TEST);
```

Once again, we iterate through the defined markers and do the drawing appropriate to the ones that are detected.

```
for (int i=0; i < nya.markers.length; i++){
   if (nya.markers[i].detected){
```

When a marker is detected, the first thing that needs to be done is to call the begin-Transform() method for the marker. This sets up a 3D transformation matrix with coordinates oriented to the marker. This means that the 3D drawing will all happen with respect to the position of this marker. If the marker moves or rotates, the entire coordinate space will move or rotate correspondingly:

```
nya.markers[i].beginTransform();
```

The next few lines draw the objects. In this case, there is a transformation first in the z direction (upward) in order to situate the objects on top of the markers. Then, depending on which index *i* represents (that is, which pattern), either a box is drawn (in the case of the Hiro marker) or a sphere is drawn (in the case of the Kanji marker):

```
translate(0,0,20);
if (i == 0){
   stroke(255,200,0);
   box(40);
}else{
```

```
                                   stroke(0,200,255);
                                   sphere(25);
                               }
```

When the 3D drawing is finished, it's necessary to end the transformation by calling the endTransform() method on the marker object:

```
                           nya.markers[i].endTransform();
                               }
                           }
                       }
```

Finally, the example sketch prints frame rate information in the upper-left corner of the window. Use this to compare the performance of P3D to OpenGL on your computer. Use whichever one gives the highest frame rate.

```
               hint(DISABLE_DEPTH_TEST);
               textFont(font2d,10.0);
               textMode(SCREEN);
               fill(100,100,0);
               text("frame rate = " + frameRate, 10, 10);
               textMode(MODEL);
               hint(ENABLE_DEPTH_TEST);
           }
```

You've now seen the basics of working with markers, and you're well on your way to making your own AR sketches.

Controlling Transformations with Multiple Markers

In this section, you'll look at a more sophisticated example that makes use of the same method of animating OBJ files that you saw in Chapter 5. This example also shows you how you can get a degree of interactivity by using multiple markers to control different parameters in the scene.

For this example, print copies of the three markers shown in Figure 6.3. You'll also need to add to the sketch the PAT files for each pattern, the camera data file, all the OBJ and MTL files, and the JPEG texture file. You can find all the necessary files at this book's web page. Also, I recommend building a simple lazy Susan turntable as described in Chapter 1 in order to make rotating the turn marker easier.

Figure 6.3

Three markers for the example

Now, create a new sketch and type the code shown in Listing 6.1. (The full sketch can be found among the support files for this chapter.)

LISTING 6.1:

A complete sketch for controlling an animated 3D AR character

```
import codeanticode.gsvideo.*;
import jp.nyatla.nyar4psg.*;
import saito.objloader.*;


GSCapture cam;
NyARMultiBoard nya;
OBJModel annie ;
PFont font;
PVector move;
PVector xypos;


OBJModel[] anim;
int animFrames = 20;
int animFrame;
boolean animOn= true;
float turn = 0.0;
float prevangle = 0.0;


void setup() {
   size(800,600,P3D);
   colorMode(RGB, 100);
   font=createFont("FFScala", 32);
   cam=new GSCapture(this,width,height);
   cam.play();
String[] patts = {"samarker16.pat",
      "walkmarker16.pat",
      "turnmarker16.pat"};
   double[] widths = {80,80,80};
   nya = new NyARMultiBoard(this, width, height,
      "camera_para.dat",patts,widths);
   print(nya.VERSION);
   nya.gsThreshold = 120;//(0<n<255) default=110
   nya.cfThreshold = 0.4;//(0.0<n<1.0) default=0.4

   String filename = "";
   anim = new OBJModel[animFrames];
   for(int i = 1; i <= animFrames; i++){
      if(i < 10){
```

continues

A complete sketch for controlling an animated 3D AR character

```
                filename = "sa_00000" + i + ".obj";
            }else{
                filename = "sa_0000" + i + ".obj";
            }
            anim[i-1] = new OBJModel(this, filename,
                "relative", TRIANGLES);
            anim[i-1].enableDebug();
            anim[i-1].scale(15);
            anim[i-1].translateToCenter();
            anim[i-1].enableTexture();
        }
        xypos = new PVector(0, 0);
        move = new PVector(0, -1);
    }
    void drawMarkerPos(int[][] pos2d){
        textFont(font,10.0);
        stroke(100,0,0);
        fill(100,0,0);
        for(int i=0;i<4;i++){
            ellipse(pos2d[i][0], pos2d[i][1],5,5);
        }
        fill(0,0,0);
        for(int i=0;i<4;i++){
        text("("+pos2d[i][0]
            +","+pos2d[i][1]
            +")",pos2d[i][0],pos2d[i][1]);
        }
    }
    void draw() {
        if (cam.available() !=true) {
            return;
        }
        background(255);
        cam.read();
        hint(DISABLE_DEPTH_TEST);
        image(cam,0,0);
        if (nya.detect(cam)){
            for (int i=0; i < nya.markers.length; i++){
                if (nya.markers[i].detected){
                    drawMarkerPos(nya.markers[i].pos2d);
                }
            }
            if(nya.markers[1].detected){
            animOn = true;
            }else{
                animOn = false;
            }
```

```
        hint(ENABLE_DEPTH_TEST);
        if (nya.markers[0].detected){
            nya.markers[0].beginTransform();
            noStroke();
            rotateX(radians(-90));
            if(nya.markers[2].detected){
                turn = nya.markers[2].angle.z;
                rotate2D(move, turn-prevangle);
                prevangle = turn;
            }
            translate(xypos.x, xypos.y, 50);
            rotateY(turn);
            if(animOn){
                anim[animFrame].draw();
                xypos.add(move);
                animFrame++;
                if(animFrame == animFrames){
                    animFrame = 0;
                }
            }else{
                anim[17].draw();
            }
            nya.markers[0].endTransform();
        }
    }
}
void rotate2D(PVector v, float theta) {
    float xTemp = v.x;
    v.x = v.x*cos(theta) - v.y*sin(theta);
    v.y = xTemp*sin(theta) + v.y*cos(theta);
}
```

When you run the sketch, position the camera and markers so that the sketch can recognize all three markers. You should see a scene like the one shown in Figure 6.4. The character will walk forward when the walk marker is in view and will stop when you conceal the walk marker (for example, by putting your hand over it). Rotating the turn marker slightly will make the character turn right and left.

Much of this sketch is made up of things you've seen in this chapter and the previous chapter, but there are some important new elements. If some parts of the code aren't clear to you, review this chapter and Chapter 4, "Creating a Low-Poly Animated Character," to refresh your memory. Now let's look a bit closer at the new things introduced in this code.

Figure 6.4

The AR character walking around the table

After the usual boilerplate of importing necessary libraries and declaring variables, the first really new elements here are the declarations of the *move*, *xypos*, *turn*, and *prevangle* variables. The *move* and *xypos* variables are PVector objects. They store vector information. In general, PVectors can be two- or three-dimensional vectors. In this case, they will be two-dimensional in order to represent the 2D space in which the character is able to walk around freely (the character won't move up and down, so 3D isn't necessary). The floats *turn* and *prevangle* will be used to rotate the character using the rotation of the turn marker. You'll see how that's done shortly. For now, it's just necessary to declare the variables:

```
PVector move;
PVector xypos;
float turn = 0.0;
float prevangle = 0.0;
```

Creating the pattern array happens in the same way as in the previous example, but it's worth noting that here we're using three different patterns: samarker16.pat, walkmarker16 .pat, and turnmarker16.pat. Of course, as always, these must be added to the sketch's data directory. (Drag the files directly into your sketch editor window to do this quickly.) Setting up three patterns instead of two is simply a matter of adding another element to the array. However, be sure that the widths array created in the next line also has the same number of elements.

```
String[] patts = {"samarker16.pat",
    "walkmarker16.pat",
```

```
        "turnmarker16.pat"};
    double[] widths = {80,80,80};
```

Loading the OBJ files into an array is done exactly as you saw in Chapter 5. Once again, all of the OBJ files must be present in the sketch's data directory. There are 20 OBJ files and 20 corresponding MTL files for this animation. They should all be moved into the data directory.

The setup ends with the creation of the two 2D vectors you'll be using to keep track of the character's position on the ground and its direction of movement:

```
    xypos = new PVector(0, 0);
    move = new PVector(0, -1);
```

The beginning of the draw() function is similar to what you saw in the previous example. The difference is that now there are three markers to consider and each is used in a different way. The walk marker is stored in *nya.markers[1]*. This will make the character walk when it's visible, and it will stop the character walking when it's concealed. To do this, we use the *animOn* Boolean variable, which has the same effect that it did in the Chapter 5 example. Here we toggle the animation on and off based on whether *nya .markers[1].detected* returns a true or a false value:

```
        if(nya.markers[1].detected){
        animOn = true;
        }else{
            animOn = false;
        }
```

The next chunk of code deals with the Shootin' Annie character marker, which controls the coordinate space of the model. This is basically the home base for the character. It has to be visible in order for the character to be displayed, and if it moves, the model's whole coordinate space will move. All the animation should happen with respect to this marker.

This marker is set up just like both markers in the multimarker example shown previously in this chapter. The rotateX() command is necessary to get the character turned head-up. We don't draw the character just yet, though. The translation and rotation depend on the state of the turn marker, which is evaluated next:

```
        if (nya.markers[0].detected){
            nya.markers[0].beginTransform();
            noStroke();
            rotateX(radians(-90));
```

This code evaluates the turn marker, which is stored in *nya.markers[2]*. If the marker is found, its z rotation angle is accessed (nya.markers[2].angle.z) and passed to the *turn* variable. This difference between this value and the previous rotation of the character is used as the argument for the rotate2D() function, which is defined at the end of the sketch. This function takes a 2D vector and rotates it by a certain angle (expressed in radians). After rotating, the current *turn* value is passed to *prevangle* so that the next frame will add the difference to this rotation. This is a simple way to deal with the steering of the character. Unfortunately, it's a bit oversimplified, and the rotation will be miscalculated at some points. This is because the angle value stored in `nya.markers[2].angle.z` ranges only from –180 to 180 degrees (–pi to pi in radians). This will cause flipping at the point where the values 180 and –180 meet. A slightly more complex solution would store an absolute rotation value as a float and use this for the *turn* value. Updating this absolute rotation value requires doing a bit of arithmetic with the marker's angle values and keeping track of what happens when the value switches from 180 to –180, or vice versa. This modification to the code is left as an exercise.

```
if(nya.markers[2].detected){
    turn = nya.markers[2].angle.z;
    rotate2D(move, turn-prevangle);
    prevangle = turn;
}
```

Now that you've established the value of *turn*, you can translate and rotate the character appropriately. The character is placed in the 3D space using `translate()`, with the *xypos.x*, *xypos.y* values for x and y and 50 for the z value, which simply moves the character up enough to seem like it's standing level with the marker plane. The `rotateY()` function turns the character the value of *turn*:

```
translate(xypos.x, xypos.y, 50);
rotateY(turn);
```

The next chunk of code handles the case in which animation is turned on. If *animOn* is true, then the object representing the current frame is drawn, the *move* vector value is added to the *xypos* vector value, and the frame is incremented (until it hits 20; then it's returned to 0). If *animOn* is not true, then the frame isn't incremented; the x,y position of the model is not altered; and the frame-17 object is drawn. You could, of course, use a separate standing-still object for this.

```
if(animOn){
    anim[animFrame].draw();
    xypos.add(move);
    animFrame++;
    if(animFrame == animFrames){
        animFrame = 0;
    }
}else{
    anim[17].draw();
}

void rotate2D(PVector v, float theta) {
    float xTemp = v.x;
```

```
    v.x = v.x*cos(theta) - v.y*sin(theta);
    v.y = xTemp*sin(theta) + v.y*cos(theta);
  }
```

With what you've learned in this chapter, I'm sure you can think of a variety of interesting experiments to create interactive AR sketches. In the next chapter, we'll take things a step further, creating a sketch that interacts even more closely with the world by means of an electronic sensor and the Arduino microcontroller.

CHAPTER 7

Interacting with the Physical World

Until now, we've taken the concept of "reality" in augmented reality to mean essentially live video. The camera has been the only "sensory" input about the real world to which your sketches have had access. But AR can potentially take advantage of a much wider range of sensors. Working with such sensors to create software that interacts with the world more closely is part of physical computing. Physical computing has enjoyed a huge boom lately in part because of the availability of inexpensive, easy-to-use hardware programming interfaces called microcontrollers. The best known of these is the Arduino microcontroller. In this chapter, you'll see how to use Arduino to incorporate input from a simple pressure sensor into an AR sketch.

In this chapter, you'll learn about the following topics:

- **Physical computing with Arduino**

- **Sensors and circuits**

- **Communicating between Arduino and Processing**

Physical Computing with Arduino

Physical computing involves creating (usually) software-based systems that interact with the physical world using electronic sensors as input and motors, lights, or other electrical actuators as output. Physical computing has been around in some form for nearly as long as computers themselves. Many everyday appliances and electronic systems are good examples of physical computing; home alarm systems, motion-sensitive shop doors, smart refrigerators, and many more commonplace items all incorporate simple programming that takes data from sensors and/or causes something to change in the physical world.

For the most part, the appliances you deal with from day to day don't have a programming interface that is accessible to users. (It's a little-known fact that the world's most widely installed operating system is the Japanese real-time operating system TRON, specifically its industrial derivative ITRON, which is the embedded operating system for almost all Japanese-made electronic goods, from alarm clocks to synthesizers to washing machines.) For this reason, physical computing has long remained the realm of industrial developers and serious electronics buffs.

With the rise of open microcontroller projects such as Wiring, Gainer, and Arduino, this has changed. These projects all have the same goal: to enable ordinary developers to take their projects beyond the confines of their computers and to let digital-media creators think outside of the box, literally. In this book, we look at the most widely used and best supported of these projects, Arduino.

The Arduino Microcontroller

Arduino is a specification for microcontrollers and a programming language and environment for controlling them. Arduino microcontrollers are small, portable input/output (I/O) boards that include the basics of a programmable computer: a small central processing unit (CPU), ports for receiving and emitting electrical impulses, a means of getting power, and a way to connect to a computer in order to have software uploaded to it. Different members of the Arduino family vary in their size, processor specifications, number of input and output ports, and other specifications, but all of them are programmable in the same way using the Arduino programming environment. Conveniently, the Arduino programming environment is based on Processing, so you will notice a lot of familiar elements in the environment and language. You can download the Arduino programming environment from the Arduino website at `http://arduino.cc`. Like Processing, it is available for all major operating systems.

The I/O board I used for the project in this chapter is shown in Figure 7.1. It's the Arduino Duemilanove, which is Italian for two thousand and nine, so you can guess what year it came out. As of this writing, the equivalent I/O board is the Arduino Uno. The main difference that is relevant here is the labeling on the inputs and outputs. I'll assume you are using the Uno, so I'll be sure to be clear about the input and output labels you should look for.

In addition to the multipurpose Uno, there is a wide variety of other Arduino boards for more specialized use. Big boards, small boards, wireless and Bluetooth boards, boards with minimal components designed for embedding, and wearable boards can all be found on the hardware page of the official Arduino website at `http://arduino.cc/en/Main/Hardware`. You can even use the specifications on the website to build your own board from scratch from basic components, if you're so inclined.

The much easier alternative is to buy an Arduino board. You can find a list of vendors that sell Arduino on the Arduino website: `http://arduino.cc/en/Main/Buy`.

Figure 7.1

The Arduino Duemilanove

Once you've got your Arduino I/O board and a suitable USB cable, follow the instructions at `http://arduino.cc/en/Guide/HomePage` for your operating system to see how to connect the board to your computer and install the drivers.

Other Hardware You'll Need

In addition to the I/O board, you'll need a few other components in order to complete the project described in this chapter, or any other physical computing project, for that matter.

The first thing you'll need is a solderless prototyping board, or *breadboard*. A breadboard is a plastic board with a pattern of perforations like the ones shown in Figure 7.2.

Figure 7.2

Diagram of a breadboard

By inserting the ends of wires into the holes, it's possible to build circuits that can be easily changed. Electricity is conducted between the holes, as shown in the diagram. The long *bus strips* shown horizontally along the top and bottom of the diagram are used to provide power to the circuit and to connect the ground. The rows of the breadboard shown running vertically in the diagram are connected as indicated.

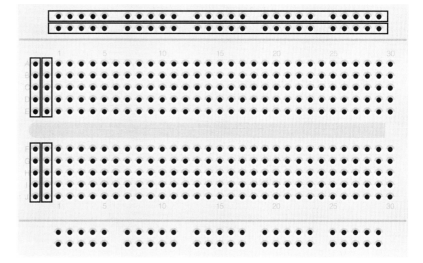

You will also need a USB cable to connect your Arduino to your computer, some jump wires to build your circuit, a 180Ω (ohm) resistor, a half-inch force-sensitive resistor, and either some small alligator clips or a soldering iron and solder to connect the sensor to the jump wires. If you are using the Arduino Uno, your USB cable should have a USB B-type connector on the end that connects to the I/O board and a standard USB A-type connector on the end that connects to your computer. Jump wires are stiff, solid wires that can be easily inserted into the holes on a breadboard and your I/O board. Resistors are important components for building circuits because they enable you to control the flow of electricity through the circuit. Finally, the force-sensitive resistor is the sensor that will be used in this example to collect data from the physical world. This part is shown in Figure 7.3. It is also sometimes referred to as a *pressure sensor* because its resistance changes when pressure is applied to it. This term is more commonly used for barometric pressure sensors, though, which are a completely different thing, so I won't use this term here.

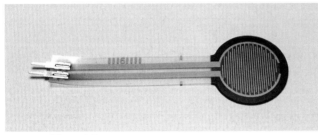

Figure 7.3

A force-sensitive resistor

You can buy all the parts online individually or in kits. Two excellent resources for all the parts you need are www.sparkfun.com and www.adafruit.com. Several kits are available from these and other vendors. Adafruit's kit, the *Adafruit ARDX - v1.3 Experimentation Kit for Arduino (Uno) - v1.3*, is a great way to get started with Arduino, and it includes almost everything you will need to carry out the project in this chapter, including the force-sensitive resistor. If you don't buy a kit, I still strongly recommend that you buy a variety of resistors, a few small alligator clips, and a handful of light-emitting diodes (LEDs) in order to follow some of the online introductory Arduino tutorials and to help with testing your circuits. If you get more serious about physical computing, a soldering iron and a digital multimeter will be next on your shopping list.

Building a Toy AR Scale

In this chapter, you'll see how to build a simple AR scale using the force-sensitive resistor. This project is intended to be a simple and inexpensive example of how an AR application can be used to report physical data in an interesting way. In fact, the force-sensitive resistor is *not* accurate enough to be used as a real scale. If you want to build a real AR scale, you will need to purchase a more sophisticated digital scale to use as a sensor.

To calibrate the toy scale and give it a numerical range to report, I used two calibration weights: a 100-gram weight and a 200-gram weight. This is about the range in which the force-sensitive resistor can give something like an accurate reading. I bought my own calibration weight set, shown in Figure 7.4, in Japan, and the same cheap educational set may or may not be easily available elsewhere. You can buy individual 100g and 200g weights online from www.americanweigh.com/index.php?cPath=113. Otherwise, you can "calibrate" your scale using other small objects of about the same weights.

For this project, I've also created a specialized AR marker, shown in Figure 7.5. I created this using the scale icon from the Noun Project, which you can find at http://thenounproject .com/. This ambitious project is a great resource for icons and pictographs representing a wide variety of concepts. Using this image, I created the marker and pattern files as described in Chapter 1, "Getting Started with Augmented Reality." Note that, in most cases, you can get away with printing your markers at a smaller size than 100 percent and still get decent performance.

Once you've got your parts all together, you're ready to get started building your circuit and putting together your physical AR sketch.

Figure 7.4

Calibration weights

Figure 7.5

A new marker

Sensors and Circuits

It's far beyond the scope of this book to describe the details of how electronic circuits work. There is a lot to learn, and without a basic knowledge of how electricity works, troubleshooting can be difficult. I recommend following a few getting started tutorials on the Arduino website (http://arduino.cc). You should at least try to get to the point where you can turn an LED on and off with a button before continuing with this section.

To set up the circuit for this project, use the jump wires to connect the Arduino I/O board, the breadboard, and the sensor as shown in the diagram in Figure 7.6. Do this with Arduino unplugged from the USB port of your computer. It's always best to do your wiring without the power source connected to avoid short-circuits or shocks. Figure 7.7 shows a photograph of the wires connected to the Arduino board. If you are using the Arduino Uno I/O board, your Analog In 0 port will be labeled A0. Otherwise there is no practical difference between the boards. Figure 7.8 shows the wires and the resistor arranged on the breadboard. Figure 7.9 shows the wires connected to the sensor. I've soldered them, but you can use small alligator clips. As you can see in the photograph, I also added a small handmade pad on top of the sensor to distribute the weight of what I put on top of it. I made this by slicing off the end of a cylindrical rubber eraser, which was ideal. A slice of 0.5″ dowel would also work.

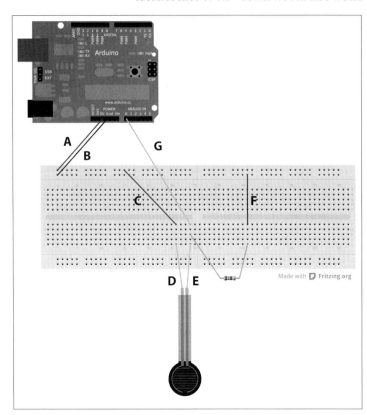

Figure 7.6
A circuit diagram for the project

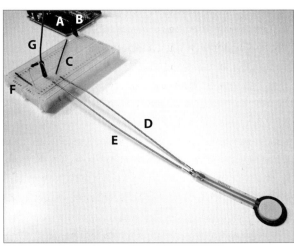

Figure 7.7
Wires connected to the Arduino microcontroller

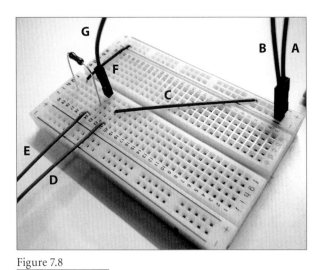

Figure 7.8
Wires connected to the breadboard

Figure 7.9
Wires connected to the sensor

Let's take a closer look at what's happening in this circuit. Look again at the circuit diagram in Figure 7.6. The wires labeled A and B extending from the 5V and Gnd holes, respectively, are the power supply (5 volts) and the ground for the circuit. You can think of the electricity as flowing from the power supply, through the circuit, and to the ground. These wires connect to the bus strips that run horizontally along the top of the breadboard in the diagram. Since all the holes in each bus strip are connected, this means that any hole in the topmost strip can act as a 5V power supply and any hole in the second strip from the top is a ground connection.

Knowing that, you can see that the wire labeled C on the breadboard extends from the power supply bus strip to a shared row with wire D to the sensor. Electricity flows from this contact through the sensor (force-sensitive resistor). After that, the flow is split. Part of the current goes through the resistor and to the ground via wire F; the other part goes to the Analog In 0 (or, on the Uno, A0) input port via wire G. The amount of current flowing into this port is measured as the input for Arduino.

When the force-sensitive resistor is not pressed, its resistance is high, so less current can flow through it. The low current then flows through the resistor for the most direct path to ground. When you press the force-sensitive resistor, its resistance is reduced, resulting in a greater flow of electricity than can easily pass through the resistor. This forces some of the current down the path to the analog input port. The harder the sensor is pressed, the greater the current is that flows into the analog input port.

This is all there is to the circuit. Once you've set this up, you can go on to program the Arduino microcontroller and write your Processing sketch to handle the input from Arduino.

Communicating Between Arduino and Processing

To program your Arduino microcontroller, you use the Arduino programming environment, which you should download from `http://arduino.cc` and install if you haven't already. When you run the Arduino software, you will see an interface very similar to the Processing editor you used in previous chapters. This is no coincidence. Like Processing, Arduino is designed to be straightforward and accessible to people with relatively little experience in programming hardware, and the similarities in design underscore the fact that the two are intended to work well together.

The superficial similarity between the Arduino and Processing interfaces can conceal some important differences in how the two operate. As you've seen, Processing sketches run on your computer. Like other processes on your computer, they can be executed and halted. The execution of a Processing sketch is done using the Run button in the editor. Arduino works differently. With Arduino, the code you write in the editor is never executed on your computer. Rather, it is verified and compiled and then uploaded via USB to the Arduino microcontroller. Once the software has been installed on your Arduino board, it executes constantly as long as the Arduino board is provided with power. The software stays on your Arduino board until another sketch has been uploaded, at which time the previous sketch is overwritten. This is important to realize. Once the sketch has been uploaded to the board, the only way to change the board's behavior is to upload something else over it. Simply pressing the Stop button on the Arduino editor will have no effect on how the software installed on the board behaves.

The code for interfacing between Arduino and Processing in this example is adapted from examples on the Arduino tutorial page at `http://arduino.cc/en/Tutorial/ HomePage`, in particular the "Graph" example, which was written by David A. Mellis and modified by Tom Igoe and Scott Fitzgerald. Tom Igoe wrote the Processing code for that example.

Arduino and the Serial Monitor

The project you'll create involves both an Arduino program to communicate with the Arduino board and a Processing sketch to handle the AR side of things on your computer. The Arduino program sends data to the Processing sketch by means of your computer's serial port. You'll use a special library in Processing to read the input from the serial port in real time. On the Arduino side, sending data from the sensor input is the only thing Arduino needs to do. The Arduino code is very simple. This is all there is to it:

```
void setup() {
    Serial.begin(9600);
}
void loop() {
    Serial.println(analogRead(A0));
}
```

Figure 7.10

The Arduino editor and code

Simply enter the code in the editor as shown in Figure 7.10. Just by looking at the code and comparing it to a Processing sketch you can probably get a rough idea of what's happening. The setup() function in Arduino is analogous to the setup() function in Processing. It is executed only once, when Arduino is powered up or reset. It is used to set values and modes that will be used throughout the sketch. In this case, the Serial .begin(9600); line of code opens the serial port and sets the rate of data transmission to 9600 bits per second. This is a commonly used speed for demonstration sketches in Arduino, although it is possible to set it at higher or lower rates. It's fine for the purposes of this project.

You've probably already guessed that the loop() function is analogous to the draw() function in Processing. It also makes sense that it would be differently named because Arduino doesn't draw anything to a screen on its own—it simply executes commands repeatedly. This function calls the `Serial.println()` method to print a line to the serial port. The argument of the function is `analogRead(A0)`, which reads and returns the value of the Analog In port 0 (or A0 on the Uno) on your Arduino I/O board.

To upload and execute the code, connect the board to the computer (once again, instructions for doing that for your operating system can be found at `http://arduino.cc/en/Guide/HomePage`) and click the Upload button shown in Figure 7.11.

Figure 7.11

The Upload button

If there are no errors in your code, it should upload without a problem. Once uploaded, it will begin executing. Values from the I/O board's Analog 0 input will be fed repeatedly to the computer's serial port via USB. You can see this happening in real time by using Arduino's serial monitor. Open the serial monitor by clicking the Serial Monitor icon shown in Figure 7.12. The serial monitor will look like Figure 7.13. Note the values coming through the serial monitor and how they change when you press your finger against the force-sensitive resistor.

Figure 7.12

The Serial Monitor icon

You will use these values to calibrate the scale. Place a 100-gram weight on the scale and note the value coming through the serial port, and then do the same with the 200-gram weight. As mentioned previously, the force-sensitive resistor is not very precise, so the values may vary. When I set up the project, the values were 3 and 32, respectively, so those are the values I used in Listing 7.1 in the next section.

Figure 7.13

The Serial Monitor

The Processing Code

Now you have all you need to create the toy AR scale in Processing. Start up a new Processing sketch, and enter the code in Listing 7.1. You can unplug your Arduino board while you enter the code and then connect the board before running the sketch.

LISTING 7.1:

The Processing code

```
import codeanticode.gsvideo.*;
import jp.nyatla.nyar4psg.*;
import processing.serial.*;

Serial myPort;
GSCapture cam;
NyARMultiBoard nya;
PFont font;
```

continues

LISTING 7.1: *(continued)*

The Processing code

```
String inString = null;
float low = 3.0;
float high = 32.0;
float weight;


void setup() {
   size(640,480,P3D);
   println(Serial.list());
   myPort = new Serial(this, Serial.list()[1], 9600);
   myPort.bufferUntil('\n');
   font = loadFont("crystal-lightning-64.vlw");
   cam=new GSCapture(this,width,height);
   cam.play();

   String[] patts = {"scale16.pat"};
   double[] widths = {80};
   nya = new NyARMultiBoard(this, width, height,
      "camera_para.dat", patts, widths);
   print(nya.VERSION);
   nya.gsThreshold=120;
   nya.cfThreshold=0.4;
}


void draw(){

   if (cam.available() !=true) {
      return;
   }
   cam.read();
   hint(DISABLE_DEPTH_TEST);
   image(cam,0,0);
   hint(ENABLE_DEPTH_TEST);
   if(nya.detect(cam)){
      if (nya.markers[0].detected){
         nya.markers[0].beginTransform();
            textFont(font,25.0);
            textAlign(CENTER);
            fill(50, 255, 0);
           translate(0,50,80);
           rotateX(radians(180));
           rotateX(radians(90));
```

```
                text(weight, 0, 0, 0);
             nya.markers[0].endTransform();
          }
       }
    }
    void serialEvent (Serial myPort) {
       inString = myPort.readStringUntil('\n');
       if (inString != null) {
          inString = trim(inString);
          float val = float(inString);
          weight = 100+((val-low)*(100/(high-low)));
       }
    }
```

Let's take a closer look at what's going on in the code.

The first few import commands are familiar. You can probably already predict that the new one introduced here imports the library for handling serial port connections. The next line of code declares the variable *myPort* to be an object of the class Serial. This will do the work of gathering the incoming data from the serial port:

```
import processing.serial.*;
Serial myPort;
```

Recall that your Arduino sketch sent the data to the serial port using a println command. This means that the data coming in from the serial port is in the form of a string. For this reason, the variable *inString* of class String is created to hold the input strings from the serial port as they come in:

```
String inString = null;
```

Next we declare some floats. The low and high values will be used for converting the serial port values into weights between 100 and 200 grams. Previously, you used the serial monitor to establish what values corresponded to the two weights. Use those values here:

```
float low = 3.0;
float high = 32.0;
float weight;
```

The next chunk of code occurs within *setup()*. The first line prints a list of the available serial ports. The next line opens the serial port corresponding to your Arduino board. Note that the index you should use for Serial.list()[1] depends on where your Arduino board appears in that list. In my case, the Arduino board is the second in the list (the first in the list is a USB mouse); therefore I use the index 1. If the Arduino board is the first in the list, you should use the index 0.

```
println(Serial.list());
myPort = new Serial(this, Serial.list()[1], 9600);
```

The next line tells Processing to buffer the input from the serial port until it sees a new line. Remember that the Arduino code used the `println()` method to send its values, which always ends with a new line. (You saw the new lines print in the serial monitor, which is why the values lined up down the left of the monitor.)

```
myPort.bufferUntil('\n');
```

The rest of `setup()` should be familiar to you. It's the same sort of thing that you've seen in previous AR examples. Skipping ahead to the point in `draw()` where the marker has been detected, you can see where the text is written to the screen. These are all just standard transformations to position the text in a nice way above the scale, positioned with respect to the marker. The `text()` function is then called to print the value of *weight*:

```
nya.markers[0].beginTransform();
    textFont(font,25.0);
    textAlign(CENTER);
    fill(50, 255, 0);
    translate(0,50,80);
    rotateX(radians(180));
    rotateX(radians(90));
    text(weight, 0, 0, 0);
nya.markers[0].endTransform();
```

Finally, a special function is used, `serialEvent()`, which is defined as part of the Processing Serial library. Like `setup()` and `draw()`, `serialEvent()` is called at predetermined times during the execution of your sketch. Specifically, this function is called whenever data comes in via the serial port (a serial event). The data up until the new line is passed to the *inString* variable, which is trimmed (to get rid of the new line symbol), converted to a floating point number, and then used to calculate the weight based on a conversion using the low and high values you set previously as constants in the beginning of the sketch:

```
void serialEvent (Serial myPort) {
    inString = myPort.readStringUntil('\n');
    if (inString != null) {
        inString = trim(inString);
        float val = float(inString);
        weight = 100+((val-low)*(100/(high-low)));
    }
}
```

This is all there is to the sketch. To test it, set the sensor and the marker as shown in Figure 7.14. If all is working as it should, the scale should display 0 if there is nothing on it.

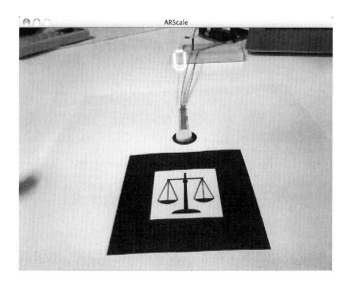

Figure 7.14

The scale with nothing on it

If the scale is properly calibrated (that is, if your high and low values have been set correctly), you should be able to get readings of 100 and 200 for your 100-gram and 200-gram weights, respectively, as shown in Figure 7.15. Once that's working, you can experiment with weighing other small items between those two weights, such as the small bottles shown in Figure 7.16.

Figure 7.15

Correct values for the weights

Figure 7.16

**Weighing some
small bottles**

At this point, you should have a sense of the interesting potential applications of combining AR with physical computing. This example is only a toy and not very useful for real-world applications. However, you can see that, with the appropriate sensors, any number of worthwhile physical qualities can be reported using an AR interface. Weight, distance, temperature, radioactivity, or other measurable values could be presented using wearable displays. If you consider the possibilities of adding Bluetooth or wireless networking, many possibilities open up for combining physical computing with AR on mobile platforms.

CHAPTER 8

Browser-Based AR with ActionScript and FLARManager

Browser-based applications enable you to deliver AR content to anyone with an Internet connection and open up many interesting possibilities for AR games, campaigns, and artwork. To create the kind of rich web content necessary for doing this, you'll now turn to the world of Flash programming with ActionScript and explore some powerful open source tools for creating AR applications in this environment.

In this chapter, you'll learn about the following topics:

- ■ **The FLARManager AR toolset for ActionScript**

- ■ **Getting FLARManager up and running**

- ■ **Creating your own projects**

The FLARManager AR Toolset for ActionScript

So far in this book, you've learned how to put some interesting AR concepts into practice. You can show people what you have in mind, or you can create installation-based AR experiences that incorporate physical computing features. However, Processing has some unfortunate limitations with respect to AR applications. One important one is that AR applications cannot easily be exported to a browser-based environment. This has to do with some incompatibilities between external libraries, and it may be fixed in the future. Already, standard Processing sketches can be easily exported to browser-ready Java applets. However, the libraries needed to do AR don't play well with this export process.

An excellent solution for creating browser-based AR is to use Adobe's ActionScript language to create Flash-based interactive content. You can do this using Adobe's open source Flex SDK programming framework. The Flex SDK framework is a very powerful set of development tools for creating all sorts of software, but it excels particularly in creating rich Internet applications.

FLARToolKit for ActionScript 3 is one of the families of ARToolKit ports based on the NyARToolKit port for Java mentioned in Chapter 1, "Getting Started with Augmented Reality." FLARToolKit itself is available for download at `www.libspark.org/wiki/saqoosha/FLARToolKit/en`. However, there is an easier way to use FLARToolKit than downloading it directly on its own. The FLARManager framework available at `http://words.transmote.com/wp/flarmanager/` is a much more accessible way to create Flash-based AR applications.

FLARManager incorporates a selection of tracking libraries, including the FLARToolKit and several others. FLARManager also enables you to work with any of a variety of 3D frameworks for Flash, including Papervision3D, Away3D and Away3D Lite, Alterna3D, and Sandy 3D. This gives you a range of options with which you can work to find the right combination for the application you want to make and the tools you have at your disposal. This flexibility can be a great advantage. Another great advantage of FLARManager is that the tools have been brought together in a relatively easy-to-use package. You can quickly compile and run the sample projects and applications to get a sense of how things are done and what is possible.

Although anyone can follow the steps in this chapter, a working knowledge of ActionScript 3 and a degree of comfort in reading object-oriented library APIs will be a must if you want to take what you learn here and do anything further with it. You've seen a simple introduction to the concept of classes, objects, and methods in Chapter 2, "Introduction to Processing," but it's a bit of a leap from that to picking up a new object-oriented programming language quickly. If browser-based AR applications are something you want to pursue once you've finished reading this book, then I strongly suggest you take some time to learn the fundamentals of object-oriented programing with ActionScript.

Getting FLARManager Up and Running

To use the FLARManager framework, you need a programming environment suitable for Flash programming. There are several options. The most widely used is Adobe's own Flash Builder, which is available for download from Adobe's website at www.adobe.com/products/flash-builder.html. Flash Builder is a powerful, feature-rich integrated development environment (IDE). Flash Builder has several advantages. For one thing, it is based on the Eclipse IDE (in fact, Flash Builder is also available as a plug-in for Eclipse itself). For this reason, the interface is automatically familiar to developers who work with Eclipse. Eclipse is the world's most widely used open source IDE and can be used for developing for a wide variety of programming languages and platforms. If Flash Builder is your first experience with an IDE, you'll find it easy to transition to Eclipse. The ARMonkeyKit introduced in Chapter 9, "Prototyping AR with jMonkeyEngine," and the Android SDK introduced in Chapter 10, "Setting Up NyARToolkit for Android," are also based on Eclipse, so you'll recognize a lot of similarities. (You can even use Eclipse to program with Processing, if you begin to find the Processing IDE restrictive.)

Another advantage is that Flash Builder is available for both Windows and Mac. The biggest disadvantage of Flash Builder is that it is not open source or free of charge. The trial version is functional for 60 days, after which you must buy a license. Special rates and free versions may be available under certain conditions to educators and students. You can learn more about those offers from Adobe's website. In general, however, you will need to pay to use Flash Builder.

A very good open source alternative is FlashDevelop, which you can download from www.flashdevelop.org. FlashDevelop is an IDE with most of the core functionality of Eclipse; you can edit your code, organize your projects, and build and run applications with FlashDevelop. The interface is not as universally familiar as Eclipse, but then again, an IDE is an IDE at the end of the day, once you get a bit of experience as a developer. A bigger disadvantage of FlashDevelop is that it is not available at all for the Mac platform. If you're a Mac user, you should install Flash Builder and then make sure you get through this chapter in the next 60 days! After that, you can decide whether you want to pay for the license or try to find alternate tools for developing your Flash applications. Linux users will need to find alternate tools anyway, but if you're a Linux user, I assume you're pretty used to that.

Installing and Preparing FLARManager

If you haven't done so already, download the FLARManager package from http://words.transmote.com/wp/flarmanager/ and unzip the ZIP file. You should find the directory FLARManager_v1_1_0 in the directory you created by unzipping the archive. This version is also included among the downloadable support files for this book, in case the officially available FLARManager version has changed in the meantime. Place this directory wherever you'd like the project to reside on your hard drive.

In the directory FLARManager_v1_1_0\resources\flarToolkit\patterns, you'll see 12 PNG image files. These are AR markers for the included FLARManager sample projects. You should print these images. I also recommend making a note on the back of each marker indicating which image is which. Doing so will make it easier to keep track when you are experimenting with applications that make use of multiple markers.

In the next two sections, I describe how to get your FLARManager project set up from scratch in both Flash Builder and FlashDevelop.

Setting Up the Project in Flash Builder

Download, install, and run Flash Builder. The initial layout of the work area will appear as shown in Figure 8.1. If you're familiar with Eclipse, you'll notice that it is essentially identical to Eclipse aside from the logos. You'll also notice that the Flash Builder start page occupies the main window. There are some useful links on this start page, and you may want to return to it later if you want to go further in learning Flash Builder. You can always bring up the start page by choosing Help → Start Page from the main menu bar. As is typical with most applications, the main menu bar is located along the top of your screen on the Mac, and across the top of the Flash Builder window in Windows. For now, close the Start Page by clicking the little white X on the tab at the top of the window.

Figure 8.1

Flash Builder when you first open it

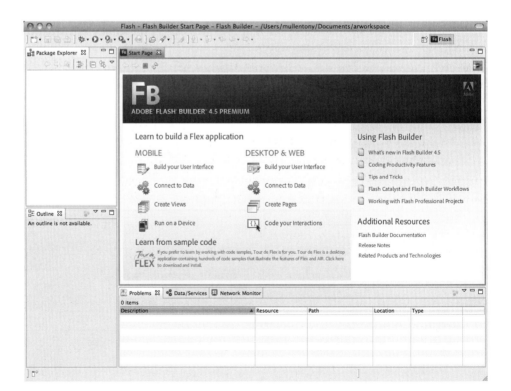

From the File menu in the main menu bar, choose Import Flash Builder Project, as shown in Figure 8.2. In the dialog box, choose the Project Folder radio button and click Browse to navigate to the FLARManager directory that you unzipped before, as shown in Figure 8.3. Click Finish. Another dialog box will open asking you to choose the Flex SDK version. The default is Use Default SDK (currently "Flex 4.5"). Leave this option selected and click OK.

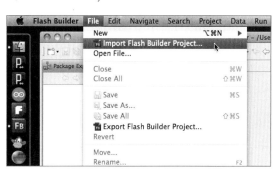

Figure 8.2
Importing a project

Figure 8.3
Selecting the project folder

When the project opens in Flash Builder, its directories and files will be displayed in the Package Explorer window to the left side of the work area. Click the little triangles to the left of the directory names to display the contents of the directories. Drill down to display the contents of FLARManager/ src/(default package), as shown in Figure 8.4. Note that the icon of the ActionScript file FLARManagerExampleLauncher.as is labeled with a small blue dot. This indicates that the application in this file is the one that will be built and run by default when you click the run button 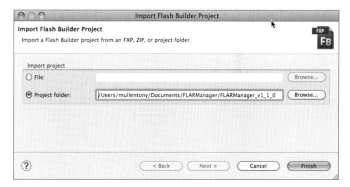 in the Flash Builder header bar. Make sure that your camera is connected to your computer, and then click the run button.

When you click the run button, Flash Builder will try to build your project. If all goes well, it will fail with three errors the first time you run it, because the necessary HTML templates have not been created. You will see an error report reading Errors (3 Items) in the Problems tab in the window below the main editor window. If you click on the triangle to the left of this error report, the three errors will be displayed, each reading "Cannot create HTML wrapper. Right-click here to recreate folder html-template." Follow that instruction, and right-click on one of the errors; then choose Recreate HTML Templates, as shown in Figure 8.5. This will fix these errors. Click the run button again, and the project should build without a hitch. If you still have problems or if there

Figure 8.4
The Package Explorer window

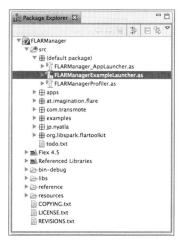

were other errors than the three described here when you first ran the project, make sure that you imported the project correctly and that the project directories are organized correctly in the Package Explorer.

Figure 8.5

Re-creating the HTML templates

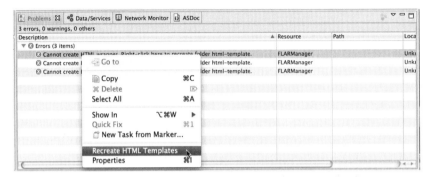

After the project builds, it will run immediately in your default web browser. A dialog box will come up in your browser to request permission from the user for the application to access the webcam, as shown in Figure 8.6. This dialog box is a security feature, and it is shown any time a Flash application requests access to the camera or microphone from the browser. Click Allow to enable the application to access the camera. When you do so, your camera will activate. Hold one of the markers so that it is visible to the camera (any of the markers you printed in the previous section will do). You should see a character appear and walk in place on top of the marker, as shown in Figure 8.7.

If you've gotten this far in Flash Builder, you can skip the next subsection and go straight to the section "A Tour of the FLARManager Examples."

Figure 8.6

The camera-access dialog box

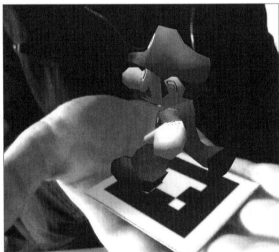

Figure 8.7

Your first browser-based AR app

Setting Up the Project in FlashDevelop

If you're working with FlashDevelop, download, install, and run the software. You also need to make sure that you have installed the open source Flex SDK from Adobe, which can be downloaded from here:

    http://opensource.adobe.com/wiki/display/flexsdk/Flex+SDK

You also need to be sure to have Flash Player 10 or above installed. You can get that from here:

    www.adobe.com/support/flashplayer/downloads.html

The FlashDevelop interface is shown in Figure 8.8. Create a new project by selecting New Project from the Project menu in the menu bar, as shown in Figure 8.9.

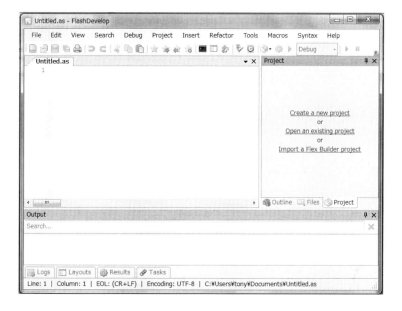

Figure 8.8

The FlashDevelop interface

A New Project window will open where you can select the type of project template and give the project a name and location, as shown in Figure 8.10. Choose Flex 3 Project, and enter your project name in the Name window. (Any name will do, but use a name that indicates that this is a FLARManager project.) Choose the location of the project in the Location field. If you want FlashDevelop to create the project directory for you, make sure the Create Directory For Project check box is selected and then click OK.

Figure 8.9

Creating a new project in FlashDevelop

Figure 8.10

Setting up the new project

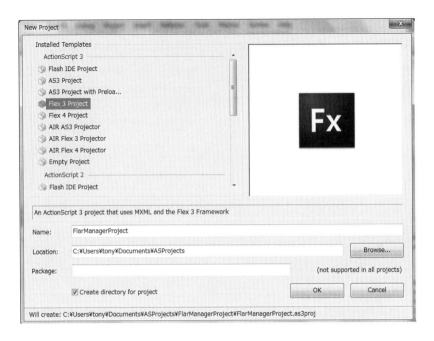

Figure 8.11

The basic Flex 3 project in the Project viewer

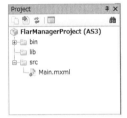

An empty Flex 3 project will be created. You can look at the structure of the project in the Project viewer window, as shown in Figure 8.11. Double-clicking directory names will display the directory's contents. A few files, such as the Main.mxml file in the src directory, have been created automatically.

To bring the FLARManager content into the project, you can simply drag and drop the necessary directories from the

Figure 8.12

Dragging the contents of FLARManager into the project

FLARManager_v1_1_0 directory into the Project viewer window in FlashDevelop. Drag all the files and directories into the top-level project directory. When you do this, you'll be asked whether you are sure you want to overwrite the src directory. Click Yes. The resulting project listing should look the one shown in Figure 8.12.

You need to make a few changes to run the project. First, delete the Main.mxml file that was created automatically by right-clicking on the filename in the Project viewer and choosing Delete, as shown in Figure 8.13. Instead of Main.mxml, you want FLARManagerExampleLauncher.as as the main application file to be compiled. Set this file to compile by right-clicking the filename and choosing Always Compile from the menu, as shown in Figure 8.14.

Figure 8.13

Deleting `Main.mxml`

Figure 8.14

Choosing the main file to compile

FlashDevelop will look for the necessary libraries in a directory called `lib`. However, the FLARManager project has the libraries in a directory called `libs`. Fix this by first deleting the directory `lib` that was created automatically. Then rename your `libs` directory to `lib`, as shown in Figure 8.15. Be careful that you delete the empty directory and not the one with all your libraries in it.

Even though you've got the directory named properly, the contents of `lib` are in compiled form and they need to be included in the project's library manually. Do this by going through the `lib` directory and for each SWC file, right-click the file and choose Add To Library, as shown in Figure 8.16.

Once you've got the libraries added, make sure your camera is connected and then build and run the application by clicking the little blue triangle button in the toolbar across the top of the FlashDevelop workspace. If all goes correctly, the application shown in Figure 8.7 will run directly in the Flash Player. This is a bit different from the default behavior that Flash Builder users see, where the application runs in

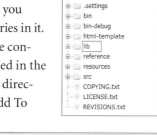

Figure 8.15

Renaming the `lib` directory

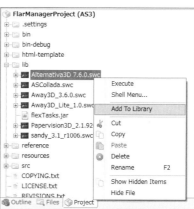

Figure 8.16

Adding the necessary SWC files to the library

the default web browser. An HTML file will be created in your project's bin directory, which you can then open in a browser.

A Tour of the FLARManager Examples

The preceding two sections cover most of the significant differences between running the project in FlashDevelop and Flash Builder. You can open a file for editing by double-clicking the filename in the Project viewer window and the Package Explorer window in FlashDevelop and Flash Builder, respectively. Editing code in the text editor windows is mostly self-explanatory, although both IDEs have their shortcuts and features with which you might want to get better acquainted. Adding assets to the resources directory is done by dragging and dropping in the same way for both IDEs. For the remainder of this chapter, I'll focus on things that should be essentially the same in both environments, such as editing the code. For simplicity's sake, when talking about files and directories in the project tree, I will refer to the Package Explorer. If you're using FlashDevelop, however, you should understand this as referring to the Project viewer window.

We'll turn to the code now to see how to run the various tutorial examples and sample applications included in the FLARManager package.

As noted previously, the file being built and executed when you click the run button is FLARManagerExampleLauncher.as, which, as its name implies, is the launcher for the example applications. Double-click that filename in the Package Manager to open the file in the text editor.

For the moment, you can ignore the first few lines of the code. The main content of this file is contained inside the public class definition of FLARManagerExampleLauncher. That code is as follows:

```
//simply uncomment whichever tutorial/example you would like to launch.
//simple tutorials for 2D, 3D, and 3D external models
//this.addChild(new FLARManagerTutorial_2D());
//this.addChild(new FLARManagerTutorial_3D());
this.addChild(new FLARManagerTutorial_Collada_Away3D());
//this.addChild(new FLARManagerTutorial_Collada_PV3D());
//2D and 3D examples using only FLARManager and native AS3
//this.addChild(new FLARManagerExample_2D());
//this.addChild(new FLARManagerExample_Flash3D());

//3D examples using third-party 3D frameworks
//this.addChild(new FLARManagerExample_Alternativa3D());
//this.addChild(new FLARManagerExample_Away3D());
//this.addChild(new FLARManagerExample_Away3DLite());
//this.addChild(new FLARManagerExample_PV3D());
//this.addChild(new FLARManagerExample_Sandy3D());
//miscellaneous examples
//this.addChild(new FLARManagerExample_2D_Loader());
//this.addChild(new FLARManagerExample_Widescreen());
```

You should notice immediately (thanks in part to the color-coded syntactic highlighting of your IDE, which turns all comments green by default) that all the lines but one in this function are commented out by double slashes (//) at the beginning of the line. This means that the lines are not executed, just as in Processing and many other programming languages. The one line that is not commented out calls the example that runs when you execute the program.

By default, the line of code that is not commented is as follows:

```
this.addChild(new FLARManagerTutorial_Collada_Away3D());
```

This code creates an object of class `FLARManagerTutorial_Collada_Away3D`. You can think of that as a mini-program being called inside this program. As its name suggests, `FLARManagerTutorial_Collada_Away3D` is an example program showing how animated 3D content in Collada (Collaborative Design Activity) format can be run in FLARManager using the Away3D rendering engine.

Figure 8.17

Colored cubes in the 3D examples

To see the actual code that gets run here, look in the Package Manager under the `src/examples` directory. You'll see 13 files there, all corresponding to lines that are commented out in `FLARManagerExampleLauncher.as`. Double-click `FLARManagerTutorial_Collada_Away3D`, and the file will open in the text editor. Later, we'll look more closely at this code. For now, let's see what some of the other examples do.

To look at the 13 examples one by one, you simply uncomment the line of code in `FLARManagerExample Launcher.as` corresponding to the example you want to see, and comment all the other lines of the code. Each time you uncomment one of the lines, build and run the project to see the example. For each example, note the result.

Many of the examples are variations on the same theme of cubes placed on the marker. Be sure to try each example with multiple markers, as shown in Figure 8.17. Different markers correspond to different-colored cubes. The code for creating the cubes is found in classes defined in the `src/examples/support` directory, and it is shared by several of the examples. The `FLARManagerExample_Flash3D` example is shown in Figure 8.18. This uses the native Flash 3D API to draw a textured plane over the marker (all markers behave the same way in this example).

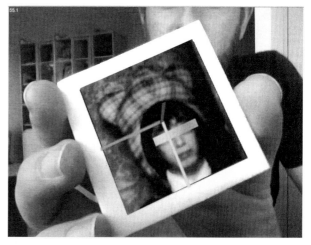

Figure 8.18

A textured 3D plane using Flash3D

Figure 8.19 shows the `FLARManagerTutorial_Collada_PV3D.as` example, which uses the Papervision3D engine and its Collada loader to display an animated 3D model in the Collada DAE file format. Likewise, the first example you saw when you initially installed and ran FLARManager was `FLARManagerTutorial_Collada_Away3D.as`, which also used a Collada file to load an animated 3D model. The difference is that the latter example uses the Away3D 3D engine for Flash.

In addition to the simple example files, the FLARManager package includes some more complete applications for you to study. To run these applications, you need first to change the default build application from `FLARManagerExampleLauncher.as` to `FLARManager_AppLauncher.as`. Simply right-click on the name of this file (located in `src/(default package)/`), and choose Set As Default Application in Flash Builder, as shown in Figure 8.20. In FlashDevelop, choose Always Compile.

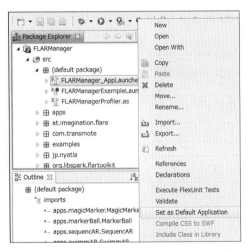

Figure 8.20

**Setting the
AppLauncher as the
default application
in Flash Builder**

This launcher application works the same as the example launcher. There are four function calls corresponding to four different sample applications, and you uncomment the one you want to run. The four applications are called MarkerBall, MagicMarker, SequencAR, and WhackAMole. In the MarkerBall application, shown in Figure 8.21, you use a marker to control a bar to hit colored balls into the correspondingly colored wall of the square. MagicMarker is an AR spray paint program that enables you to draw directly in the browser window by moving markers around (Figure 8.22). Different markers draw with different colors. The SequencAR application works like a simple beat box. You line up different markers in a sequence, as shown in Figure 8.23, to create a looping sequence of drum sounds. Finally, the WhackAMole application is a game that enables you to use the AR marker to whack a famously unpopular CG movie character over the head with a mallet.

These applications are your best references for continued study once you complete this chapter, so be prepared to read the code closely!

Figure 8.21

The MarkerBall game

Figure 8.22

Graffiti in your browser

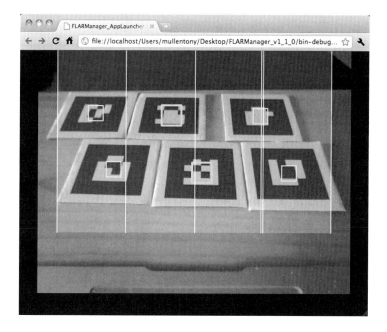

Figure 8.23

An AR beat box

Creating Your Own Projects

As much fun as it is to play with the ready-made examples from the FLARManager package, what you really want to do is to create your own. In this last section, you'll look at how to get your own 3D animated model into a Flash AR application and also take a cursory look at simple tweaks you can make to existing examples to add interesting interactivity. Although you'll be fiddling with the code here, this is by no means intended as a substitute for learning ActionScript. If you want to go much further in creating your own Flash applications, you'll want to sit down and study it properly. Think of this section as a basic icebreaker, where you can get a feel for what's going on in the code.

Creating a New Example

You're going to take a big shortcut here and simply adapt an existing example to use your own animated 3D model and to add a bit of extra interactivity. I think this is always a good way to learn new languages and APIs, and it will save you from having to learn all of ActionScript from the ground up, while still covering some interesting points in using FLARManager specifically.

To get started, copy the file FLARManagerTutorial_Collada_Away3D.as in your project and rename it to **FLARManagerTutorial_Collada_Away3D_annie.as**. Don't let your IDE do any automatic class-name fixing for the time being.

Double-click FLARManagerTutorial_Collada_Away3D_annie.as in your Project viewer window to open it up in your text editor. You will need to edit two lines to make the class definition consistent with the filename. Edit line 41 from

```
public class FLARManagerTutorial_Collada_Away3D extends Sprite {
```

to

```
public class FLARManagerTutorial_Collada_Away3D_annie extends Sprite {
```

Also, edit line 61 from

```
public function FLARManagerTutorial_Collada_Away3D () {
```

to

```
public function FLARManagerTutorial_Collada_Away3D_annie () {
```

Finally, open the file FLARExampleLauncher.as in the text editor, and add this line inside the FLARExampleLauncher() public function definition:

```
this.addChild(new FLARManagerTutorial_Collada_Away3D_annie());
```

Once you've done this, you can move on to adding the 3D content you'll need for the new example.

Exporting and Importing 3D Content

If you want to use your own animated 3D models in FLARManager applications, the first thing you need to do is to export them to a file that can be imported into your ActionScript project and rendered by one of the 3D engines available to FLARManager.

Unfortunately, and as much as it pains me to say this, at the time of this writing it's not as straightforward to do this as it should be.

First, a bit of explanation. Collada is an XML-based open format for representing 3D content. In principle, Collada files should be able to encode everything that your 3D software is able to produce, making it possible to transfer 3D content, including models, materials, textures, and animations, from one 3D environment or application to another. The extension for Collada files is .dae.

Both the Papervision3D and Away3D engines are able to do a good job of handling correctly formed Collada (DAE) files. As you have already seen when running the FLARManagerTutorial_Collada_PV3D and FLARManagerTutorial_Collada_Away3D examples in the previous section, both engines can render textured, animated 3D models imported from DAE files. Both of those animated models were exported from 3D Studio Max using that software's standard Collada exporter.

Blender also has Collada export functionality, and the good news for Blender users is that improving this functionality is a scheduled project for the 2011 Google Summer of Code. By the time you read this, the Collada exporter may be much improved. However, as of this writing, neither the 2.58 exporter nor the 2.49 exporter can be relied on to export DAE files that read correctly in Papervision3D or Away3D. Bummer!

Fortunately, there is a workaround, inelegant though it is. You can export your animation from Blender 2.49 to the FBX format and use Autodesk's free-of-charge FBX Conversion software to output a well-formed DAE file that will read more or less correctly in Away3D. (This method still does not read correctly in Papervision3D, unfortunately.)

I'll describe this method of creating your Collada file and importing it into Away3D. By the time you are reading this, things may have changed (improved, hopefully!), so I recommend you experiment with exporting your content from Blender 2.5.

Creating Collada Files

The most reliable way to create Collada files suitable for use in Away3D is to start by exporting the model to the FBX format. This can be done in either Blender 2.49 or Blender 2.58; FBX export for both versions works well. Select the model you want to export, and choose File → Export → Autodesk FBX (.fbx) from the header menu, as shown in Figure 8.24. The Blender File Browser window will open, and you can select where the exported file is saved. The filename should have the .fbx extension. You can find the annie.fbx file among the support files for this chapter.

Figure 8.24

Exporting the Shootin' Annie model to FBX in Blender 2.58

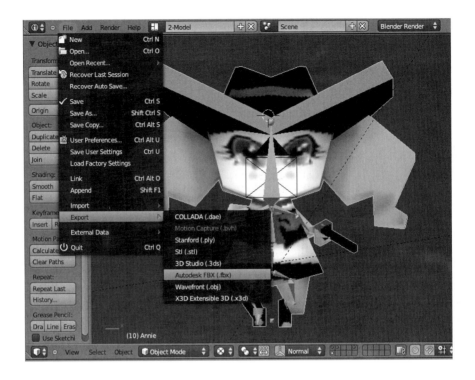

To convert the FBX file to a Collada (DAE) file, you will need Autodesk's proprietary but free-of-charge FBX Converter software. You can download the software from Autodesk's website here:

http://usa.autodesk.com/adsk/servlet/pc/item?id=10775855&siteID=123112

The interface of the Autodesk FBX Converter is shown in Figure 8.25. As you can see in the toolbar along the top of the window, several tools are incorporated in this suite. Before you use the FBX Converter to convert the file to DAE, it's a good idea to use the FBX Viewer to view your FBX file and make sure it looks the way you want it to. Do this by clicking Add FBX Viewer. In the FBX Viewer window, click File in the lower-left corner of the window, and then navigate to the FBX file you just created and select it. Figure 8.26 shows the display of the annie.fbx file. You can change the camera angle, the viewing mode, the display mode, and the speed of the animation display, among other characteristics, by using the buttons along the bottom edge of the window.

When you are satisfied that the FBX file was exported properly, close the FBX Viewer and open your FBX file in the FBX Converter, as shown in Figure 8.27. In the Destination Format drop-down menu on the right side of the window, choose DAE Collada and then click Convert.

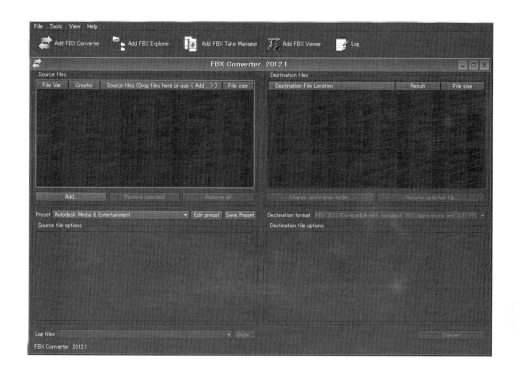

Figure 8.25

The Autodesk FBX Converter

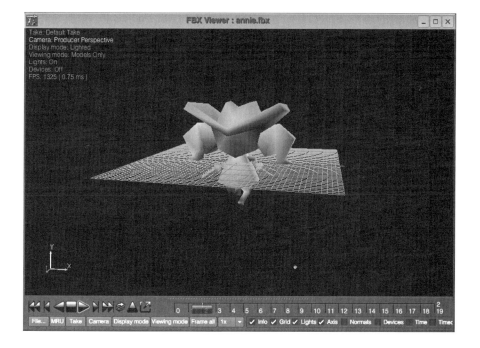

Figure 8.26

Viewing the FBX file

Figure 8.27

**Converting your file
from FBX to Collada**

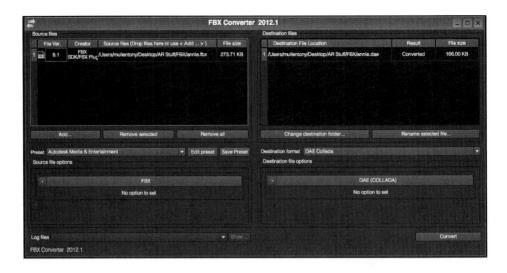

Drag the DAE file and the texture JPEG image from your desktop into the resources/ assets directory of your FLARManager project, as shown in Figure 8.28.

Figure 8.28

**Dragging the files
into the project**

You now need to change the code to refer to the appropriate file in the assets directory. Turn on line numbering in the Text Editors preferences window (Window → Preferences → General → Editors → Text Editors), and then change line 55 from

```
[Embed(source="../resources/assets/mario_tex.jpg")]
```

to

```
[Embed(source="../resources/assets/SA_small_color.jpg")]
```

This will point to the appropriate image file for the texture.

Next change line 57 from

```
[Embed(source="../resources/assets/mario_testrun.dae",
mimeType="application/octet-stream")]
```

to

```
[Embed(source="../resources/assets/annie.dae",
mimeType="application/octet-stream")]
```

This will point to the correct DAE file on your filesystem.

Next change line 108

```
model.materialLibrary.getMaterial("FF_FF_FF_mario1")
.material = new BitmapMaterial(Cast.bitmap(Charmap));
```

to

```
model.materialLibrary.getMaterial("SmallSAMatt__SA_small_color_jpg_ncl1_1")
.material = new BitmapMaterial(Cast.bitmap(Charmap));
```

This will tell the program how to find the material information from the DAE file. You might wonder why the argument in this last line of code is AnnieMat__SA_small_color_jpg_ncl1_1. This is a material ID generated by the DAE file creation process. You can find this string by opening your annie.dae file in the text editor window and doing a search for the string material id.

Once you've made these changes, build and run the program. You should see the animated model of Shootin' Annie running along on top of your marker.

Adding Interactivity

The code for this example does not distinguish between markers. Any of the 12 available markers will be treated the same. Whichever one is recognized will get the character drawn on top of it. In this section, you'll make some changes such that only one of the markers will act as a placement for the model, and another marker will be used to rotate the model similarly to the example you worked on in Chapter 5, "3D Programming in Processing" (although without translating the model). Specifically, we'll use the marker with pattern ID 0 (from the file patt001.png) and the marker with pattern ID 5 (from the file patt006.png) shown in Figure 8.29. Note that the pattern IDs are counted from 0, whereas the file-names begin with patt001 and

Figure 8.29

Markers with pattern IDs 0 and 5

count upward, so you need to subtract 1 from the index in the filename in order to find a pattern's ID number.

To use a second marker for the purpose of rotating the object, it's necessary to create a FLARMarker object to store the data of that marker. Do that by declaring a second variable of type FLARMarker around line 50, just after where the object activeMarker is declared. Call the new variable *rotationMarker*, and declare it with this line of code:

```
private var rotationMarker:FLARMarker;
```

Now that you've got this variable to work with, you can go ahead and rewrite some important functions to deal with both markers separately The first function that needs to be rewritten is the onMarkerAdded() function, which tells the program what to do when the recognition algorithm spots a new marker in the viewport. The code in the demo application is as follows:

```
private function onMarkerAdded (evt:FLARMarkerEvent) :void {
    trace("["+evt.marker.patternId+"] added");
    this.modelContainer.visible = true;
    this.activeMarker = evt.marker;

}
```

So, what's happening here? The first line simply declares that this is a definition of a function called onMarkerAdded(), and that it takes an argument of a FLARMarkerEvent and will be represented as the variable *evt* in the function definition:

```
private function onMarkerAdded (evt:FLARMarkerEvent) :void {
```

The next three lines of code are executed when the function is called upon, recognizing a marker. The first thing is a trace command, which is the rough equivalent of the println command you saw earlier in Processing; it prints values to your debugger interface so that you can see what's happening with the variable values. In this case, it tells you which marker is added by accessing the *evt.marker.patternId* value. This is the patternID value of the marker associated with the marker event *evt* that was passed into the function as the argument. That is to say, this is the patternID value of the marker that has just been recognized. The marker patternIDs are set when the marker pattern files are originally created. In this case, the patternIDs of the default marker patterns are numbered from 0 to 11, with 0 corresponding to the image in file patt001.png.

The next line, this.modelContainer.visible = true;, sets the model to be visible in the display. Finally, this.activeMarker = evt.marker; sets the value of *this.activeMarker* to the marker that was just recognized.

To add some of the interactivity you played with in Chapter 5, we want to treat patterns differently here. If the pattern with patternID 0 is seen, we want it to provide the basis for the model's coordinate space (which is what *this.activeMarker* does). However, if the pattern with patternID 5 is seen, we want it to cause the model to rotate according to the marker's rotation. This is why we introduced the *rotationMarker* variable.

To assign the markers to the correct variables, we need to add some conditional `if` statements that test for the `patternID` of the recognized marker. The function needs to be rewritten as follows:

```
private function onMarkerAdded (evt:FLARMarkerEvent) :void {
    trace("[" + evt.marker.patternId + "] added");
    if (evt.marker.patternId == 0)
    {
        this.modelContainer.visible = true;
        this.activeMarker = evt.marker;
    }
    if (evt.marker.patternId == 5)
    {
        this.rotationMarker = evt.marker;
    }
}
```

As you can see, the `if` statements ensure that the *this.activeMarker* value and the *this.rotationMarker* are set only if the appropriate patterns are seen. The model will be set to visible only if pattern 0 is recognized.

The next function that needs to be rewritten is `onMarkerUpdated()`. This function is called for every frame (redraw) of the window in cases where a marker that has been previously recognized is still recognized. If a marker is visible in the window persistently for more than a single frame, the code in this function will be executed. The content here isn't much different from `onMarkerAdded()`. I've added a trace of the rotation around the z-axis of the rotation marker.

```
private function onMarkerUpdated (evt:FLARMarkerEvent) :void {
    if (evt.marker.patternId == 0)
    {
        this.modelContainer.visible = true;
        this.activeMarker = evt.marker;
    }
    if (evt.marker.patternId == 5)
    {
        trace("rot: "+ this.rotationMarker.rotationZ + ".");
    }
}
```

Another marker-handling function needs to be rewritten. This is the `onMarkerRemoved()` function, which handles what happens when a marker disappears from view or is no longer recognizable to the recognition algorithm.

The new function is analogous to `onMarkerAdded()`, but in reverse. If the patternID is 0, the model is set not to be visible with the line `this.modelContainer.visible = false;` and the active marker is set to null. If the rotation marker (patternID 5) disappears, then the *this.rotationMarker* value is set to null. It's very important to do this. If your program does not know that these variables are null, it will try to access information about the marker's position onscreen even when the marker is not visible, which will crash your program.

```
private function onMarkerRemoved (evt:FLARMarkerEvent) :void {
    trace("["+evt.marker.patternId+"] removed");
    if (evt.marker.patternId == 0)
    {
        this.modelContainer.visible = false;
        this.activeMarker = null;
    }
    if (evt.marker.patternId == 5)
    {
        this.rotationMarker = null;
    }
}
```

Finally, you need to change the function onEnterFrame(), which is called for every new frame (redraw) of the program. The new function is as follows:

```
private function onEnterFrame (evt:Event) :void {
    if (this.activeMarker) {
        this.modelContainer.transform =
        AwayGeomUtils.convertMatrixToAwayMatrix(this.activeMarker.➥
transformMatrix);
        this.modelContainer.moveBackward(50);
        if (this.rotationMarker) {
            this.modelContainer.roll(-this.rotationMarker.rotationZ);
        }
    }

}
```

There are two conditional if statements in this function. The first one is if (this.activeMarker), which simply checks whether *this.activeMarker* is null. If it's not null, the marker is visible and the rest of the code is executed. The model is positioned based on the active marker's transform matrix, and the other conditional if statement checks whether *this.rotationMarker* is null. If this marker is not null, the model is rotated based on the rotation marker's rotation. This is done by setting the *roll* value of the model container. The Away3D engine uses the variables *pitch*, *yaw*, and *roll* to control rotation around the three axes.

When you've got this code written, execute your application. You should be able to rotate the character using the marker as a "steering wheel," as shown in Figure 8.30.

Figure 8.30

Rotating the character with the second marker

Custom Markers for FLARManager

To create FLARManager applications that are truly your own, you will want to create your own markers. Again, you can use tarotaro's online marker generator as described in Chapter 1. This can be found at

```
http://flash.tarotaro.org/blog/2009/07/12/mgo2/
```

You can create pattern files as described in Chapter 1. Choose either 8×8 or 16×16 marker segments. Lower numbers of marker segments enable quicker and more robust recognition if the images used are sufficiently distinct at that resolution. Don't use higher than 16×16 marker segments. Also note that, when using more than one marker in a given application, all markers must be set to the same resolution. When you've created your pattern files, drag and drop them into the project under a subdirectory of /resources. The sample patterns are located in the directory /resources/flarToolkit/patterns/pat8, but you can put them wherever you like.

Finally, you need to edit the flarConfig.xml file to tell your application where to find the patterns and what their resolution is. This is found in the /resources/flar directory in your project. In both Flash Builder and FlashDevelop, if you double-click flarConfig .xml, it will open in the built-in XML editor. You can also edit the XML in a plain text editor, but this is a bit more challenging.

The pattern configuration data to be edited is shown in the Flash Builder XML editor in Figure 8.31. As shown in the figure, the path for the pattern settings is flar_config/ trackerSettings/flarToolkitSettings/patterns. You need to set the resolution to be either 8 or 16, depending on the resolution you used to create your pattern files for the markers. Below this, an arbitrary number of patterns is listed. The figure shows the default sample

Figure 8.31

Pattern configuration data

pattern configuration, so there are 12 patterns. Under each pattern node in the XML file is a path attribute. (The figure shows this for the first pattern, which shows the relative path to the corresponding pattern file, beginning with ../resources.) The patternID of the pattern is derived from the order in the XML of the patterns. The first one has a patternID of 0, the next one has a patternID of 1, and so on.

When you've placed your pattern files in the project and added their paths to the flarConfig.xml file, you're ready to access them by their patternID and use them in your programs.

Troubleshooting and Further Information

With so many interdependent technologies, and so many of them under active development, there are a lot of places where things can go wrong. It's not always easy to know where to look for help. Of course, the place to start is in the documentation that comes with the software or that is available on the website where you downloaded the software. Studying the API will help you understand the functions and classes that are available to you and how they work. Frequently encountered problems may be discussed in README files or code comments. However, there are times when these sources are not enough, and you will want to ask somebody for help.

For FLARToolKit-related questions, including FLARManager questions, the FLARToolKit userz group at Google Groups is a good resource. You can find that here:

```
http://groups.google.com/group/flartoolkit-userz
```

If you're using the Away3D engine and run into trouble, you may find the information that you need at the Away3D website at `http://away3d.com`, or you may want to turn to the Away3D Google Groups forum here:

```
http://groups.google.com/group/away3d-dev
```

For questions about Papervision3D, you can start with the Papervision3D website here:

```
http://blog.papervision3d.org/
```

The Papervision3D forum is temporarily down as of this writing. It may be up again by the time you read this. In any case, there is a great interactive Papervision3D demo in its place at the moment, so it's worth checking out here anyway:

```
www.forum.papervision3d.org/
```

You can ask questions about Collada and DAE files here:

```
https://collada.org/public_forum/
```

Finally, if your problem deals with Blender export functionality, the Python Support room at the `Blenderartists.org` forum is a good place to try:

```
http://blenderartists.org/forum/forumdisplay.php?11-Python-Support
```

There are solutions for most problems, but some of them require a bit of patience and perseverance to get to, so don't give up!

The Complete Code

The complete code for the `FLARManagerTutorial_Collada_Away3D_annie` class follows. For reasons of space and clarity, the comments and authorship information from the code files are not reprinted here. FLARManagerTutorial_Collada_Away3D_annie is adapted directly from the FLARManagerTutorial_Collada_Away3D class created by Eric Sokolofsky, which is part of the FLARManager package available at http://transmote.com/flar. A write-up describing the original tutorial file can be found at

http://words.transmote.com/wp/flarmanager/inside-flarmanager/
loading-collada-models

This code should be contained in a file called FLARManagerTutorial_Collada_Away3D_ annie.as, which should be located in the src/examples directory of your FLARManager project. The line this.addChild(new FLARManagerTutorial_Collada_Away3D_annie()); must be added to the FLARManagerExampleLauncher public function in the file FLARManagerExampleLauncher.as. The Collada file annie.dae must be in the resources/ assets directory, as should the file SA_small_collor.jpg. Listing 8.1 provides the code for the class.

LISTING 8.1:

The complete code for *FLARManagerTutorial_Collada_Away3D_annie*

```
package examples {
    import away3d.animators.Animator;
    import away3d.animators.BonesAnimator;
    import away3d.containers.ObjectContainer3D;
    import away3d.containers.Scene3D;
    import away3d.containers.View3D;
    import away3d.core.utils.Cast;
    import away3d.events.Loader3DEvent;
    import away3d.lights.DirectionalLight3D;
    import away3d.loaders.AbstractParser;
    import away3d.loaders.Collada;
    import away3d.loaders.Loader3D;
    import away3d.loaders.utils.AnimationLibrary;
    import away3d.materials.BitmapMaterial;

    import com.transmote.flar.FLARManager;
    import com.transmote.flar.camera.FLARCamera_Away3D;
    import com.transmote.flar.camera.FLARCamera_PV3D;
    import com.transmote.flar.marker.FLARMarker;
    import com.transmote.flar.marker.FLARMarkerEvent;
    import com.transmote.flar.tracker.FLARToolkitManager;
    import com.transmote.flar.utils.geom.AwayGeomUtils;
    import flash.display.Sprite;
    import flash.events.Event;
    import flash.geom.Rectangle;
    import flash.geom.Vector3D;
    import flash.utils.getTimer;
```

```
public class FLARManagerTutorial_Collada_Away3D_annie extends Sprite {
    private var flarManager:FLARManager;
    private var view:View3D;
    private var camera3D:FLARCamera_Away3D;
    private var scene3D:Scene3D;
    private var light:DirectionalLight3D;

    private var activeMarker:FLARMarker;
    private var rotationMarker:FLARMarker;
    private var modelLoader:Loader3D;
    private var modelContainer:ObjectContainer3D;
    private var modelAnimator:BonesAnimator;

    [Embed(source="../resources/assets/SA_small_color.jpg")]
    private var Charmap:Class;
    [Embed(source="../resources/assets/annie.dae",
    mimeType="application/octet-stream")]
    private var Charmesh:Class;


    public function FLARManagerTutorial_Collada_Away3D_annie () {
        this.addEventListener(Event.ADDED_TO_STAGE, this.onAdded);
    }

    private function onAdded (evt:Event) :void {
        this.removeEventListener(Event.ADDED_TO_STAGE, this.onAdded);
        this.flarManager
            = new FLARManager("../resources/flar/flarConfig.xml",
            new FLARToolkitManager(), this.stage);
        this.addChild(Sprite(this.flarManager.flarSource));

        this.flarManager.addEventListener(FLARMarkerEvent.MARKER_ADDED,
            this.onMarkerAdded);
        this.flarManager.addEventListener(FLARMarkerEvent.MARKER_UPDATED,
            this.onMarkerUpdated);
        this.flarManager.addEventListener(FLARMarkerEvent.MARKER_REMOVED,
            this.onMarkerRemoved);
        this.flarManager.addEventListener(Event.INIT,
            this.onFlarManagerInited);
    }
    private function onFlarManagerInited (evt:Event) :void {
        this.flarManager.removeEventListener(Event.INIT,
            this.onFlarManagerInited);
        this.scene3D = new Scene3D();
        this.camera3D = new FLARCamera_Away3D(this.flarManager,
```

continues

LISTING 8.1: *(continued)*

The complete code for *FLARManagerTutorial_Collada_Away3D_annie*

```
            new Rectangle(0, 0, this.stage.stageWidth,
                this.stage.stageHeight));
        this.view = new View3D({x:0.5*this.stage.stageWidth,
            y:0.5*this.stage.stageHeight,
            scene:this.scene3D, camera:this.camera3D});
        this.addChild(this.view);
        this.light = new DirectionalLight3D();
        this.light.direction = new Vector3D(500, -300, 200);
        this.scene3D.addLight(light);
        var collada:Collada = new Collada();
        collada.scaling = 20;
        var model:ObjectContainer3D =
            collada.parseGeometry(Charmesh)
            as ObjectContainer3D;

model.materialLibrary.getMaterial("SmallSAMat__SA_small_color.jpg_ncl1_1").
material
            = new BitmapMaterial(Cast.bitmap(Charmap));
        model.mouseEnabled = false;
        model.rotationX = 90;
        this.modelAnimator =
            model.animationLibrary.getAnimation("default").animator
            as BonesAnimator;

        this.modelContainer = new ObjectContainer3D();
        this.modelContainer.addChild(model);
        this.modelContainer.visible = false;
        this.scene3D.addChild(this.modelContainer);

        this.addEventListener(Event.ENTER_FRAME, this.onEnterFrame);
    }

    private function onMarkerAdded (evt:FLARMarkerEvent) :void {
        trace("[" + evt.marker.patternId + "] added");
        if (evt.marker.patternId == 0)
        {
            this.modelContainer.visible = true;
            this.activeMarker = evt.marker;
        }
        if (evt.marker.patternId == 5)
        {
            this.rotationMarker = evt.marker;
        }
    }
```

```
    private function onMarkerUpdated (evt:FLARMarkerEvent) :void {
        if (evt.marker.patternId == 0)
        {
            this.modelContainer.visible = true;
            this.activeMarker = evt.marker;
        }
        if (evt.marker.patternId == 5)
        {
            trace("rot: "+ this.rotationMarker.rotationZ + ".");
        }
    }


    private function onMarkerRemoved (evt:FLARMarkerEvent) :void {
        trace("["+evt.marker.patternId+"] removed");
        if (evt.marker.patternId == 0)
        {
            this.modelContainer.visible = false;
            this.activeMarker = null;
        }
        if (evt.marker.patternId == 5)
        {
            this.rotationMarker = null;
        }
    }


    private function onEnterFrame (evt:Event) :void {
        if (this.activeMarker) {
            this.modelContainer.transform =
                AwayGeomUtils.convertMatrixToAwayMatrix(this.activeMarker.
transformMatrix);
            this.modelContainer.moveBackward(50);
            if (this.rotationMarker) {
                this.modelContainer.roll(-this.rotationMarker.rotationZ);
            }
        }
        if (this.modelAnimator) {
            this.modelAnimator.update(getTimer() * .005);
        }
        this.view.render();
        }
    }
}
```

CHAPTER 9

Prototyping AR with jMonkeyEngine

jMonkeyEngine is a powerful, Java-based game engine capable of creating interactive 3D content for a variety of uses. jMonkeyEngine provides a lot of high-level functionality for creating games and organizing assets and interactions. The ARMonkeyKit is a framework built on the jMonkeyEngine, and it incorporates the NyARToolKit AR libraries to provide a powerful toolset for prototyping AR applications on Windows.

In this chapter, you'll learn about the following topics:

- Introducing jMonkeyEngine and ARMonkeyKit

- Exploring ARMonkeyKit

- Thoughts from the developer

Introducing jMonkeyEngine and ARMonkeyKit

jMonkeyEngine is an open source, Java-based game engine for people who want a versatile, powerful platform for creating 3D games and interactive environments. jMonkeyEngine is composed of a collection of libraries, known collectively as *jME*, and an optional SDK, called jMonkeyPlatform, that provides higher-level tools and a user-friendly interface based on the NetBeans IDE, a popular open source IDE and widely used alternative to Eclipse. Programming with jMonkeyEngine requires a certain degree of comfort with object-oriented programming in Java, but it is intuitive and fairly accessible as a game engine.

ARMonkeyKit is a framework for rapid prototyping of AR applications, based on the jME libraries and NyARToolKit. AR researcher Adam Clarkson created ARMonkeyKit. The idea behind ARMonkeyKit is to bring the AR power of NyARToolKit together with the accessible 3D game programming tools of jMonkeyEngine.

Both projects are released under open source licenses. The latest version (3.0) of jMonkeyEngine is released under the permissive BSD-2 license. This license allows you to use the software in any way you wish, including incorporating the code into non–open source projects, something that is forbidden by GPL-style "copyleft" licenses. The ARMonkeyKit (like the NyARToolKit it incorporates) is released under the GPL.

Versions and Distinctions

jMonkeyEngine is an interesting and exciting project in its own right and, if you're interested in 3D game programming (including for the Android platform), you should definitely check it out at http://jmonkeyengine.org. You can download the jMonkeyPlatform, which includes the full set of libraries and SDK tools shown in Figure 9.1. Numerous tutorials are available that will help you learn jMonkeyEngine 3.0, which is the current version, in alpha release as of this writing.

Figure 9.1

The jMonkey-Platform

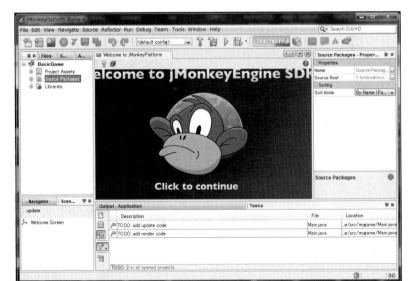

However, at present, ARMonkeyKit is based on an older version of the jME libraries, version 2.0. Information about using jME 2.0 is harder to come by, and the higher-level SDK tools based on the NetBeans IDE are not available for ARMonkeyKit. Rather, the ARMonkeyKit is distributed as an Eclipse project directory. A break in development and change in personnel between versions 2.0 and 3.0 of the jME meant that the API changed rather significantly.

There are plans to upgrade the ARMonkeyKit to conform to jME 3.0, but it is not possible to say where development on this will be by the time this book is published. The best way to delve into programming with ARMonkeyKit is to download the currently available version as described later in this chapter and to study the code. The code includes a lot of helpful comments, so with some effort you should be able to find your way around. This chapter will help to get you started.

Regarding the OS

jMonkeyEngine is available for any platform that can run Java, and the jMonkeyPlatform runs smoothly on both Windows and Mac OS X. However, the ARMonkeyKit uses libraries that enable integration between QuickTime video and Java to handle camera video. As of version 10.6, Snow Leopard, OS X no longer supports the QuickTime/Java libraries on which ARMonkeyKit depends.

This is not to say that ARMonkeyKit can't be run on Mac OS X. Although some necessary libraries are deprecated, it is likely that, with some effort, you can find the ones you need and get them working on your OS X system. However, the creator of ARMonkeyKit explicitly makes no claims about OS X support, and I personally ran out of patience in my efforts to set up the environment on OS X. For that reason, I'm following the creator's lead and considering ARMonkeyKit to be, for all intents and purposes, Windows-based at present. For Mac users determined to take a shot at getting ARMonkeyKit set up on their system, I'll offer what pointers I can.

Preliminaries

To use the ARMonkeyKit, you will need some resources installed on your system in advance. Some of these you probably have already installed for exercises in previous chapters.

Java Development Kit

You need an up-to-date Java Development Kit (JDK6), but you probably already have it. The JDK was also required to use Processing, so if you have gotten this far in the book, you should have already installed the JDK. If you do need to install it, find the appropriate package for your platform here:

```
www.oracle.com/technetwork/java/javase/downloads/index.html
```

If you are using a 64-bit version of Windows 7, don't install 64-bit Java. Stick with the 32-bit version or you will have problems.

Java Media Framework

The Java Media Framework (JMF) is a framework for enabling Java applets and applications to incorporate video and other media. This is not a default part of the JDK, so it is likely you don't yet have it installed. You can get it here:

`www.oracle.com/technetwork/java/javase/tech/index-jsp-140239.html`

Eclipse IDE

Eclipse is the world's most widely used open source, general-purpose IDE, and it is extremely popular for Java development. It is not the basis for the jMonkeyPlatform, which is based on another IDE, NetBeans, but ARMonkeyKit is distributed as an Eclipse project, making Eclipse the most straightforward option for developing with ARMonkeyKit. As mentioned in Chapter 8, "Browser-Based AR with ActionScript and FLARManager," Flash Builder is based on Eclipse, and the two share similar user interfaces. Furthermore, your installation of Eclipse for this chapter will also be useful in Chapter 10, "Setting Up NyARToolkit for Android," if you want to build NyARToolKit for Android. The Android SDK is also designed around Eclipse.

You can download Eclipse from `www.eclipse.org`. Choose a recent version (Galileo, Helios, or Indigo are all okay), and download either the Classic package or the Eclipse for Java Developers package for your platform. Follow the instructions to install Eclipse.

Subversion Client

Subversion (SVN) is one of several popular version control and release management systems for software development. It enables multiple developers to access and alter a code base without interfering with each other's work. Using SVN, software project managers create *repositories* where the code is stored and from where developers or users can check out the software, downloading a local copy of the software for themselves. Typically, open source software projects are hosted on a version control server of some kind, and contributing developers access the software using a client for the version control software.

For software projects with a large user base, it's customary to make the software available via simple download. However, in the case of some smaller projects, this may require more effort and time than it's worth. In these cases, people who want the software can often access it using the appropriate version control client. In the case of ARMonkeyKit, you can download the package using SVN.

The details for checking out a repository in SVN depend on the client you use, which in turn depends on your OS, because different clients are available for different platforms. Likewise, the process of installing SVN depends on your OS. For Windows, I recommend TortoiseSVN, available at `http://tortoisesvn.net/downloads.html`. TortoiseSVN includes all you need to use SVN, nicely incorporated into the Windows desktop environment.

If you're a Mac user and you've decided to throw caution to the wind and try to get ARMonkeyKit up and running on your system, I suggest the free 30-day trial version, which is easily the simplest to install and most user-friendly GUI-based SVN client available for Mac. You can find it at `www.versionsapp.com`.

Another alternative is to use Subclipse, an SVN client that integrates directly into Eclipse. You can learn about that here: `http://subclipse.tigris.org`.

QuickTime 7

You will need QuickTime 7, if you don't already have it. You can download that here:

`www.apple.com/quicktime/download`.

WinVDIG

Windows users will need WinVDIG installed. This is a video digitizer for enabling QuickTime to communicate with your webcam hardware under Windows. The ARMonkeyKit requires version 1.0.1. Note that this is *not* the most recent version. Changes made since version 1.0.1 cause problems for the current version of ARMonkeyKit. You can download WinVDIG at `www.eden.net.nz/7/20071008`.

Installing ARMonkeyKit

To get ARMonkeyKit running on your system, you need to do two things: First, check out the SVN repository. Next, import the downloaded directory as a project into Eclipse.

Checking Out the Code

To check out the ARMonkeyKit code from the SVN repository, first install TortoiseSVN. When you've done this, you'll find that some new SVN-related menu entries have been added to the standard Windows menu that comes up when you right-click over the desktop or over an open directory window. Specifically, an SVN Checkout entry and a TortoiseSVN submenu appear, as shown in Figure 9.2.

Choose SVN Checkout from this menu, and the Checkout dialog box will open, asking you for the URL of the repository and the local directory where you want the code to reside on your computer. The URL of the ARMonkeyKit repository is

`http://armonkeykit.googlecode.com/svn/trunk`

Figure 9.2

TortoiseSVN menu entries

Enter this into the URL field, and enter the local location you want to use for the Checkout directory, as shown in Figure 9.3. (Note that on my Japanese operating system, backslashes appear as yen signs.)

Figure 9.3

The Checkout dialog box

Another dialog box will display the progress of the Checkout box and list the files as they are downloaded to your computer. When it's finished, as shown in Figure 9.4, click OK. Your revision might not match the one in the figure exactly. This shouldn't be a problem.

Figure 9.4

Completing the checkout

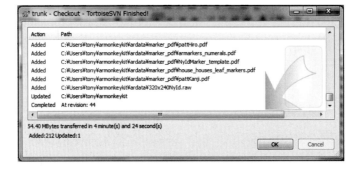

The Windows icon for the newly created directory will appear, as shown in Figure 9.5. It looks like an ordinary directory, except that it has a green circle with a white check mark on it, indicating that it has been successfully updated.

This directory now contains the complete ARMonkeyKit project.

Figure 9.5

The local SVN directory icon

Importing the Project into Eclipse

Start Eclipse. If this is your first time opening Eclipse, you'll see the Welcome screen first. Click the workbench icon shown in Figure 9.6. The first time you use Eclipse, you'll also be asked to create a workspace. The default for this is a directory called workspace in your home directory. Confirm this and continue on to the Eclipse workbench.

In Eclipse, choose File → Import, as shown in Figure 9.7. If you recall working in Flash Builder from Chapter 8, you should find the Eclipse workbench familiar. The process of importing a project is also similar. On the Select screen of the Import wizard, select Existing Projects Into Workspace and click Next, as shown in Figure 9.8.

Figure 9.6

The workbench icon

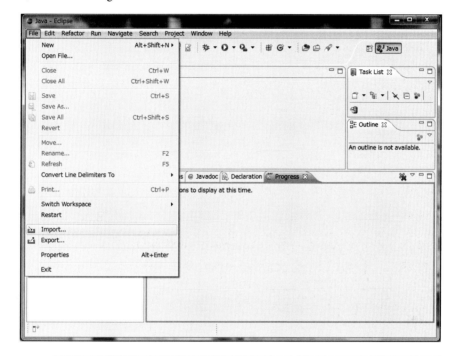

Figure 9.7

Importing in Eclipse

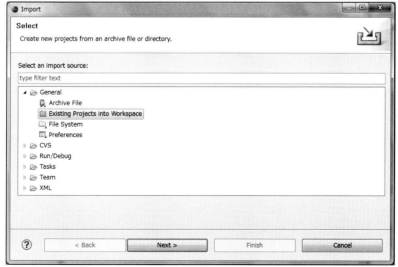

Figure 9.8

Importing an existing project into the workspace

On the Import Projects screen, click Browse by the Select Root Directory field to navigate to the directory you just created for ARMonkeyKit, as shown in Figure 9.9. Click Finish.

Figure 9.9

Importing an existing project into the workspace

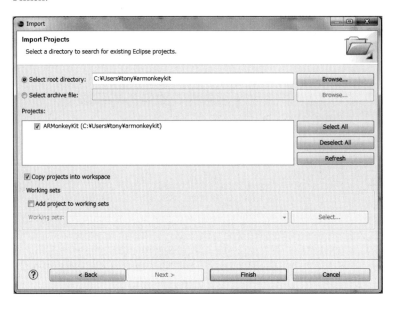

Figure 9.10

The project file tree in the Package Explorer

You should now see the project directory tree displayed in the Package Explorer window of the Eclipse workbench, as shown in Figure 9.10. You can look at the contents listings of directories and subdirectories by clicking the little triangle icons to the left of the directory names. Take some time to poke around in here to get a sense of what is in the project.

Before you attempt to run the project, there are some errors you may need to address. ARMonkeyKit makes some calls to deprecated API functions. By default, Eclipse is set up to produce an error for these cases. You need to tell Eclipse to ignore them. With the ARMonkeyKit project directory selected in the Package Explorer, choose Properties from the Project menu. In the Properties window, under Java Compiler, open Errors/Warnings and change the Forbidden Reference drop-down menu selection from Error to Ignore, as shown in Figure 9.11.

If you are working with a Windows 7 64-bit system, you may also have problems with the QTJava.zip library in your build path. In the Properties window, go to Java Build Path and click on Libraries to view any missing libraries. In Figure 9.12, the little × on the library icon next to QTJava.zip indicates that the library is missing. To fix this, click Edit and change the path for QTJava.zip to

`C:\Program Files(x86)\QuickTime\QTSystem.`

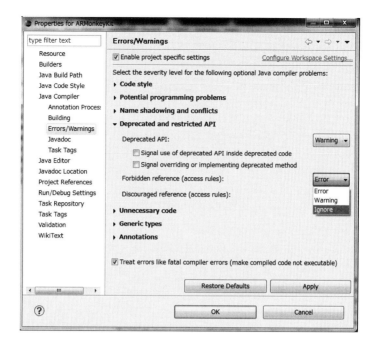

Figure 9.11

Ignoring forbidden references

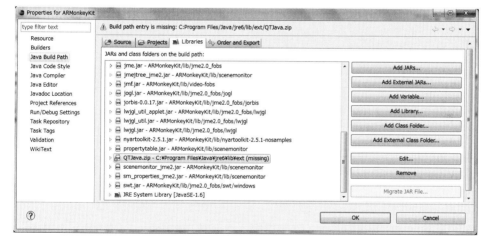

Figure 9.12

Missing library reference for `QTJava.zip`

Next, click the little triangle next to `QTJava.zip`, and check the path for the Native Library Location, as shown in Figure 9.13. If it reads

    C:/Program Files/QuickTime/QTSystem,

edit it to read

    C:/Program Files(x86)/QuickTime/QTSystem.

Figure 9.13

Checking the Native Library Location

Doing so will ensure that the 32-bit version of the library is used, and it should eliminate any remaining build errors. If you're still having build-path problems, go back and make sure that you have downloaded and installed the 32-bit versions of all the necessary Java tools.

If you're still following along on OS X, I can tell you that the QTJava.zip library should reside on your system in /System/Library/Java/Extensions. Beyond this, I'm afraid you're on your own. If you do manage to get ARMonkeyKit up and running on OS X, by all means, post the steps you took on the Web and send me a link. I'll post it on the website that accompanies this book.

Exploring ARMonkeyKit

If all has gone well, you should now have ARMonkeyKit compiling without errors in Eclipse. Don't worry if you have some warnings. To run the project, be sure your webcam is connected (the program will crash if it cannot find a camera), and then choose Run As → Java Application from the Run menu, as shown in Figure 9.14.

Figure 9.14

Running the project as a Java application

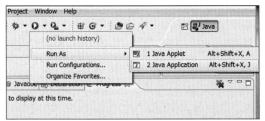

The project includes multiple applications, several of which are demonstrations of functionality. The first time you run the ARMonkeyKit project, you'll see a window like the one in Figure 9.15, asking you to choose which application to run. Once you've chosen one of these, it will become the default run configuration. If you want to see the list again when you run the project, you can choose Run As by right-clicking on the ARMonkeyKit project in the Package Explorer. You can also run individual examples in the same way by selecting them in the Package Explorer and right-clicking; then select Run As → Java Application.

For now, you'll look at a specific example. I think the most responsive and straightforward example is the ARMaggie application, which demonstrates loading of OBJ models. Choose the ARMaggie application shown in the list (it may not appear in the same order as shown in the Figure 9.15, but you will find it in the list).

Figure 9.15

Choosing the application to run

An OBJ Model-Loading Example

When you run an ARMaggie, the first thing you'll see is the Select Display Settings dialog box shown in Figure 9.16. You can choose the display dimensions or set the application to display in full-screen mode here. There is also a drop-down menu for selecting the OpenGL library to use, but you will not be changing this. For the time being, you can just leave all the settings at their default values and click OK.

The ARMaggie application is a simple example application that features an OBJ-format model that follows the movements of the Hiro pattern marker. By this time, you should have a Hiro marker printed up, so you can use that with this application. Once you've confirmed the display settings, two windows will appear. The main application window is shown in Figure 9.17.

Figure 9.16
Setting the display settings

Figure 9.17
The application window

By default, this application is configured to use the head-up display (HUD) format to display the camera video. This shows the camera video content in a small window in the lower-left corner of the window. When you hold the Hiro marker in view of the camera, the character will appear larger in the main window. This is not how you have seen camera video displayed in previous examples, but it is easy to edit the code to switch the camera display to fill the whole window, in which case the model will appear to rest on the marker. You'll see how to do this when you look at the code of the application.

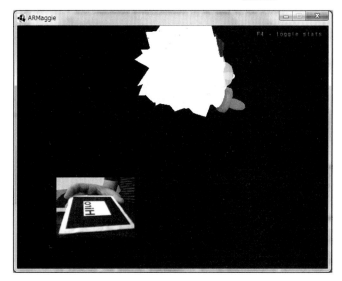

Before looking at the code, however, there's something else important to understand. In addition to the main application window, a second window came up when you ran the application. This is the Scene Monitor shown in Figure 9.18. It's important to check this window because the scene graph and its nodes form the basis of how jMonkeyEngine (and, by extension, ARMonkeyKit) organizes the content of a scene.

Figure 9.18
The Scene Monitor

Scene Graph and Nodes

The concepts of the scene graph and nodes are some of the most important things to understand in using jMonkeyEngine and ARMonkeyKit. The scene graph is a tree-structured collection of objects representing 3D assets or attributes in the scene. Some of the nodes of the tree are group nodes, which in turn contain child nodes with more specific data associated with them. jMonkeyEngine parses the data in the tree structure in such a way that the 3D assets in the scene graph affect each other according to their position in the scene graph. For example, a Light node attached to the Root node would provide lighting data for the scene and illuminate nodes representing models at the same level of the tree.

Figure 9.19

The Light node

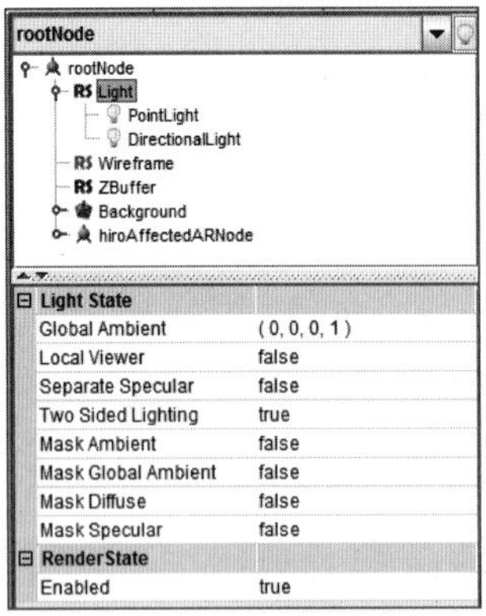

Figure 9.20

The PointLight node

Figure 9.21

The DirectionalLight node

Nodes are attached and detached from the scene graph in the code, as you will see in more detail later in this chapter. Values displayed for each node in the Scene Monitor can be edited directly in the Scene Monitor for runtime debugging, and they can, of course, also be set in the code. The Scene Monitor itself can be set to display or not to display when the application is run by means of a line of code. You'll see how all of this is done shortly, but first let's delve a little further into what the Scene Monitor shows.

If you click on the Light node in the Scene Monitor tree display, as shown in Figure 9.19, you'll see the general Light value settings. There are a lot of possible value settings at each node of the tree—some of them are not used in this example—but some of the values will probably be intuitively clear just from a glance. The Global Ambient value is the color setting (in RGBA) of the global ambient light. In this case, with R, G, and B values set to 0, this is black, meaning there is no global ambient light, only the specific light sources represented by child nodes of the Light node. Two Sided Lighting is turned on, enabling mesh surfaces to be lit from both front and back. Finally, the Light node is set to have rendering enabled.

The child nodes of Light represent a point light and a directional light, with the values displayed in Figure 9.20 and Figure 9.21, respectively. These are the lights that actually illuminate the scene. A *point light* is a light source where the light emanates in all directions from a single point. The direction of the light is determined by the location of the point, which is set here in the Location value. In this case, the x coordinate of the point light is 50, and the y and z coordinates are 0, so the light is placed directly on the x-axis. By contrast, the directional light does not have a location specified. Directional light affects an entire scene in the same way, coming from the same direction (in this way, it mimics a very faraway light source such as the sun, with practically parallel rays). Both of the light sources have Ambient, Diffuse, and Specular values in RGBA format. Try editing these values by clicking on the value field directly and manually entering numerical values (in the case of RGBA values, the values should be between 0.0 and 1.0). You will see the color of the lights change. You can also disable either of the lights or both of them by switching the Enabled value to false.

The Wireframe node shown in Figure 9.22 contains values for wireframe drawing of the scene. You can set the thickness of the line and toggle antialiasing (smoothing) and rendering. You can also determine whether front faces, back faces, or both are drawn in wireframe. Drawing front faces in wireframe has the effect of a typical wireframe-style render appearance, whereas drawing back-face wireframes has the effect of a simple toon-style contour line when the front faces are rendered solidly. You can see the difference between front-face wireframe rendering and back-face wireframe rendering in Figure 9.23.

Figure 9.22
The Wireframe node

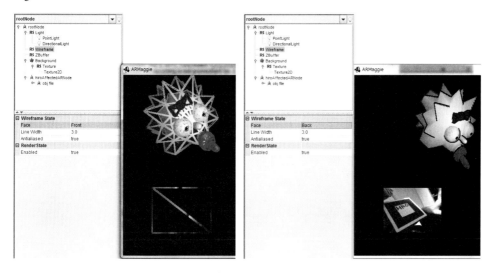

Figure 9.23
Front-face and back-face Wireframe options

The ZBuffer node contains settings that affect the way transparent objects are drawn over other objects along the z-axis of the view, as shown in Figure 9.24. The Test Function determines whether a pixel is drawn to the z buffer or not based on its alpha value.

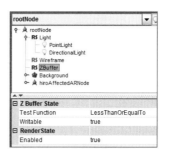

Figure 9.24
The ZBuffer node

The Background node shown in Figure 9.25 represents the plane on which the camera video is projected. This is the first node we've looked at that includes a spatial. A *spatial* is an object in jME that takes up space in the 3D world and can have location, rotation, and scale. Note that the term "object" here is used in the same sense of object-oriented programming, where an object is simply an instance of a class. Thus, objects in general are data and not necessarily spatial entities. This is as opposed to the Blender term "object," which refers to things in space. The Background object is a spatial because it is a mesh object. The 2D texture is contained on a child node, shown in Figure 9.26, which holds a variety of values concerning the mapping and positioning of the texture, its alpha and RGB combine properties, and other details.

The next node, the Hiro-affected AR node shown in Figure 9.27, is the first node we've seen that is not a jMonkeyEngine native node type. Rather, as you can probably guess, it is a node type specific to ARMonkeyKit, which in this application has been defined as the node that handles all 3D content that is affected by the Hiro marker. All the spatials inhabiting child nodes of this node will have their position and rotation governed by the Hiro marker. This is the node that contains the data about the position and orientation of the marker-affected spatial node. You can use these variables if you want to control something in the application using the position or rotation of the marker.

Drilling down a bit deeper, you can see that the content of the Hiro-affected node is an OBJ file, which makes up a single node, shown in Figure 9.28 with five child nodes, each labeled MAGGIE.

These five child nodes each represent portions of the mesh that together make up the 3D character object. Although there are no textures on this object, each of the mesh portions are associated with their own material, and each of

Figure 9.25

The Background node

rootNode	
Geometry	
Num Vertices	4
Num Normals	4
Num Texture Coords	4 (1 units)
Spatial	
Name	Background
Translation	(160, 120, 0)
Rotation	(0, 0, 1, 0)
Scale	(1, 1, 1)
Bounding Volume	None
Cull Hint	Never
Light Combine Mode	Off
Texture Combine Mode	CombineClosest
Normals Mode	NormalizeIfScaled
Collidable	true
Z Order	0
RenderQMode	QUEUE_ORTHO
Spatial Locks	
Lock Bounds	false
Lock Meshes	false
Lock Shadows	false
Lock Transforms	false
Lock Branch	false

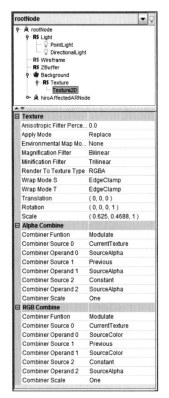

Figure 9.26

The Texture 2D node

Texture	
Anisotropic Filter Perce...	0.0
Apply Mode	Replace
Environmental Map Mo...	None
Magnification Filter	Bilinear
Minification Filter	Trilinear
Render To Texture Type	RGBA
Wrap Mode S	EdgeClamp
Wrap Mode T	EdgeClamp
Translation	(0, 0, 0)
Rotation	(0, 0, 0, 1)
Scale	(0.625, 0.4688, 1)
Alpha Combine	
Combiner Funtion	Modulate
Combiner Source 0	CurrentTexture
Combiner Operand 0	SourceAlpha
Combiner Source 1	Previous
Combiner Operand 1	SourceAlpha
Combiner Source 2	Constant
Combiner Operand 2	SourceAlpha
Combiner Scale	One
RGB Combine	
Combiner Funtion	Modulate
Combiner Source 0	CurrentTexture
Combiner Operand 0	SourceColor
Combiner Source 1	Previous
Combiner Operand 1	SourceColor
Combiner Source 2	Constant
Combiner Operand 2	SourceAlpha
Combiner Scale	One

Node	
Num Children	1
Spatial	
Name	hiroAffectedARNode
Translation	(-74.7535, 229.1059, -...
Rotation	(0.3983, 0.6785, -0.59...
Scale	(1, 1, 1)
Bounding Volume	Bounding Sphere
Cull Hint	Never
Light Combine Mode	CombineFirst
Texture Combine Mode	CombineClosest
Normals Mode	NormalizeIfScaled
Collidable	true
Z Order	0
RenderQMode	QUEUE_SKIP
Spatial Locks	
Lock Bounds	false
Lock Meshes	false
Lock Shadows	false
Lock Transforms	false
Lock Branch	false

Figure 9.27

The Hiro-affected AR node

these materials in turn has its ambient, diffuse, and specular color settings, as well as other material attribute values.

The first of these mesh portions is shown in Figure 9.29. This portion of the mesh represents the character's eyes. It is the only part of the mesh that is partially transparent (as you can see when looking at the character) and, for this reason, it is the only portion that has a blend child node, as shown in Figure 9.30. Like the other mesh parts, it has a material node, as shown in Figure 9.31. Note that the Ambient and Diffuse values for the material are all (1, 1, 1, 0.7), meaning they are white with slightly over half-opacity value.

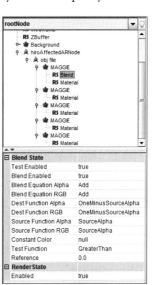

Figure 9.30

Blend node for transparency of the character's eyes

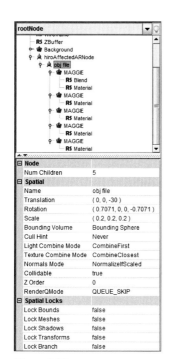

Figure 9.28

The OBJ file node

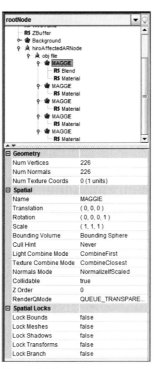

Figure 9.29

Mesh node representing the character's eyes

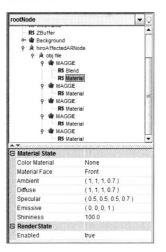

Figure 9.31

Material node for the character's eyes

Choose the other mesh nodes to see if you can determine which nodes correspond to which parts of the character object. The second to last, for example, shown highlighted in Figure 9.32, has material color values of (0.7, 0, 0, 1). This represents slightly less than fully bright red, so you can surmise that it is the pacifier. Try clicking on the RGBA values and editing them directly, as shown in Figure 9.33. If you enter RGBA values (0, 1, 0, 1) as shown, you will see the pacifier turn bright green.

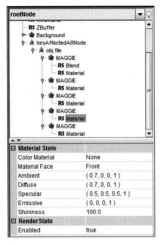

Figure 9.32

Values for the pacifier material node

Figure 9.33

Changing the ambient color of the pacifier

By now you should have a fairly clear idea of the overall meaning of the scene graph and of how nodes interact with each other. It should be clear that attaching a node to the scene graph is the equivalent of introducing its contents to the scene, and detaching the node removes its contents from the scene. Understanding this will be helpful in the next section as you take a look at the application's code.

Studying the Code

To study the example further, open the `ARMaggie.java` code in the Eclipse text editor by locating it in the Package Explorer, as shown in Figure 9.34. The full path to the file is `ARMonkeyKit/src/armonkeykit.examples.patternmarkers.modelloading/ARMaggie.java`.

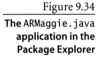

Figure 9.34

The `ARMaggie.java` application in the Package Explorer

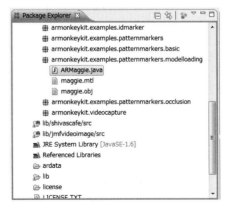

Double-click on the filename in the Package Explorer to open the file in the text editor. Toggle line numbers on by right-clicking on the left margin of the text editor and choosing Show Line Numbers from the menu, as shown in Figure 9.35.

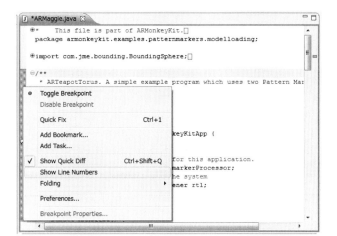

Figure 9.35

Toggling line numbers on

To walk through the code, we'll start at the end. This is where the `main()` function is defined, which makes it possible for this file to be run as a freestanding application. The `main()` function begins on line 129:

```
public static void main(String[] args) {
    ARMaggie app = new ARMaggie();
    app.setConfigShowMode(ConfigShowMode.AlwaysShow);
    app.start();
}
```

The first line of the content of the function creates a new object of type `ARMaggie()`, called `app`. This is the application itself. The second line sets the application to show its display options dialog box on startup. This is set to `AlwaysShow`. To turn off the display options dialog box (the application will start up with default values, rather than letting the user set them), this should be changed to `NeverShow`. Finally, the `start()` method is called. This is a method defined in the jME class `BaseGame`, from which the `ARMaggie` class inherits its attributes and methods. Object methods here are just like the ones you learned about in Processing. They are functions that are defined with respect to specific classes, and they are called from instances of objects by appending the method call to the object name, separated by a period, as in the line `app.start();`.

Next, we'll return to near the top of the file, where the definition of the `ARMaggie` class begins on line 37, as follows:

```
public class ARMaggie extends ARMonkeyKitApp {
```

This line declares the class and states that the class *extends* `ARMonkeyKitApp`. This is a commonly used feature of object-oriented programming languages such as Java. It means that the `ARMaggie` class will have all the same variables and methods associated with it as the `ARMonkeyKitApp` class, plus whatever has been added to `ARMaggie`. If the values of variables or methods from `ARMonkeyKitApp` are not defined (overridden) in `ARMaggie`, then they will default to their values from the definition of `ARMonkeyKitApp`.

`ARMonkeyKitApp`, in turn, extends the jME class `BaseSimpleGame` (you can see this by looking at line 70 of the file where this class is defined, `armonkeykit.core` `.app/ARMonkeyKitApp.java`. An easy way to find the file is to click your mouse in the `ARMonkeyKitApp` (after the extends clause) and to press F3. This means that `ARMaggie` is also a subclass of `BaseSimpleGame`, and it inherits the variables and methods of that class.

Lines 41 and 43 in `ARMaggie.java` declare two variables, *markerProcessor* and *rtl*, which are instances of `ARMonkeyKit` classes for handling markers and events:

```
private PatternMarkerProcessor markerProcessor;

private NodeRotateTranslateListener rtl;
```

The definition of the `ARMaggie()` constructor, which is the special method a class uses to create an instance of itself, begins on line 47 and is empty. When an instance is created, the constructor of the super class `ARMonkeyKitApp` will be used.

The next few methods override methods from `ARMonkeyKit` with values specific to `ARMaggie`. Beginning on line 61, the `simpleInitARSystem()` method is defined to initialize the marker processor and event listener and to register the event listener to the marker processor. This enables the event listener to communicate with the marker processor so that marker movement can trigger events and influence transformations in the 3D space.

```
protected void simpleInitARSystem() {
    markerProcessor = initPatternProcessor();
    rtl = new NodeRotateTranslateListener();
    markerProcessor.registerEventListener(rtl);
}
```

The `configOptions()` method beginning on line 68 sets two configuration option values:

```
protected void configOptions() {
    showSceneViewer = true; // enable or disable SceneMonitor
    showCameraFeedAsHUD = true;
}
```

The first option, `showSceneViewer`, enables or disables the Scene Monitor that you looked at in the previous section. When this is toggled to `true`, the Scene Monitor is displayed and the scene graph and its nodes can be viewed and edited during runtime. If this is toggled to `false`, the Scene Monitor is not displayed. The second option, `showCameraFeedAsHUD`, sets the camera video to be shown as a small head-up display in the lower-left corner of the application window. If this is set to `false`, the camera video feed is displayed normally, filling the entire background. As you noticed when you ran the ARMaggie application, the head-up display option is set to `true` in this example.

The next method is a bit longer than the others, and it does a number of important things that you will probably find a bit familiar from previous chapters. The method is called addMarkers(), but what it really does is register specific marker data to the marker processor and also set up the marker-affected nodes and their child nodes containing 3D content in the scene graph.

The first few lines of addMarkers(), beginning on line 78, create a PatternMarker object called kanji. The createMarkerObject() method takes arguments representing the name of the marker, the resolution of the marker, the pattern-file location, and the size of the marker. The marker is then registered to the marker processor:

```
PatternMarker kanji = markerProcessor.createMarkerObject("kanji", 16,
    "ardata/patt.kanji", 80);
markerProcessor.registerMarker(kanji);
```

The same thing is done for the Hiro marker:

```
PatternMarker hiro = markerProcessor.createMarkerObject("hiro", 16,
    "ardata/patt.hiro", 80);
markerProcessor.registerMarker(hiro);
```

Next, on line 90 a node is created called hiroAffectedARNode. This is an object of class Node and, as you can probably guess, it represents the Hiro-affected node in the scene graph. The next line of code, line 91, attaches it to the scene graph, making it a child node of the root node.

```
Node arAffectedNode = new Node("hiroAffectedARNode");
rootNode.attachChild(arAffectedNode);
```

Beginning on line 97, the node containing the character mesh is initialized and the object is loaded. The spatial node is then positioned, given a bounding-shaped object, and rotated to the desired orientation. Finally, on line 105, the maggie node is attached to the arAffectedNode, creating the node structure that you saw displayed in the Scene Monitor.

```
Node maggie = ObjectLoader.loadObjectFromFile("maggie",
    this.getClass().getResource("maggie.obj"));
maggie.setLocalScale(.2f);
maggie.setModelBound(new BoundingSphere());
maggie.updateModelBound();
maggie.setLocalTranslation(0, 0, -30);
maggie.setLocalRotation(Rotate.PITCH270);
arAffectedNode.attachChild(maggie);
```

Finally, the arAffectedNode needs to be associated with the event listener, which is done for the Hiro-affected node on line 112:

```
rtl.associate(hiro, arAffectedNode);
```

Between reading this code and studying the Scene Monitor, you should begin to have a sense of how the scene graph works and how to attach different kinds of assets and render states to it.

Other Functionality

ARMonkeyKit is usable but incomplete at the present. Run the different example applications to get a sense of what functionality is currently supported. Figure 9.36 shows the ARVideoPlayer application, which uses a video texture on a plane.

Figure 9.36

**A video-
textured plane**

More advanced functionality, such as supporting animated models and an update to the jME 3.0 API, are pending. So keep your eyes on ARMonkeyKit for potentially useful developments in the future.

Thoughts from the Developer

For some further insight into the background of ARMonkeyKit and into the directions of AR technologies in general, I turned to Adam Clarkson, the creator of ARMonkeyKit and a PhD researcher in the field of AR at the University of Durham. You can find out more about Adam and his research at his university website here: www.dur.ac.uk/adam.clarkson/.

Q: What initially attracted you to augmented reality research?

A: After completing a Bachelor of Science degree in computer science and specializing in software engineering, I knew that I wanted to continue my academic career and move toward research. I've always had an interest in the creative side of computing and digital design, and I wanted to continue looking at novel methods of content creation and delivery. I had heard a little about augmented reality, but like most people, I was more familiar with the term *virtual reality*, probably thanks to the media and films!

On applying to do my Masters by Research, my supervisor suggested that I might want to look into augmented reality, as it was an area that seemed to mesh closely with what I had done in the past and where I wanted to go. From the moment that I started,

I was hooked. The more I read, the more I saw the immense possibility of this technology, which has been around for a while but is becoming infinitely more possible with the hardware we have easily available today.

Q: What motivated you to begin creating the ARMonkeyKit?

A: The first thing that I noticed when starting my research was that there were only a limited number of frameworks available to enable developers to build AR systems. Of these, many required quite a lot of groundwork and a sound understanding of AR principles in order to get up and running. Throughout my degree, I had used Java almost exclusively for desktop applications, and as I felt comfortable with it as a language, I decided to see whether there were many frameworks out there for AR in Java.

Although I did find one or two, they were quite early in development and still posed a rather large barrier to entry. Add to that the fact that they usually required the use of native video libraries and OpenGL calls to render the graphics, and I saw potential for a new framework.

ARMonkeyKit was devised to satisfy the need for a rapid prototyping framework for AR applications written in Java that used the popular JMonkeyEngine as a video framework. ARMonkeyKit allows people to build a full AR application in a short amount of time, without worrying about the technicalities of AR systems and using a video library with which they are no doubt already familiar.

While the software is a piece of research, it is stable and usable, and as more and more reports came through from people using it and thanking me, it spurred on the development even though my research has moved away from the use of fiducial image markers, on which ARMonkeyKit is founded.

[Author's note: "Fiducial" or "fiduciary marker" refers to a physical object or pattern used as a point of reference for computer vision. It is a technical term for the markers used in AR.]

Q: Can you tell us a little bit about your own research or the research of others in your department?

A: The research that provided a base for ARMonkeyKit was largely an experiment into what different interaction techniques can be applied to augmented reality aside from the standard ideas of looking at a marker through a camera. This led to me looking at using markers as input devices, so occluding a marker from the scene triggered a button press, and also looking at controlling other things using markers.

The eventual path of the research was to follow the traditional approach and allow virtual content to be attached to markers, but then to take a diversion in terms of the camera. Instead of having the notion of a "see-through" system, where the user moves a camera and sees the object in place in the real world, I displayed everything on a monitor and attached a virtual camera to a fiducial marker. In doing this, the user could control the viewpoint shown onscreen by moving this fiducial, allowing them to explore other content freely. The example application here was to introduce a novel way of navigating around 3D models of buildings, where you aren't necessarily bothered about seeing the "real world" as well as the content attached to the fiducials.

Some would instinctively argue that by not introducing virtual content into the real world in an obvious manner, this is not augmented reality, but it is still making full use of AR technologies: the spatial relationship between markers, and the provision of a tangible interface for virtual content.

As I mentioned previously, all of this started out as a Masters by Research degree for myself and, at that time, I was the only person in our department actively researching augmented reality. However, as I progressed I quickly realized that I didn't want this to be a one-year project, and so I transferred to a PhD course.

With this came a fairly large shift in my research direction. With the extra time afforded to me through doing a PhD, I began to look past the fiducial marker–based approaches and started to look at augmented reality in unprepared environments. While I think there is great potential in marker-based AR applications, they are restricted to controlled environments, and my curiosity for the research area led me to question what happens when you can't introduce a fiducial, or you don't know the dimensions of the space you are in. After plenty of research, this is how I came across PTAMM [parallel tracking and multiple mapping], which is the system I am now extending as part of my PhD research.

As for my PhD, it is mainly concerned with providing a means of natural content placement for markerless AR systems. PTAMM is providing the base, but my extension is looking at the ways in which people want to interact with an environment to add content and how the technology can facilitate that.

Q: What have been your experiences working with the PTAMM tools?

A: As a concept, PTAMM is still something that I find awesome. While the creators specify that it be designed for use in mapping small workspaces, I have successfully mapped whole offices with it. The mapping itself takes a bit of time, and can be frustrating on that scale, but it is certainly doable. There are some issues that are introduced when you use the program on this scale, such as map points drifting away from where they should be due to multiple perspectives of the same area. However, this is a small price to pay when you are using the software out of its comfort zone, as it were.

The PTAMM library itself is nothing short of fantastic. From a programming point of view, and with regard to extending the functionality, which is my aim, it is a solid base on which to work. It is obvious that a great deal of thought has been put into the design of the data structure that underpins the system, and that is crucial for me as the data set can get very large when you are mapping areas as large as I am attempting to map!

The other thing that I find impressive about the PTAMM tool is its ability to work with almost any camera I have thrown at it. A five-minute calibration using the built-in tool, and you are ready to go with a new camera. On that front, I have found the best results to be using a wide angle lens camera as suggested in the documentation. I've been using it for a number of months now with a camera and a head-mounted display, and I really think that wherever markerless tracking in augmented reality goes, PTAMM will be right there with it.

Q: What do you think are some of the most interesting AR-related technologies or applications out there right now?

A: In terms of what is available on the market right now, Microsoft's Kinect has to be one of the best examples of camera-based tracking. While it may seem like a novelty on the face of it, the technology that is underpinning every aspect of it is very promising for the future of augmented reality—especially at the price point for which you can pick one up.

As an outright augmented reality system, I'd have to choose applications such as Layar and other similar mobile apps. Mobile AR is a great platform, and it is something that I intend to get involved in sooner rather than later. The power of smartphones now provides such a perfect base that it would be foolish not to take full advantage of them. In addition to this, it's refreshing to see that QR codes are being used more and more in advertising campaigns. I even saw one on a TV advertisement last night, which will provide a gateway and make more and more people aware of the idea of fiducials and prepare them for when augmented reality really hits the market hard.

I do reserve a special mention for the marketing on the recent *Star Trek* film (2009), which was one of the first augmented reality apps I saw. It is a model that has become more commonplace now, that a brochure or a printable document from a company's website bears a fiducial, and it allows you to view more content by holding it in front of you webcam. This kind of AR might not be pushing the bounds of the technology, but it is getting it into the mass market and I find that to be very interesting in proving the validity of AR as an interaction technique.

Q: Where do you see AR going in the future? Are there any especially exciting directions you imagine things moving in?

A: Mobile. It's all going to be about mobile, in my opinion. Until they perfect a contact lens that has a display built in, or regular glasses that can be used as a display medium, but even then I think it will be a smartphone powering the display. I also think that as technologies like PTAMM become stronger, more stable, and faster at mapping, we will see the end of fiducial-based AR. While it has a great place in the early development of the technology and particularly the commercial market, I see the fiducial as a stepping stone on to content being placed more naturally into environments.

I also think there is an obvious future in learning and training applications. By being able to replicate certain situations in a real environment but making use of virtual content, it is possible to provide a better stage for learning. Take the medical profession, for example. Medicine is often at the forefront of new technologies in all areas, and augmented reality is no different. By enabling a surgeon to practice techniques using real equipment but on a virtual patient, you give them more learning time in a safe environment. Additionally, with the right display technology, AR can be used to provide useful feedback to a surgeon during an operation on a real patient.

I mentioned Layar as an example of a very successful mobile app that is out at the minute. I think apps such as these are already providing the basis for the future of augmented reality. There are thousands of people out there using apps like Layar that don't have a clue that they are using augmented reality technology, and they probably wouldn't know what it was if you asked them. This is the future for me. AR should be an enabling technology, a transparent layer that the general consumer sees as a natural interaction between their virtual content and the world around them. Be it in an office space where virtual 3D models are placed on a meeting table and discussed, videos are viewed by looking at a wall, or on the move picking up navigation information and estimated arrival times, it will eventually become a natural part of task completion. Apps like Layar might be there already, and that's just proving that augmented reality certainly has a big future ahead.

CHAPTER 10

Setting Up NyARToolkit for Android

Smartphones represent a major milestone on the road to AR ubiquity with their integrated camera and display, constant connectivity, and near universal adoption. Android has become one of the most popular mobile platforms in the world. It is open source and Java-based, and the Android SDK is very well supported and documented, making it an ideal place to begin with mobile AR application development. This chapter will show you the basics of getting an AR application up and running on an Android-based mobile device.

In this chapter, you'll learn about the following topics:

- Android and the Android SDK

- NyARToolkit for Android

- Going further with Android

Android and the Android SDK

The last few years have seen smartphones become the standard for mobile devices. *Smartphones* are handheld computers capable of running a vast array of third-party applications created under (to various degrees) open development models. Cameras are standard on these phones, as are displays with all the functionality of small computer monitors. Because they are connected to wireless phone networks, they have access to the Internet almost all the time. Location-aware functionality is standard, and accelerometer-based tilt and direction sensitivity is also common.

All of these features, plus the fact that nearly everybody has a smartphone, make smartphones a natural fit for many kinds of AR applications. Location- and direction-aware applications such as junaio, Wikitude, and Layar can provide powerful location-annotation services. Meanwhile, computer vision–based AR applications, such as those described in this book, can take advantage of the device's camera and constant connectivity to augment the user's view with 3D content anywhere.

Android is Google's open source, Java-based mobile operating system. Because it is an open platform, it is not associated with a specific device. Rather, a wide variety of devices on a variety of mobile carriers run Android. Handsets from HTC, Samsung, Motorola, and numerous other smaller players all use Android as their OS. In 2010, Android shot to near the top of the list of the most widely adopted operating systems.

Developers interested in creating applications for Android have an excellent set of resources available to them in the well-supported and well-documented Android SDK. In this chapter, you'll see how to set that up in Eclipse and how to run the NyARToolkit sample application on your Android hardware.

What You'll Need

There are a few requirements for following along with this chapter, both in terms of hardware and software.

Hardware

The most important thing you'll need to have on hand to get the most out of this chapter is an Android device. Any Android smartphone that runs Android version 2.1 or later should do for the version of NyARToolkit you'll be working with in this chapter. If you have an older Android version, you can use an older version of NyARToolkit, but the details of getting it to run might be slightly different from what is presented here.

This requirement is a bit exceptional. Typically, Android development does not absolutely require having an Android device on which to develop. The Android SDK includes emulator software that enables you to run Android applications on your desktop without any external hardware. However, at present the emulator does not have the capability to access your computer's camera directly as though it were the device's camera.

Earlier versions of the NyARToolkit (version 2.52) for Android had some limited support for viewing in the emulator that has since been dropped (hopefully temporarily). This was a rather convoluted setup. Rather than getting video directly from the computer's webcam hardware, the NyARToolkit environment could be set up to receive a stream of video frames from the Web via HTTP. You could then run a separate webcam broadcaster, which would create a web server on your machine whose sole purpose was to stream your camera's video to a URL. Currently, no version of NyARToolkit works out of the box (without a lot of fairly advanced Java tweaking) with the emulator, but if you are a skilled Java hacker, you can search online for how to display webcam content in the Android emulator, and you will find several code samples that should help you set this up yourself.

Figure 10.1

A Huawei IDEOS Android phone

There are plenty of easier ways described throughout this book to run AR applications on your desktop, though. This chapter's main focus is getting the NyARToolkit up and running on a mobile device.

My own Android device is the Huawei IDEOS shown in Figure 10.1. It's the least expensive Android handset I could find, and it's one of the only ones available where I live (Japan) without restrictive (and usually permanent) SIM card locking. It's far from a 3D powerhouse, but it's sufficient to run graphical applications such as NyARToolkit. It runs Android v2.2. NyARToolkit version 3.0 should run on any Android device running v2.1 or later.

Software

The software you'll need is all available free of charge, and much of it is open source. Some of it is also likely already installed on your computer if you have been working through other chapters of this book.

You will need the Java Development Kit (JDK) 6. If you have been working with Processing or ARMonkeyToolkit, then you should already have this installed, and you shouldn't need to worry about it. If not, it is available from `www.oracle.com/technetwork/java/javase/downloads/index.html`.

Install the version for your platform. If you are on a 64-bit version of Windows 7, though, do not install the 64-bit version of the JDK6. Go with the 32-bit version instead.

You will need a fairly recent version of Eclipse (versions Galileo, Helios, and Indigo are all okay). If you have previously worked with ARMonkeyToolkit, you should already have this installed. If not, get it here: `www.eclipse.org/downloads/`. Download either the Classic configuration or the Eclipse for Java Developers configuration.

Finally, you'll need to download the Android SDK. You can find it here: `http://developer.android.com/sdk/index.html`. Download the SDK archive, and unzip it to an accessible place on your hard drive. Your computer's home directory is a good choice.

You'll also need the Android Development Tools (ADT) Plug-in for Eclipse, but you will download and install this plug-in from within Eclipse, as discussed in the next section.

Setting Up the Android SDK in Eclipse

Once you've downloaded and unzipped the Android SDK, you'll need to prepare your Eclipse environment to use it. This also involves installing the Android Development Tools Plug-in.

To do this, start Eclipse. From the Help menu, choose Install New Software, as shown in Figure 10.2. When you do this, the Install dialog box shown in Figure 10.3 will open. To the right of the field labeled Type Or Select A Site, click the Add button to add a new site from which to download software.

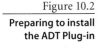

Figure 10.2

Preparing to install the ADT Plug-in

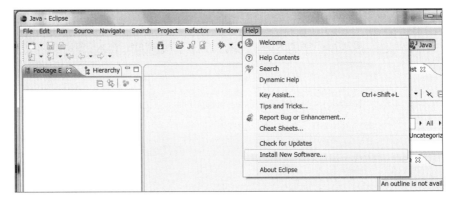

Fill in the fields of the Add Site dialog box as shown in Figure 10.4. For the Name field, enter **ADT Plugin**. For the Location field, enter the URL

`https://dl-ssl.google.com/android/eclipse/`.

Then click OK.

The Install dialog box should now look like Figure 10.5, with the Work With field displaying the URL you just entered and Developer Tools displayed in the software window. If you click the triangle icon to the left of Developer Tools, you will see a more detailed listing of the contents. Click Next.

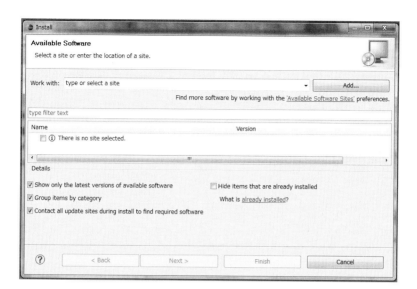

Figure 10.3

Choosing software to install

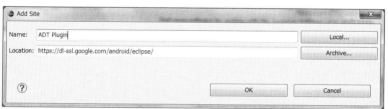

Figure 10.4

Entering the location for the ADT Plug-in

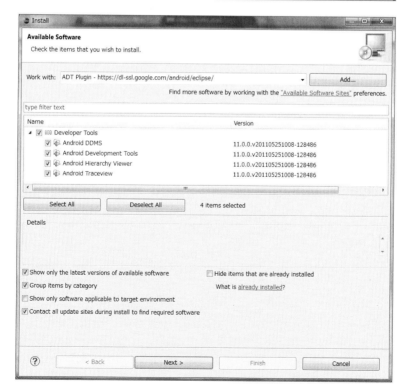

Figure 10.5

Selecting Developer Tools for download

You'll go through some more standard boilerplate dialog boxes. When you're asked to review the items for download, click Next. When you're asked to review the licenses, choose the "I accept the terms of the license agreements" radio button and click Next. When you're asked to restart Eclipse, click Restart Now.

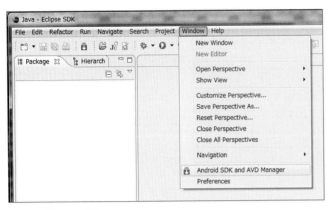

If all went as it should have, then you should now have the Android Development Tools Plug-in installed in Eclipse. You can verify this by making sure that the Android SDK and AVD Manager entry is present in the Window menu, as shown in Figure 10.6. Open this now to finish downloading the necessary packages.

In the Android SDK and AVD Manager, choose Available Packages, as shown in Figure 10.7. This shows all the Android packages and revisions available for download. Check both Android Repository and Third Party Add-Ons.

Figure 10.6

The Android SDK and AVD Manager in the Window menu

You don't need all the third-party add-ons, but there's no particular benefit in picking and choosing. Downloading them all is simpler. Click Install Selected, choose the Accept All radio button in the license confirmation dialog box, and then fix yourself a cup of coffee while the whole shebang installs.

Figure 10.7

Browsing available packages

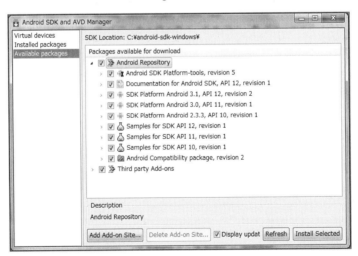

Once you've installed all the packages, there's one more thing you haven't yet done to set up your Android development environment: Eclipse still doesn't know where you put the Android SDK directory that you downloaded at the beginning of this section. Open Preferences from the Window menu, and click on Android for the Android Preferences window. Beside the field labeled SDK Location, click the Browse button and navigate to the location of your Android SDK directory, as shown in Figure 10.8. When you've done so, click Apply.

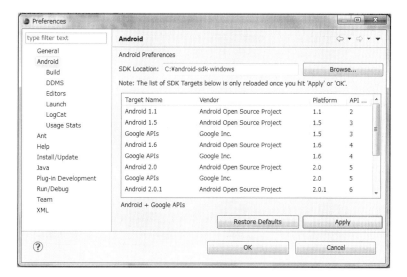

Figure 10.8

The SDK Location field in the Android preferences

Creating a Virtual Device

An Android Virtual Device (AVD) is a platform to which Android apps can be built so that they run in the desktop emulator. To run an Android app in the emulator, you must first define at least one AVD and set parameters, such as the Android version that it runs, its memory allotment, and various other optional specifications.

Although you can't test the camera behavior through the emulator, setting up an AVD is a standard part of preparing to do any Android development. In this case, it will at least enable you to ensure that the application builds and runs without show-stopping errors before connecting your hardware and building to the device.

Figure 10.9

Adding a virtual device (AVD) in the ADT Plug-in

You add an AVD using the Android SDK and AVD Manager that you used to install and revise packages previously. You can access this via the Android SDK and AVD Manager entry in the Window menu, as described in the previous section. In the Android SDK and AVD Manager, click Virtual Devices to see the list of virtual devices (which is empty by default), as shown in Figure 10.9. To add a new virtual device, click New.

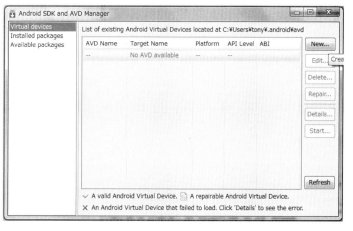

A Create New Android Virtual Device window will open, as shown in Figure 10.10. Give your AVD a name in the Name field. Since you will be creating only one AVD for

Figure 10.10

Virtual device settings

the time being, you can name it something simple, like **My_AVD**. Of course, if you want to use the emulator to test an application for various Android device configurations, you should give the AVD a descriptive name. For this one, set the Target either to Android 2.1 or Android 2.2. I set it to Android 2.2 because that's the version used by my handset. The other values can all be left exactly as they are. When you click Create AVD, you'll see the AVD appear in the list of devices in the AVD Manager, as shown in Figure 10.11.

You're now ready to begin running software in the emulator.

Figure 10.11

A device in the AVD Manager

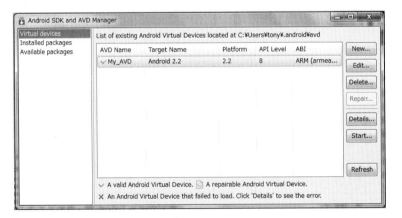

NyARToolkit for Android

NyARToolkit for Android is another port of the same NyARToolkit that you've encountered in several guises throughout this book. You saw the NyARToolkit for Processing and the FLARToolkit, which was in turn based on NyARToolkit. All of these are ports or variations of the original ARToolkit from HitLab at the University of Washington.

NyARToolkit for Android is developed by the Japan Android users group, and unfortunately very little exists in terms of organized online documentation; what little does exist is mostly written in Japanese. For this reason, if you want to go much further than the introductory steps of this chapter, you will need to immerse yourself in Java programming for the Android environment in order to study the code directly. You can download the latest package from `http://sourceforge.jp/projects/nyartoolkit-and/`. As of this writing, the latest available version is version 3.0.0. Download the file `NyARToolkit_Android_v3.0 .0-1os2.1.zip` and unzip it in an accessible place on your hard drive to get started.

Importing and Running the Project

Importing an existing project into Eclipse is straightforward. Choose File → Import to bring up the Select screen of the Import wizard, shown in Figure 10.12. Select Existing Projects Into Workspace, as shown in the figure, and click Next.

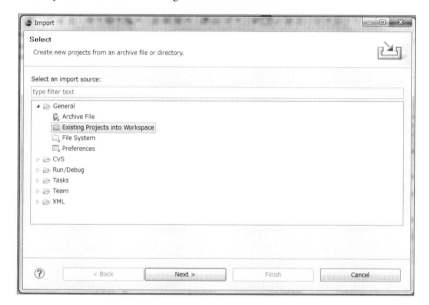

Figure 10.12

The Select screen of the Import wizard

On the next screen, Import Projects, click Browse and navigate to your unzipped NyARToolkit directory, as shown in Figure 10.13. Make sure Copy Projects Into Workspace is checked, and click Finish.

At this point, your mileage may vary somewhat depending on your own computer's configuration. If no errors are reported right off the bat, you can skip the next few troubleshooting steps and go straight to running the Android application in the emulator. However, when I initially imported NyARToolkit version 3.0 on my system, 413 errors popped up immediately. You can see any errors by clicking on the Problems tab in your Eclipse desktop, as shown in Figure 10.14.

Figure 10.13

**Importing the
project**

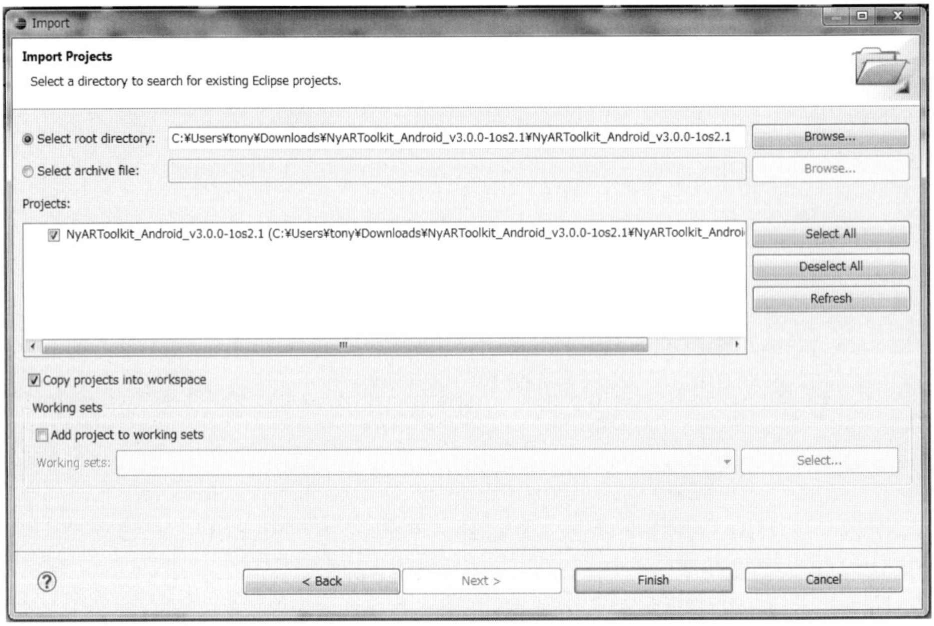

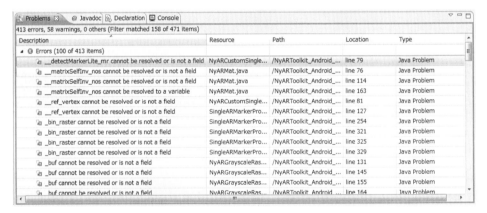

Figure 10.14

A ton of errors

None of the errors' descriptions give much of a hint as to the actual problem here, but it turns out that, in my case, all 413 of these errors originate from the same simple cause: the text encoding is incorrect, making problems for code files that incorporate Japanese-language comments.

If you don't read Japanese, you probably don't see a huge difference between the two encodings shown in Figure 10.15, but there's a big difference. The first one is utter gibberish, and the second one is properly commented code (as a hint to be able to recognize the difference, note that the gibberish one is a more densely packed–looking series of symbols and includes diamonds, arrows, and other noncharacter symbols). To see the files causing the errors, double-click on the Resource column for the error in the Problems window. It is likely that you'll see garbled Japanese.

Figure 10.15

Gibberish vs. Japanese

```
NyARCustomSingleDetectMarker.java

/**
 * 蜀◆K髢訂諛−縺ァ縺吶◆
 * 縺薙髢訂諛−縺ャ縲》his縺ョ蟒梧ヮ。蛻◆浩蠖「諠◆∵蟷励Oク蛷代縺」縲縺溘縺呈羲讙−蟷励ャ縺吶◆
 * @param i_coord
 * @param i_vertex_index
 * @throws NyARException
 */
protected void updateSquareInfo(NyARIntCoordinates i_coord,int[] i_vertex_index)
{
    NyARMatchPattResult mr=this.__detectMarkerLite_mr;
    //深エ驛ュ蠎ァ譓吶°縺蛾ゥ♪蟶ヲ縺ク縺闍医↓蛻画蜊
    NyARIntPoint2d[] vertex=this.__ref_vertex;   //C隱◆エ蝟↑繧峨縺、繝ゥ縺ェ繧峨縺」蜷ァ縺◆〒蟶溿潯」◆
    vertex[0]=i_coord.items[i_vertex_index[0]];
    vertex[1]=i_coord.items[i_vertex_index[1]];
    vertex[2]=i_coord.items[i_vertex_index[2]];
    vertex[3]=i_coord.items[i_vertex_index[3]];
```

```
NyARCustomSingleDetectMarker.java

/**
 * 内部関数です。
 * この関数は、thisの二次元矩形情報プロパティを更新します。
 * @param i_coord
 * @param i_vertex_index
 * @throws NyARException
 */
protected void updateSquareInfo(NyARIntCoordinates i_coord,int[] i_vertex_index)
{
    NyARMatchPattResult mr=this.__detectMarkerLite_mr;
    //輪郭座標から頂点リストに変換
    NyARIntPoint2d[] vertex=this.__ref_vertex;   //C言語ならポインタ扱いで実装
    vertex[0]=i_coord.items[i_vertex_index[0]];
    vertex[1]=i_coord.items[i_vertex_index[1]];
    vertex[2]=i_coord.items[i_vertex_index[2]];
    vertex[3]=i_coord.items[i_vertex_index[3]];
```

To fix the problem, choose Edit → Set Encoding, as shown in Figure 10.16. In the Set Encoding dialog box, click the Other radio button and choose UTF-8 from the drop-down menu, as shown in Figure 10.17.

Unfortunately, although it is possible to set a default encoding for all text files in a project, I have found that this seems to work only for newly created files. I haven't found a way to switch all existing files to UTF-8 in one stroke. (I invite readers who know how this can be done to contact me to let me know.) This means that each file must be switched individually by calling it up in the editor and changing the encoding as described previously. The good news is that you will find that many of the errors are in the same files, so there are far fewer than 413 files that need to be changed.

Figure 10.16

The Set Encoding menu entry

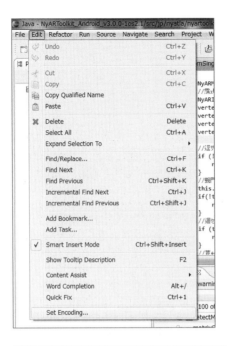

Figure 10.17

Setting the encoding to UTF-8

If an error does not seem to go away when you change the file's encoding, simply ignore it and change the encoding of the other files. Once all the problematic files have

Figure 10.18

Running as an Android project

been set to UTF-8, all the problems should disappear. When there are no more errors, run the project by clicking the ▶ icon. In the Run As dialog box, choose Android Application, as shown in Figure 10.18.

If everything has been configured correctly, running your application from Eclipse in this way should automatically start the emulator, install the application, and execute the application on the AVD in the emulator. Of course, you already know that the result won't be quite what you might hope for. The emulator has no access to a camera, so the video content is displayed as a standard animated placeholder of a moving plane over a black-and-white-checkered background, as shown in Figure 10.19. It's not very exciting to look at, but you should be pleased to have gotten this far; the application is running without problems. You can now set up your device to see it do what it's supposed to do. Shut down the emulator, and turn your attention to your Android device.

Figure 10.19

Running in the emulator

Setting Up Your Device

Setting up an Android device for development can be very simple or somewhat more complicated. In this respect, Mac OS has the advantage over Windows, at least in my own experience with the IDEOS, which a bit of investigation has shown me is at least somewhat general to other Android handsets. On Mac OS X, you should simply be able to plug and play. First, set your Android device to enable USB debugging. Go to Settings → Application → Development to find the USB debugging toggle switch, and make sure it's turned on. Then simply connect your Android device to your computer's USB port, and run your application again. Your Eclipse/ADT development environment should automatically recognize the presence of an Android device and install and run the application on your device. It's that easy! (Developers accustomed to working with iOS development will be especially impressed by how easy it can be to install software on a smartphone from a Mac.)

For whatever reason, Windows systems may require you to install a driver for your Android phone before you get to plug and play as you can with Mac OS X. Where you get this driver depends entirely on your hardware, so I can't give you specific instructions. I can give you a few hints that might help shorten your Google time, though. In the case of my IDEOS phone, the Windows driver can be found on the phone itself. Getting at the driver is a bit unintuitive. When you connect the phone to upload the driver, both USB debugging and data sharing should be disabled. This will cause the phone to be displayed as an external drive containing the driver. Install the driver, and then turn USB debugging back on to run the software.

Finally, with the device connected by USB, run the application. The application will be installed in your phone (you may have to wait a few minutes), and it soon should start running. You'll see a video display of the camera view, and when you point your camera at a Hiro or kanji marker, you'll see an animated Android droid character, as shown in Figure 10.20.

Congratulations! You've managed to install and run an AR application for Android!

Figure 10.20
NyARToolkit on IDEOS

Going Further with Android

NyARToolkit for Android is under active development, and it remains in a state of constant flux, with new features being added (and occasionally dropped) with regularity. It's very much a tool for programmers, and you will need to become proficient in Java development for Android in order to take advantage of it. Unlike some of the other implementations you've seen throughout this book, there isn't a simple template that an inexperienced programmer can tweak easily to make changes to the content.

3D Assets for NyARToolkit for Android

Up until recently, the NyARToolkit for Android had the quirk of depending on the Metasequoia (MQO) format for 3D assets. Metasequoia is a freeware (free-of-charge, closed source) and shareware application for 3D modeling and texturing that is popular in Japan, but much less so elsewhere. Metasequoia is available for Windows only, and it can be downloaded at `www.metaseq.net/english`. An exporter for Blender 2.58 to MQO format exists and can be found here:

`http://pr0jectze10.tuzigiri.com/simpleVC_20101030133458.html`.

NyARToolkit v. 3.0 can also import from the MD2 format, which currently has rudimentary export support from Blender 2.58. Plans are underway to implement OBJ support in NyARToolkit for Android, which will be a welcome improvement.

Learning Resources

Knowing the fundamentals of object-oriented programming in Java will make it much easier to study the NyARToolkit code yourself so that you can find out where the various functionalities are defined and how they are used. A number of Android programming books also offer gentle introductions to Java, and I recommend that you start with one of these if you plan to go further with Android development.

There are different approaches to take to learning Android development. For extending the NyARToolkit example, you'll need to know something about working with Android's OpenGL ES implementation. *Beginning Android Games* by Mario Zechner (Apress 2011) is a good place to start.

For background study of 3D development on mobile devices, *The OpenGL ES 2.0 Programming Guide* by Aaftab Munshi, Dan Ginsburg, and Dave Shreiner (Addison-Wesley Professional 2008) is a good general guide for 3D programming with OpenGL ES, the standard OpenGL implementation for mobile devices, and the one used by Android. While this guide won't necessarily give you a lot of hands-on Android programming examples, it will help to deepen your understanding of how 3D is handled on mobile devices.

Studying OpenGL ES, however, presupposes a decent level of familiarity with OpenGL. Tons of OpenGL tutorials and books are available and, in my opinion, you should study some of these if you plan to do any kind of 3D programming at all. The NeHe tutorials (`http://nehe.gamedev.net`) for OpenGL are very well known, and I highly recommend following them. I also recommend the OpenGL *SuperBible: Comprehensive Tutorial and Reference* by Richard S. Wright, Nicholas Haemel, Graham Sellers, and Benjamin Lipchak (Addison-Wesley Professional 2010).

There's a lot to learn about programming for Android, and indeed about programming for all the platforms and environments described throughout this book. I've only just scratched the surface here, but I hope that, through reading this book, you've begun to get a sense of some of the interesting possibilities of AR development. If anything here has inspired you to learn more, I've done what I set out to do. AR is an exciting and fast-moving field, and I hope that you will soon be having fun contributing to it.

Appendices

From Blender 2.49 to Blender 2.58

In Chapter 3, "Blender Modeling and Texturing Basics," and Chapter 4, "Creating a Low-Poly Animated Character," you learned to create animated 3D content in Blender. For reasons described in Chapter 3, the version chosen for that was Blender 2.49, an outdated version whose main benefit is up-to-date third-party export tools. This appendix will show you how to translate concepts from Blender version 2.49 to Blender version 2.58, the updated and much-improved version and most recent stable release as of this writing. Forward-looking users will want to learn Blender 2.58, but should be aware that export functionality for certain formats may lag behind. By the time this book is published, it is likely that a broader selection of formats will be supported.

In this appendix, you'll learn about the following topics:

- **Basics and views**
- **Mesh modeling**
- **Texturing, baking, and materials**
- **Rigging and animation**

Basics and Views

Within the Blender community, it's well known that Blender's event system and graphical user interface (GUI) have seen significant changes and improvements with the introduction of the 2.5 release series (hereafter version 2.5). For many beginners, this has been a source of confusion about where to begin studying Blender, particularly given the fact that some third-party exporters have not been rewritten yet to conform to the new (and still evolving) Python API.

The truth is, however, Blender is still Blender, and users of the 2.4 series (hereafter version 2.4) will not find it difficult to transition to version 2.5. Version 2.5 is better looking and better organized, but the underlying concepts and the way Blender handles its assets and data have not changed significantly.

Most of the tools work basically the same in version 2.5 as they did in version 2.4. Transitioning to version 2.5 is simply a matter of knowing where to look for functionality that has been moved in the interface or in some cases renamed. This appendix will tell you where functionality described in Chapter 3 and Chapter 4 can be found in Blender 2.5.

This appendix is *not* intended to be a freestanding rehash of the entire process of modeling, texturing, and animating a model as described in Chapter 3 and Chapter 4. You should follow the steps in Chapter 3 and Chapter 4, and then turn to this appendix in cases where functionality employed in those chapters is no longer where it is described in those chapters. The vast majority of steps from those chapters involving tools and hotkeys will carry over to version 2.5 without translation. This appendix will fill in the blanks.

It might help speed things up a bit if you read through this appendix quickly before trying to apply the steps from Chapter 3 and Chapter 4 to Blender 2.5. Having a general sense of the way that Blender has been redesigned between the two versions will save a little time looking for things.

The Default Desktop

The Buttons area (the area that covers the lower third of the desktop by default in version 2.4) has been entirely replaced by the Properties window, highlighted in Figure A.1. With a few exceptions, most of the functionality that was previously found in the Buttons area has migrated to the Properties window. The desktop also has a few more windows visible by default in Blender 2.5, including a Timeline window below the 3D Viewport and an Outliner in the upper-right corner, which enables an overview of scene data. The Timeline window is essentially identical to the Timeline in version 2.4, but now it is conveniently visible by default when Blender is first opened.

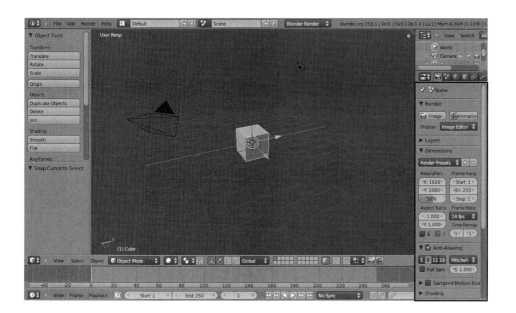

Figure A.1

The default desktop in Blender 2.58

Changing Views

As in Blender 2.4, the numeric keypad can be used to change the view of the 3D Viewport. The keys used are the same. The only difference is that Blender 2.5 starts up by default in Perspective view, whereas Blender 2.4 started up in Orthographic view. To switch to Orthographic view (which is best for modeling), you need to press 5 on the numeric keypad. As in version 2.4, all numeric keypad views can also be obtained by using the View menu on the header of the 3D Viewport, as shown in Figure A.2.

Layers

Placing objects on different layers is done with the M key, just as in Blender 2.4. The layer selection dialog box that opens looks a bit different in version 2.5, as you can see in Figure A.3, but its meaning is the same and should be self-explanatory.

Figure A.2

Switching to Front view with the View menu

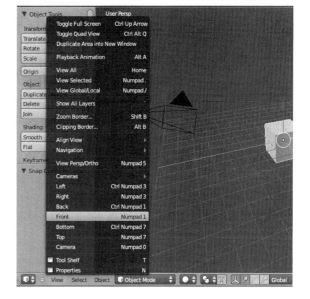

Figure A.3

Switching to Front view with the View menu

The Tool Shelf

A new feature in Blender 2.5 is the Tool Shelf, which occupies the left side of the 3D Viewport window. This can be toggled in and out of view by pressing the T key with the mouse over the 3D Viewport, as shown in Figure A.4. Note the Smooth and Flat buttons that control the way shading is calculated on the object's surface. These will come up again later in this appendix.

Figure A.4

Toggling the Tool Shelf in and out of view

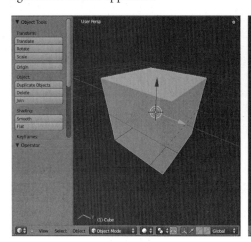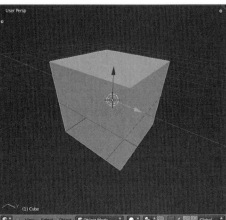

Splitting and Merging Windows

In Blender 2.4, splitting and merging windows is accomplished by clicking on the border between the windows and choosing to split or merge the windows in a dialog box. In Blender 2.5, this process is sped up. In the upper-right and lower-left corner of every window is a pattern of serrations or lines indicating the split/merge area. To split a window, click on this area in the corner of the window you want to split, as shown in Figure A.5, and drag in the direction that you want to split the window. Doing so will create two separate identical windows in the area occupied by the original window. The contents of these windows are independent and can now be selected using the Editor Type menu in the left corner of the header, just as in Blender 2.4.

Merging windows is done analogously to splitting windows, but in the opposite direction. To merge two windows, click on the split/merge area in the window corner just as you did to split the window, but this time drag the mouse into the second window you want to merge the first window into, as shown in Figure A.6. Doing so will eliminate the second window and result in the first window occupying the entire space where the two windows had been. Note that the windows edges must be aligned in the direction you want to merge the windows. If you want to merge windows horizontally, the horizontal top and bottom borders of the original windows must meet.

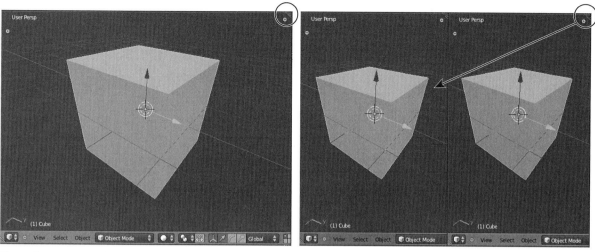

Figure A.5
Splitting a window in two

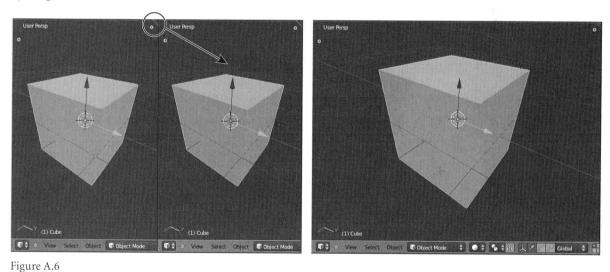

Figure A.6
Merging two windows together

Mesh Modeling

Most of the hotkeys and tools used to do the mesh modeling tasks in Chapter 3 are identical in Blender 2.5. This section points out a few superficial interface differences and a few more significant differences in where the mesh modeling–related functionality resides.

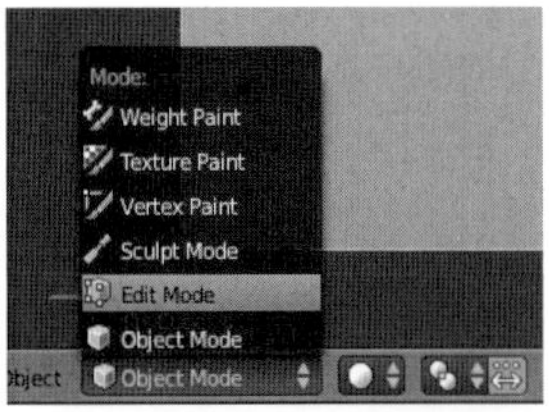

Figure A.7

Switching to Edit mode

Figure A.8

Subdivide Smooth in the Specials menu

Switching to Edit mode is done with the menu in the 3D Viewport header shown in Figure A.7, similar to Blender 2.4. In both versions, you use the Tab key.

The Subdivide Smooth command is found in the Specials menu shown in Figure A.8, which you open by pressing the W key in Edit mode, just as in Blender 2.4.

Modifiers are now handled in the Modifiers panel of the Properties window. The Modifiers panel is accessed with the wrench icon button in the Properties window header, as shown in Figure A.9. The Add Modifier button opens the menu shown in the same figure, where you can choose the modifier you want, just as in Blender 2.4.

There are some slight differences in the appearance of the Mirror modifier panel, as shown in Figure A.10. Option buttons from version 2.4 have been replaced by check boxes. Do Clipping is renamed Clipping. Otherwise, the changes are self-explanatory.

Figure A.9

Adding a Mirror modifier

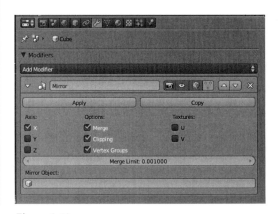

Figure A.10

The Mirror modifier panel

The Subdivision Surface (Subsurf) modifier panel appears as shown in Figure A.11. As with the Mirror modifier, the differences between versions 2.5 and 2.4 are mainly cosmetic and should be self-explanatory.

The Set Smooth functionality for smoothing the way the surface faces reflect light has been moved and renamed in Blender 2.5. There is no longer a Set Smooth button; instead there is a Smooth button located on the Tool Shelf under the Shading label, as shown in Figure A.12. The button formerly known as Set Solid is now the Flat button.

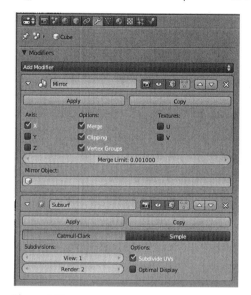

Figure A.11

The Subsurf modifier panel

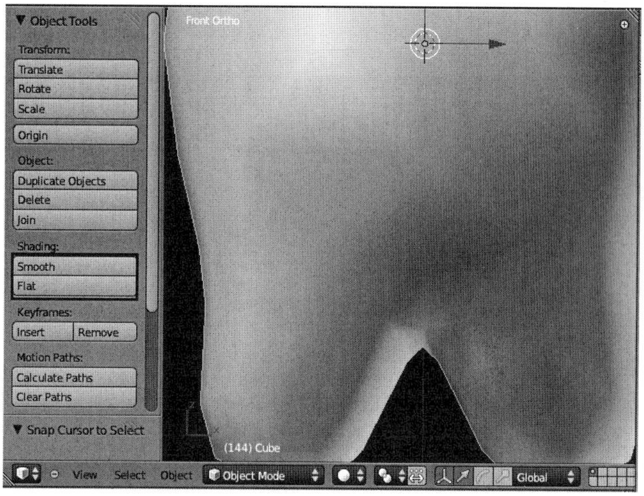

Figure A.12

Smooth and Flat Shading buttons

Texturing, Baking, and Materials

As in the case of mesh modeling, most of the hotkeys and tools are identical to version 2.4. Once again, the biggest differences are in functionality that previously was found in the Buttons area.

UV Textures and Unwrapping

In Blender 2.4, the UV texture slots are handled in the Buttons area. These have been moved to the Object Data Properties panel, accessed (when a Mesh object is selected) via the little triangular mesh-like icon in the Properties window header. The panel labeled UV Texture shown in Figure A.13 is where the UV textures are managed.

Figure A.13

The UV Texture panel

Figure A.14

Adding a UV texture

Clicking on the plus icon to the right of this panel will add a UV texture to the object. By default, the first UV texture will be named UVTex, and it will appear in the field, as shown in Figure A.14.

Adding seams to the model in preparation for UV unwrapping is done exactly as in Blender 2.4. You access the Edges menu shown in Figure A.15 by pressing Ctrl+E when in Edit mode, just as in Blender 2.4.

In Blender 2.4, the Window Type menu in the left corner of the window header is used to change the contents of windows. In Blender 2.5, the location is the same, but the icons have changed and the name of the menu is now Editor Type, as shown in Figure A.16. Some of the menu entries are also different from those in the version 2.4 menu.

You can see the header of the UV/Image Editor in Figure A.17. As you can see, there are a number of superficial differences and added data in the header. The associated UV texture, called UVTex, is shown in the header, and the empty image drop-down is in the form of a button labeled New, which you will click to create a new texture image.

Exporting the UV Layout is done just as in version 2.48, by accessing the Export UV Layout script, as shown in Figure A.18.

Figure A.15

Adding a seam with the Edges menu

Figure A.16

Choosing UV/Image Editor from the Editor Type menu

Figure A.17

The UV/Image header

Figure A.18

Exporting the UV Layout

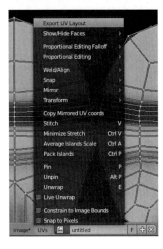

Once you've exported the UV Layout, you can work with it in GIMP exactly as described in Chapter 3.

Baking Ambient Occlusion

Setting ambient occlusion values and baking involve working in the Properties window, which is where much of the functionality of Blender 2.48's Buttons window has migrated. Turn on ambient occlusion by clicking the check box in the Ambient Occlusion panel of the World Properties window, as shown in Figure A.19.

The Bake panel is found in the Scene Properties window, as shown in Figure A.20. Select Ambient Occlusion from the Bake Mode menu, and click the Bake button to bake the ambient occlusion to a texture.

Material and Texture Settings

Material and texture values are also accessible in the Properties windows. Creating a texture for a material is done in the Texture Properties window, as shown in Figure A.21. Here, you can set the preview display to show the texture, or the material with the texture applied, or both, as shown in the figure.

Figure A.19

Ambient occlusion settings

Figure A.20

The Bake panel

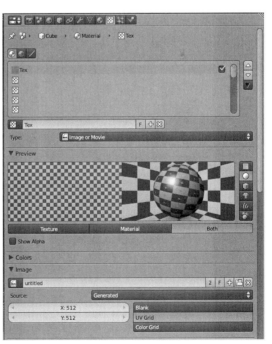

Figure A.21

Texture Properties window

Unlike in Blender 2.48, where texture mapping and influence values are set in the Material buttons area, these values are all set in the Texture Properties window in Blender 2.5, as shown in Figure A.22. In the Mapping panel, you can see the drop-down menu set to UV and, in the Influence panel, the check box next to Color is selected.

Figure A.22

Mapping and Influence panels

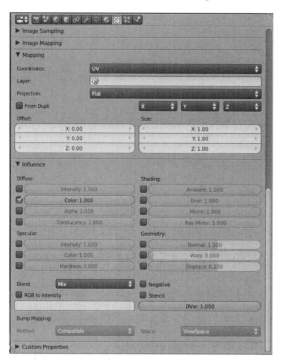

Rigging and Animation

As with the other topics covered in this appendix, there are differences in the location of functionality connected with rigging and animation. Functionality from the Buttons window has been moved elsewhere, and the Action editor has been incorporated into a more general editor, the Dope Sheet. This section will give you the details you need to know to translate the content of Chapter 4 for Blender 2.5.

Figure A.23

Adding an Armature object

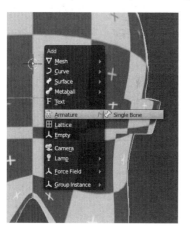

Setting Up an Armature

You add an Armature object in Blender 2.5 much the same way as you did in 2.4. Shift+A is the hotkey that brings up the Add menu. From the Add menu, select Armature → Single Bone, as shown in Figure A.23.

As in Blender 2.4, the bone is initially concealed within the mesh if it is not set to be rendered in X-Ray display mode. Setting the display mode to X-Ray is done on the Object properties tab in the Properties window, as shown in Figure A.24. Under the Display tab, select the check box next to X-Ray.

Unlike most buttons from the version 2.4 Buttons area, the X-Axis Mirror editing option has not migrated to the Properties window. Rather, the X-Axis Mirror editing option is accessible in the 3D Viewport Tool Shelf when an Armature object is selected, as you can see in Figure A.25.

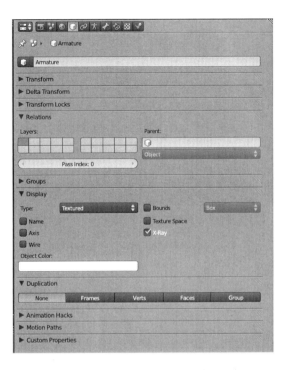

Figure A.24

Object properties for the Armature

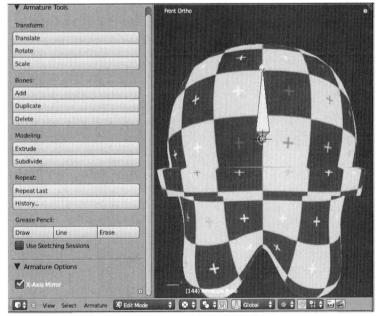

Figure A.25

Setting X-Axis mirroring

Editing of the armature proceeds identically to the way it happens in Blender 2.4. You use Ctrl+N to recalculate bone angles, although a few more options are available for this task, as shown in Figure A.26. For example, you can choose View Axis.

Figure A.26

Recalculating bone roll angles

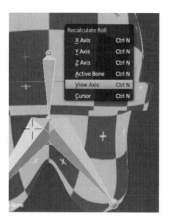

Associating the mesh with the armature uses the same hotkey, Ctrl+P, as Blender 2.4. The menu that comes up is slightly different, as you can see in Figure A.27. Armature Deform With Automatic Weights is the equivalent option to what you did in Chapter 4.

Figure A.27

Skinning with automatic weights

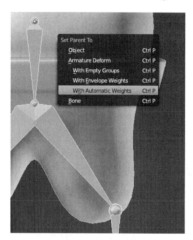

Figure A.28

Opening a Dope Sheet window

Working with the Dope Sheet

The Dope Sheet is a generalized animation editor that includes and expands on functionality from the Action editor in previous versions. Like all the other editor types, you can access the Dope Sheet using the Editor Type menu, as shown in Figure A.28.

The Action editor is accessed from the menu in the Dope Sheet header, as shown in Figure A.29. Although the Action editor looks very similar to the Dope Sheet, there are some important differences that become clearer when you work on more-complex animations. The Action editor focuses on a single object, whereas the Dope Sheet gives an overview of animation data for all objects.

You can create a new action by clicking the New button of the Action editor header, as shown in Figure A.30. Alternately, you can simply begin keying your armature, and an action called ArmatureAction will be created automatically. Keying the armature poses is done exactly the same way as in Blender 2.4: by pressing the I key over the 3D Viewport and choosing LocRot from the Insert Keyframe menu shown in Figure A.31.

When you've keyed the frames, the keyframes are represented in the Action editor as yellow or white diamonds, just as in Blender 2.4. Also similarly to Blender 2.4, you can display the keyed values of each bone's channel by clicking the little triangle to the left of the bone name. Figure A.32 shows keyframes for two bones, with one of the bone's complete location and rotation values displayed.

Copying and pasting keyframes in the Action editor is done exactly the same way as in Blender 2.4. The hotkeys and selection work essentially identically. The copy and paste buttons for poses are also in the same place in the 3D Viewport header but the icons are different, as you can see highlighted in Figure A.33.

Figure A.29

Choosing the Action editor

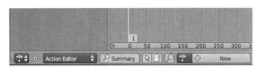

Figure A.30

The Action editor header

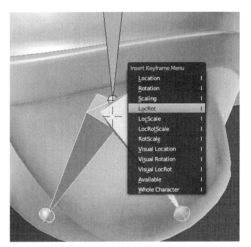

Figure A.31

Keying a pose

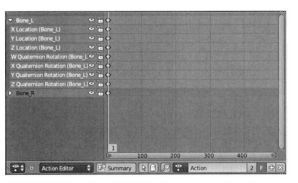

Figure A.32

Keyframes in the Action editor

Figure A.33

Pose copy and paste buttons

You now should have all the information you need to translate the processes described in Chapter 3 and Chapter 4 to the latest version of Blender. I hope it's clear that the differences are not all that insurmountable. You're not really learning a completely new piece of software, even though it might seem that way. Blender 2.5 is better organized and easier to use. As you continue learning Blender 2.5, you will also discover that it is extraordinarily configurable and customizable. For the purposes of this book, though, everything you need to know about making the switch from Blender 2.4 to version 2.5 should be here in this appendix.

File Formats and Exporting

Throughout this book, various programming environments are discussed. Each environment has different requirements in terms of the kind of 3D content it is able to handle. This appendix collects the information concerning file formats from throughout the book in one place so that you can quickly find out what file formats you need to use for the programming environment in which you're interested. In addition, this appendix includes information about how to export the file format you need from Blender.

In this appendix, you'll learn about the following topics:

- ▦ **Development environments and file formats**

- ▦ **Exporting from Blender**

Development Environments and File Formats

This section tells you which programming environment can process which file format and discusses any restrictions or complications you may encounter when using 3D assets in that particular environment.

Processing

Processing can import OBJ files using the OBJ Loader library found here:

```
http://code.google.com/p/saitoobjloader/downloads/list
```

Some efforts have been made to create import libraries for other formats, including MD2, but none of these has been developed to the same extent as the OBJ Loader library.

OBJ files do not support animation. Animated 3D models can be imported into Processing as an array of separate single-frame OBJ files, as described in Chapter 5, "3D Programming in Processing." However, this places significant demands on the memory used by the Processing sketch. For this reason, in terms of deforming textured 3D models, only very short animations featuring very low-poly models are possible in Processing at present.

FLARManager

FLARManager imports Collada (DAE) files. Collada files support animation, and FLARManager is able to handle animated 3D models in Collada format. However, there are some inconsistencies in how the files are read by the various 3D engines available to FLARManager (Away3D, Papervision), and the import functionality can be extremely sensitive to details of how the files were exported. Currently available Blender exporters for Collada may have mixed results. The best alternative is to export from Blender to FBX and to use Autodesk's proprietary, free-of-charge converter software to convert from FBX to Collada.

FLARManager also includes import support for the MD2 format.

ARMonkeyKit

ARMonkeyKit handles OBJ files. The jMonkeyEngine (JME) 3.0 platform handles animated Ogre Game Engine files, but this functionality is not yet available in ARMonkeyKit.

NyARToolKit for Android

NyARToolKit for Android traditionally imported only the Metasequoia (MQO) file format, but support is currently under development for OBJ files. Metasequoia is a free-of-charge 3D modeling and texturing application that is popular in Japan. Unfortunately, it is available only for Windows, and learning to use it is not straightforward because there is very little English-language documentation or tutorial material available. An up-to-date Blender exporter is available.

Exporting from Blender

This section presents instructions for exporting various formats from both Blender 2.49 and Blender 2.58, where exporters are available. In addition, it notes limitations in the currently available export functionality for both versions where such limitations exist.

OBJ

Export to OBJ files is well supported in Blender 2.49, and it has limited support in Blender 2.58. Like many of the export scripts discussed in this appendix, the OBJ export script is accessed via the File → Export menu, as shown in Figure B.1 (Notice the other contents of the menu. This menu contains all of the standard exporters for Blender 2.49.) Blender 2.49 support for OBJ export enables a variety of useful options, which you can select in the dialog box shown in Figure B.2. This dialog box appears after you have selected a location on your hard drive where you want to export the OBJ file(s). The Animation option in this dialog box causes the exporter to export separate OBJ and MTL (material) files for each frame in the animation range (as determined by the Start and End values in the Timeline). When exporting animation to OBJ files, it is a good idea to pick a dedicated directory in which to save the exported files.

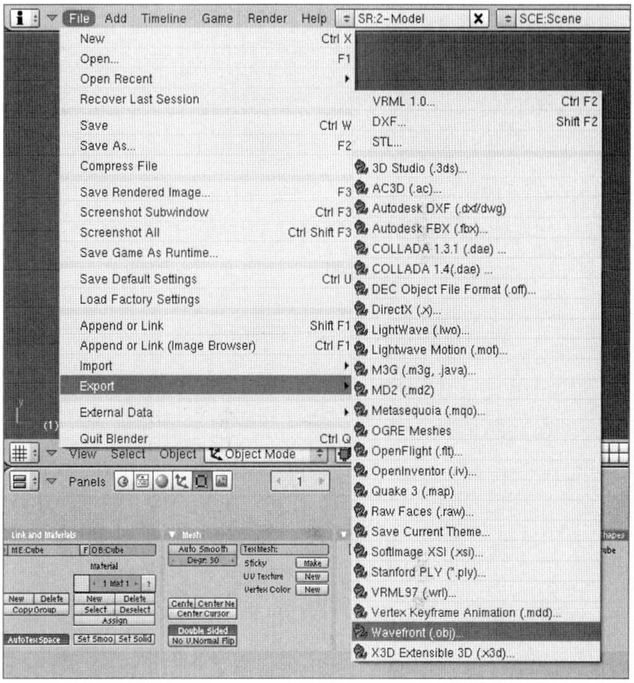

Figure B.1

OBJ Export for Blender 2.49

Blender 2.58 has OBJ export functionality enabled by default, and it can also be found in the File → Export menu, as shown in Figure B.3. Note that there are fewer export options available here than in the corresponding Blender 2.49 list. There are two reasons for this. The first is that fewer exporters exist at present. The other reason is that some exporters are disabled by default and must be enabled in the add-ons system in User Preferences. (See the "Other Formats" section of this appendix for information on doing this.)

Figure B.2

Export options in Blender 2.49

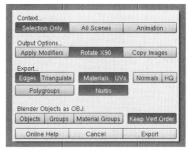

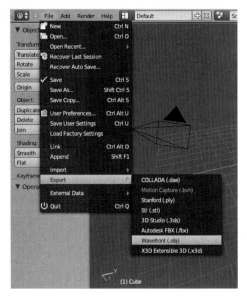

Unlike in Blender 2.49, the version 2.58 exporter does not allow you to choose any options and does not support animated export as of this writing. This may change in the near future, but OBJ is not an optimal format for exporting animation and there are no commonly used game engines that use multiple OBJ files for animation. Therefore, support for animation export to OBJ files is probably not a developer priority.

A more interesting development would be for Processing and NyARToolKit for Android to support importing animated meshes in Collada or Ogre formats, but I am not aware of any efforts to do so at this time.

Collada

Collada is an open, XML-based format for encoding 3D data, including models, textures, lighting, and animation. Collada files use the extension .dae. Collada exporters can be found in the File → Export menu of both Blender 2.49 and Blender 2.58. As with OBJ export, the version 2.49 exporter allows the selection of a number of options via the dialog box shown in Figure B.4, whereas the version 2.58 exporter exports the DAE file without any user feedback or options dialog box.

It is difficult to say where the problems lie, but I can say that, in my experience, the DAE files exported by Blender often have serious problems being read both in Papervision and Away3D, although they are not always the same problems. I found problems with animation and depth sorting with exported models. This is not necessarily due to poor exporting on Blender's side, but may be due to incompatibilities with the way Papervision or Away3D parses the files. Whatever the case, I was ultimately forced to use an inelegant work-around to export Collada files that would display correctly (or almost correctly) in Away3D. To do this, I used Blender's FBX exporter and converted from FBX to Collada using Autodesk's proprietary FBX converter software. Even using this method, I was unable to get a Collada file that rendered correctly in Papervision, which is why the example in Chapter 8, "Browser-Based AR with ActionScript and FLARManager," focuses on the Away3D engine.

Figure B.4

Collada export dialog box for Blender 2.49

Autodesk FBX

The Autodesk FBX exporter in both Blender 2.49 and 2.58 can be accessed by default through the File → Export menu. FBX export from both versions yields good results. You can check your exported FBX files by using the Autodesk FBX Viewer, shown in Figure B.5. The FBX Viewer is bundled with the FBX Converter, which can convert an animated FBX file directly to an animated Collada DAE file, as shown in Figure B.6. You can download the proprietary FBX Converter software for free from Autodesk's website here:

http://usa.autodesk.com/adsk/servlet/pc/item?siteID=123112&id=10775855

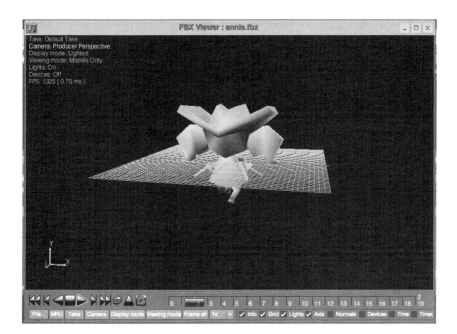

Figure B.5

Autodesk FBX Viewer

Figure B.6

Autodesk FBX Converter

As mentioned previously, the resulting DAE file displayed correctly for me using the Away3D engine in FLARManager, but I still experienced unacceptable render problems when I imported it into the Papervision 3D engine. I can't speculate on where those problems arose.

Metasequoia

Metasequoia is a Windows-only, free-of-charge 3D modeling and texturing application that is popular in Japan, but not so much outside of Japan. Because NyARToolKit was originally created (and remains primarily) developed by Japanese developers, the Metasequoia (MQO) file format was a reasonable choice for the NyARToolkit for Android.

Blender 2.49 includes an MQO exporter in the File ▸ Export menu by default. The dialog box is shown in Figure B.7. The export functionality is incomplete. (Click Options to see what I mean. You'll see a gray field with only two buttons reading Exit and Export. Some options!) However, the main item missing is the ability to export textures with the mesh. Meshes themselves export correctly, but a bug in the exporter prevents the exported mesh from having a texture, although it is fully textured in Blender.

Figure B.7

Metasequoia export dialog box for Blender 2.49

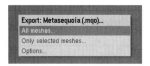

The situation is better for the Blender 2.5 series. Good MQO export scripts exist for all stable releases of the 2.5 series. However, they are not currently distributed as part of the official Blender distribution. Because the Python API has changed rapidly, this exporter has required regular updating. As of this writing, the latest version available is for Blender 2.58. You need to download it yourself and install it as an add-on. You can download the exporter here:

```
http://pr0jectze10.tuzigiri.com/index.html
```

Click on the link labeled ダウンロードリンク (download links), and then click on the link labeled Blender スクリプト (Blender scripts). Download the file called `mqo_script_258`. When you've downloaded it, unzip the script archive.

To use add-ons, you first need to place them in your Blender add-ons directory. The location of this directory depends on your system and other factors. If you don't know the

Figure B.8

Generating system info

location of your add-ons directory, the quickest way to find it is to run the System Info script from the Help menu, as shown in Figure B.8. After you do this, you will be able to open a text file with a complete listing of system info in a text editor window, as shown in Figure B.9. The addons directory is shown highlighted in Figure B.10. This is where you need to put the `mqo_script_258` directory. When you've placed the directory here, restart Blender.

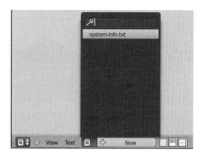

Accessing system info in the text editor

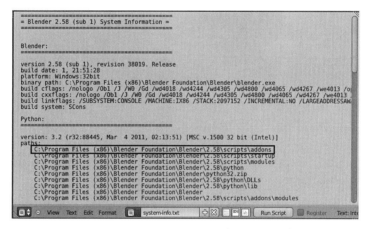

Figure B.10

The addons directory in system info

Figure B.11

Turning on the Metasequoia exporter

Click Ctrl+Alt+U to open the User Preferences window, and click the Add-Ons button to see the Add-Ons preferences. Find the Import-Export Metasequoia Format (.mqo) panel shown in Figure B.11, and click the check box to activate the add-on. You do not need to restart Blender after doing this. Close the User Preferences.

If you look in the File → Export menu now, you will see a new entry, as shown in Figure B.12, with a little plug icon to the left to show that it is an optional add-on.

With the mesh you want to export selected, simply call this exporter from the menu and choose where to save the MQO file. The export should go smoothly. Figure B.13 shows an exported mesh from Blender opened in Metasequoia.

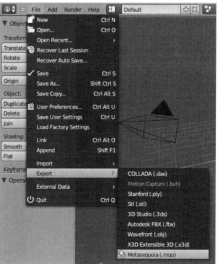

Figure B.12

The Metasequoia exporter in the Export menu

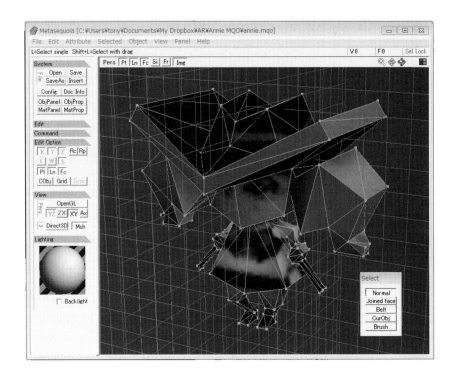

MD2

As of this writing, export to the MD2 file format is supported in Blender 2.49 but not in Blender 2.58. The exporter for MD2 can be found in the File → Export menu in Blender 2.49. When you run the exporter, you'll see the dialog box shown in Figure B.14.

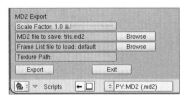

To control the length in frames and the number and names of exported actions, you can enter a Frame List file, which is an external file that tells the exporter the names of the actions you want to export, along with their start and end frames.

Ogre XML

Ogre XML is the format for animated objects used by JME 3.0. For this reason, the jMonkeyEngine community has been at the forefront of pushing for up-to-date Blender exporters. A stable exporter exists for Blender 2.49 and can be downloaded here:

```
www.ogre3d.org/tikiwiki/Blender+Exporter
```

The Ogre exporter for Blender 2.49 is very stable and fully featured. As you can see from the interface shown in Figure B.15, it includes a GUI tool for choosing actions to export by name, along with the file.

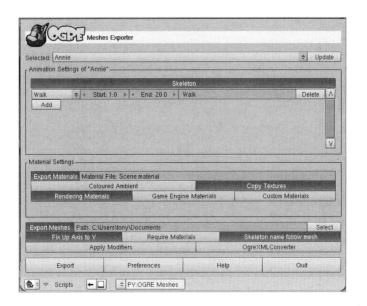

Figure B.15

Ogre XML export from Blender 2.49

The 2.5-series exporter is under development as of this writing. The latest version is written for Blender 2.57, but by the time you read this, an exporter for version 2.58 should be available. Be sure to read the installation instructions in the package's README .txt for important dependencies and where to download them:

```
http://code.google.com/p/blender2ogre/downloads/list
```

Other Formats

A fairly complete list of supported formats for Blender 2.58 can be found by looking at the Import-Export Add-ons list, as shown in Figure B.16. Access this list by pressing Ctrl+Alt+U, which brings up the User Preferences window, and then clicking Add-Ons.

Figure B.16

Import-Export Add-ons

To add the functionality of an add-on, simply select the check box on the right side of the add-on panel. Note that some add-ons are under development and their functionality may be incomplete.

Index

Index

Note to the Reader: Throughout this index **boldfaced** page numbers indicate primary discussions of a topic. *Italicized* page numbers indicate illustrations.